A Garland Series

AMERICAN INDIAN ETHNOHISTORY

Plains Indians

compiled and edited by
DAVID AGEE HORR
Brandeis University

Blackfeet Indians

ETHNOLOGICAL REPORT ON THE
BLACKFEET AND GROS VENTRE TRIBES
OF INDIANS

John C. Ewers

COMMISSION FINDINGS

Garland Publishing Inc., New York & London
1974

Copyright © 1974

by Garland Publishing, Inc.

All Rights Reserved

Library of Congress Cataloging in Publication Data

Ewers, John Canfield.
    Ethnological report on the Blackfeet and Gros Ventre Tribes of Indians.

    (American Indian ethnohistory: Plains Indians)
    At head of title: Blackfeet Indians.
    Report presented before the Indian Claims Commission, docket no. 279-A.
    Bibliography: p.
    1. Siksika Indians--History. 2. Siksika Indians--Land tenure. 3. Atoina Indians--History. 4. Atsina Indians--Land tenure. I. United States. Indian Claims Commission. II. Title. III. Series.
E99.S54E79   970.3   74-5459
ISBN 0-8240-0755-7

Printed in the United States of America

Contents

Preface	7*
The Garland American Indian Ethnohistory Series	
General Nature and Content of the Series	
David Agee Horr	9
The Indian Claims Commission, *Ralph A. Barney*	13
Introduction to the Ethnohistorical Reports	
on the Land Claims Cases, *Robert A. Manners*	17
Background Material on the Blackfeet Indians as of 1953	
Map showing 1950 location and estimated	
original range	20
Historical and Population Information	21
The Report	
Ethnological Report on the Blackfeet and Gros	
Ventre Tribes of Indians, *John C. Ewers*	23
Commission Findings on the Blackfeet Indians	203

*Garland Publishing has repaginated this work (at outside center) to facilitate scholarly use. However, original pagination has been retained for internal reference.

6

Publisher's Preface

The Garland American Indian Ethnohistory series presents original documents on the history and anthropology of many American Indian tribes and groups who were involved in the Indian Claims actions of the 1950s and 1960s. These reports were written to be used as evidence in legal proceedings to determine the aboriginal rights of various Indian groups to certain geographical regions or areas within the United States. In each case, the Indian Claims Commission issued a set of findings which are an important historical outcome of the proceedings and of the reports.

The Garland volumes include, as background material, introductory sections on the Indian Claims actions and the gathering of the ethnohistorical materials by Ralph A. Barney, Chief of the Indian Claims Section of the Department of Justice since its inception in 1946, and Robert A. Manners, Professor of Anthropology at Brandeis University. Both were professionally involved in several cases and Dr. Manners has published on the Claims actions.

Each volume also contains a brief introductory historical sketch of the tribe or group which is representative of the kind of information available at the time of the Claims actions. Much of this material was summarized in a 1650-page document (House Report No. 2503), published in 1953 by order of the House of Representatives committee investigating the Bureau of Indian Affairs. In addition to summaries on history and population, the massive government report included maps which gave the 1950 location of the various American Indian groups, largely on reservations, as well as the estimated original range occupied by the group or tribe in question. This material appears in the Garland volumes in abridged form, since it gives a picture of the kind of information available to the United States government in the 1950s on which it might have based decisions concerning the

PREFACE

American Indians had the Indian Claims actions not taken place. In addition, these brief introductory sections will help orient the general reader to the groups covered by the ethnohistorical reports.

The reports in this series have been organized into logical groupings for maximum efficiency of use. Short reports have been bound together into single volumes by tribe or by geographical area when several tribes are represented by a single report, with Commission findings bound at the end of the pertinent volume. In those cases where many reports pertain to the same group or area they may comprise several volumes which are numbered consecutively. When several volumes deal with the same set of claims, the findings appear in the final volume of that set of interrelated reports. It should be noted that, since this series is intended to present these ethnohistorical materials as documents, the reports are reproduced *verbatim*, with no additions, deletions, or other editing by the compiler of the series or the original authors.

Within the body of the reports, reference is often made to exhibit numbers. These refer to other material accepted as evidence, often in the form of excerpts from existing publications or other documents pertaining to the tribes in question. This material is not included in the volumes themselves, although a bibliography of these items usually appears in the report. These exhibits are on file in the Indian Claims Commission offices in Washington, D.C., or in the National Archives.

General Nature and Content of the Series

The formal reports contained in this series represent only part of the evidence amassed in the 370-odd court actions assigned separate docket numbers by the Indian Claims Commission. Almost since the outset, those involved with the Indian Claims' activities have voiced the opinion that the specifically researched ethnohistorical studies should not simply be filed away in some federal depository though this did become the case with these reports. The present series is the result of careful searching through more than 600 unindexed file drawers in the Indian Claims Commission, the National Archives, and elsewhere, sometimes even in the papers of the originally participating scholars.

Each claims action was an adversary proceeding with a particular Indian tribe or group as plaintiff and the United States Government, represented by the Indian Claims Section of the Justice Department, as defendant. Each side collected evidence on the nature of aboriginal use and occupancy of particular areas in order to determine which Indian groups were entitled to compensation for lands taken by the United States, either by treaty or otherwise, and just what lands were in question. Once this phase of the action was settled, the proceedings moved on to the question of the value of the lands at the time they were taken from the Indians. It is with the title phase of the Claims proceedings that the present series is concerned. Therefore the numerous appraisals of economic value are omitted.

Claims to title were settled on the basis of several types of evidence presented during hearings before the Indian Claims Commission. The expert testimony submitted included verbal and written reports by anthropologists, archaeologists, and historians. During the early days of the Commission, virtually all such testimony was oral and is preserved only in the official court transcripts. Later on, the Government required

NATURE AND CONTENT OF SERIES

its expert witnesses to submit formal written reports. The lawyers for the plaintiffs did not initially make this a requirement so that, for some cases, reports are available on the Government side but not for the Indians. Finally, the Commission did require all ethnohistorical reports to be submitted by both sides in written form. The title page of each individual report indicates whether it was submitted as an exhibit for the plaintiff (sometimes called claimant, petitioner or intervenor) or the defendant.

Since the formal reports were subject to examination by the Commissioners and by the opposing lawyers, they were carefully prepared. The specific nature of the reports did mean that some topics often included in an ethnography might be excluded. In the California cases, for example, some well-researched reports on pottery making and other craft industries were not used. On the other hand, data on political structure, kinship and property inheritance rights, and many other such topics, were often considered because they did bear upon how rights to property and power were determined within a group and the question of how the Indians originally used the land. Once the evidence was submitted and examined in the hearings, the Commissioners issued a set of Findings and Opinions, which, by themselves, are important historical documents.

The Garland series includes only the formal ethnohistorical reports and the title findings of the Commission since the entire documentation of the Claims actions is so voluminous. The lengthy hearing transcripts are uneconomic to reproduce without editing and our purpose is to present unedited documents as actually *used*. The transcript of the Kiowa-Comanche case is included because of its unique nature. The transcripts are all on file either in the Indian Claims Commission or the National Archives, and may be consulted there.

The content of this series was determined solely by those ethnohistorical reports submitted to the Commission. Therefore, American Indian tribes and groups not involved in Claims actions are not represented for various reasons. For

NATURE AND CONTENT OF SERIES

example, the Indians of the northeastern and eastern United States had lost most of their lands prior to the establishment of the country in 1776. In other instances, the tribe no longer existed in 1946 or did not submit a claim. In some cases claims were submitted, but were denied before a report was commissioned for that tribe.

The reports for the various areas covered by the Claims Act have been approached in somewhat different ways. When possible, they deal with individual tribes or named groups. This does not mean that in such cases there were no overlapping claims; however, the overall tribal situation was not so complex as to prevent an initial identification of tribal groups with specific geographic areas. By contrast, in some areas such as the eastern and north central regions, reports tend to focus on Royce areas rather than individual tribes because the aboriginal claims situation often involved recurring movement through the region by many different tribes over a relatively short time period. In these regions treaties ceding certain lands to the United States were often signed by several different tribes or perhaps only by certain parts of some of the tribes involved. Here the area reports *in toto* form an almost jigsaw-puzzle-like solution to the enormously complex tribal relationships. The Royce Area maps and designations were published in Bureau of American Ethnology, Annual Report, vol. 18, no. 2, 1896-7.

David Agee Horr

The Indian Claims Commission

Prior to the creation of the Indian Claims Commission by the Act of August 13, 1946 (60 Stat. 1049; 25 U.S.C. § 70 et seq.), no tribe of Indians could bring a suit against the United States without the special permission of Congress. This was a cumbersome and wholly unsatisfactory procedure. By the 1946 Act, Congress created a special judicial tribunal to "hear and determine" claims by Indian tribes in an effort to settle, once and for all, the claims of the Indians. The Act is unique in the true sense of the word. Never before has any government generally opened the doors of its courts to the claims of its aborigines. The Commission is authorized to consider claims by any "tribe, band or identifiable group of American Indians" that the United States in its previous dealings had not always carried out its treaty obligations, had imposed treaties upon them against their wishes, had failed to pay them adequately for their land, had failed to account properly for the expenditure of their tribal funds and, in many instances, had not been "fair and honorable" in their dealings with them.

The tribes had five years within which to file their claims and, after adjudication, they could have the Commission's decisions reviewed by the United States Court of Claims and by the Supreme Court of the United States. The Congress imposed one important limitation: the Commission could render only a money judgment in favor of the tribes. It could not return any land to them which might have been taken wrongfully, nor could it give them any land to supply a land base.

The present volumes deal with only one of the multi-faceted aspects of Indian claims litigation: the area of land occupied by the tribes prior to the coming of the white man into the area in general, or the area occupied by a particular tribe for "a long time" prior to its acquisition by the United

INDIAN CLAIMS COMMISSION

States, or their dispossession by the whites.

The land problem was confounded by different concepts inherent in the nature of the disparate cultures. The culture of the Europeans who discovered and later settled this continent was basically legalistic, particularly where land was concerned. Land was the subject of "ownership" either by the monarch or his subjects, and "titles" were the capstone of such ownership. "Ownership" in the sense of a legal right was unknown to the Indian. As Justice Black said in *Shoshone Indians* v. *United States*, 324 U.S. 335, 357 (1945):

> ... Ownership meant no more to them than to roam the land as a great common, and to possess and enjoy it in the same way that they possessed and enjoyed sunlight and the west wind and the feel of spring in the air. Acquisitiveness, which develops a law of real property, is an accomplishment only of the "civilized."

When the Europeans "discovered" the North American continent they found it inhabited by the Indians and the question of their rights aroused a great moral debate. Charles V of Spain sought the advice of the theologian Franciscus de Victoria, primary professor of sacred theology in the University of Salamanca, who suggested that since the aborigines "were true owners, before the Spaniards came among them, both from the public and private point of view," they should be treated with to secure cessions of their lands. This view obviously could not prevail if the European monarchs owned the land and could parcel it out to their subjects.

The matter came to a head in 1823 when Chief Justice John Marshall decided the famous case of *Johnson* v. *McIntosh*, 21 U.S. (8 Wheat.) 453. In 1775 the Piankeshaw Indians had sold a tract of land to various individuals. However, in 1818, the United States sold and patented the same land to William McIntosh. Thus the contest was which deed was valid. From a long and detailed examination of the history of Indian relations in this country, Chief Justice Marshall concluded that the legal title was in the United

INDIAN CLAIMS COMMISSION

States Government and that the tribes had no right to sell and convey the land (at least, without governmental consent).

However, the Indians could not be ignored, particularly in the early days when they were numerically far stronger than the few settlers huddled along the coast. From this developed the theory that while the legal "title" was in the discovering nations and later in the United States, the Indians had a right of possession based on what was characterized as their "aboriginal title."

More than thirty years ago, long before the creation of the Indian Claims Commission, the Supreme Court had occasion to lay down the rule, which was later adopted by the Commission, as to what was necessary to establish Indian title. In *United States* v. *Santa Fe Pacific R. Co.*, 314 U. S. 339, 345 (1941), the Court said:

> Occupancy necessary to establish aboriginal possession is a question of fact to be determined as any other question of fact. If it were established as a fact that the lands in question were, or were included in, the ancestral home of the Walapais in the sense that they constituted a definable territory occupied exclusively by the Walapais (as distinguished from lands wandered over by many tribes), then the Walapais had "Indian title". . . .

The determination of the "question of fact" of the aboriginal or original Indian title is what the ethnographic studies in these volumes, and the findings and the opinions of the Commission are all about. The anthropologists have dug up the facts to the extent that they were able to do so. Based on these facts the Commission has made its determination of the areas of land occupied by the various tribes under their original title or their later occupancy, and it is on the basis of these determinations of the areas of aboriginal title that these cases then go forward to determine the amount of recovery by the several tribes.

Quite understandably much of the "evidence" consists of deductions made by the witnesses from the frequently

INDIAN CLAIMS COMMISSION

meager hard facts available and, of necessity, the determinations of the Commission are based on this type of evidence. While the boundaries of the areas exclusively and actually used and occupied may not always be correct, they represent in most instances a fair approximation of the areas occupied by the various tribes aboriginally or for "a long time" on the dates when the United States acquired the land or they were permanently dispossessed of it. All in all, it has been a difficult job well done.

I cannot close this brief introduction without expressing my admiration for the many scholars on both sides who so diligently sought out the facts to present to the Commission. They did a magnificent job for which all other scholars and interested laymen should be grateful. My personal acquaintance with them has been an outstanding experience.

I am also personally happy to see these ethnographic studies and the decisions of the Commission published instead of being buried in the National Archives. They will contribute greatly to our knowledge of the American Indian.

Ralph A. Barney

Introduction to the Ethnohistorical Reports on the Land Claims Cases

The research reports and the findings contained in this compilation may prove, in the long run, to have contributed little to resolving the massive economic and social problems which confront today's Native Americans. However, it is most unlikely that any of the diligent and often dedicated sponsors of the movement that led, in 1946, to the passage of the Indian Claims Commission Act ever had such lofty expectations. What is more likely is that the proponents of the legislation, as Ralph Barney observes in his introductory remarks, had simply hoped to "clean up the mess," to put an end to the stream of suits and claims against the federal government, each of which had required Congressional approval before it could be brought to trial. But the "mess" was not so easily resolved. Some cases have been settled. Others have been heard, adjudicated and appealed to higher courts. A few, like that of "the Indians of California," may be reopened.

But when, and if, all of the claims have been resolved in the courts, the government will not have succeeded in pacifying the claimants nor in satisfying their demands for decent compensation. In short, the Act has not fulfilled even the minimal goal of putting an end to Native American claims against the United States Government.

In light of the relatively meager benefits that have so far accrued to Native Americans as a consequence of the Act of 1946, it might seem almost callous to draw attention now to the richness of the by-product of that Act as represented in the 118 volumes in this series. For whatever one may feel about the intended benefits of the Act, it is clear that the

INTRODUCTION TO THE REPORTS

scholarly fallout is stunning indeed. The materials presented in these volumes include a concentrated body of ethnohistorical research data and adversary findings unique in the record of cultural historiography and, so far as I know, in the annals of jurisprudence.

Literally hundreds of people were involved in the research and litigation that led to these reports and findings. Thousands of interviews were conducted. Extensive archaeological surveys were made. Large quantities of previously "unknown" or unexamined agency and other files, personal correspondence, photographs, diaries, and so on were uncovered and their contents incorporated in the reports. Regular archival and library resources were examined and reexamined with a thoroughness that would not have been possible without the support that both claimants and the defendant were able to provide. Then there were the adversary proceedings, which, though patently unpleasant to most of the experts, did provide an even more effective check on the quality of the research product than the customary scholarly scrutiny of one's colleagues. For where there is litigation, the experts on both sides have probably reviewed much, if not all, of the same data. Moreover, the litigous circumstances place a premium on revealing inaccuracies and/or slipshod research methods.[1]

Finally, I would like to emphasize that another apparent by-product of the Act and the research and hearings that followed its implementation may be detected in the effect that this research and its attendant litigation have had on the thinking of many Native Americans now pressing for improved economic, social and political conditions for *all* Indians in the United States. Thus, if the working-out of the Act has made only minor contributions to the welfare of a

---

[1] Some ethnohistorical and legal problems confronted by the plaintiffs' and defendant's experts and attorneys were explored at a 1954 symposium on the Claims Act (see *Ethnohistory* 2,4, pp. 287-375). The participants were Ralph A. Barney, Chief of the Indian Claims Section, Lands Division, Dept. of Justice; Donald C. Gormley of the law firm of Wilkinson, Boyden, Cragun & Barker; and anthropologists Verne Ray, Julian Steward, A. L. Kroeber, J. A. Jones and Nancy Oestreich Lurie.

INTRODUCTION TO THE REPORTS

handful of American Indians, it has apparently had a much more salutary effect on their thinking about the welfare of *all* Native Americans. For the "time immemorial" and the "exclusive occupancy" strictures of the Act resulted, in many ways, in pitting group against group to the detriment of all.[2] In most cases, the occupancy and/or use claims of one group conflicted, at least in part, with those of another or several other groups of Indians.[3] Where such joint use or occupancy was proved to the satisfaction of the Commission, none of the claimants benefitted, thus demonstrating (as I have been told by several Native Americans) the perils of division and intra-Indian competition and, by implication, the likely advantages of pan-Indian cooperation in future endeavors, political as well as legal.

This "unforeseen consequence" of the research and litigation, of the claims and counter-claims, has certainly been among the factors that have helped to persuade those Native Americans who were not already convinced of the pitfalls as well as the potential virtues of a revived "tribalism" of the need for a more unified, a pan-Indian approach to their problems. These volumes can only help to bolster the case for such unity and, thus, perhaps to enhance the political impact of Native Americans in the United States.

Robert A. Manners

---

[2] In this respect, the claim of "The Indians of California" is exceptional because an earlier case had laid the groundwork whereby a number of different groups (culturally and linguistically) were permitted to combine all of their separate land-use-and-occupation claims into one. If the Act had allowed *all* American Indian plaintiffs to combine their claims in this manner (and to share equally in the awards), and if they had been willing to do so, the resultant claims, litigation and decisions might have been, at the very least, quite interesting. . . . i.e., "The Indians of the United States vs. the United States Government for just compensation for the taking of all lands (less land held in existing reservations) between the Atlantic and the Pacific Oceans."

[3] A striking example, with which I am familiar, are the overlapping Navaho, Hopi, Walapai, Havasupai claims.

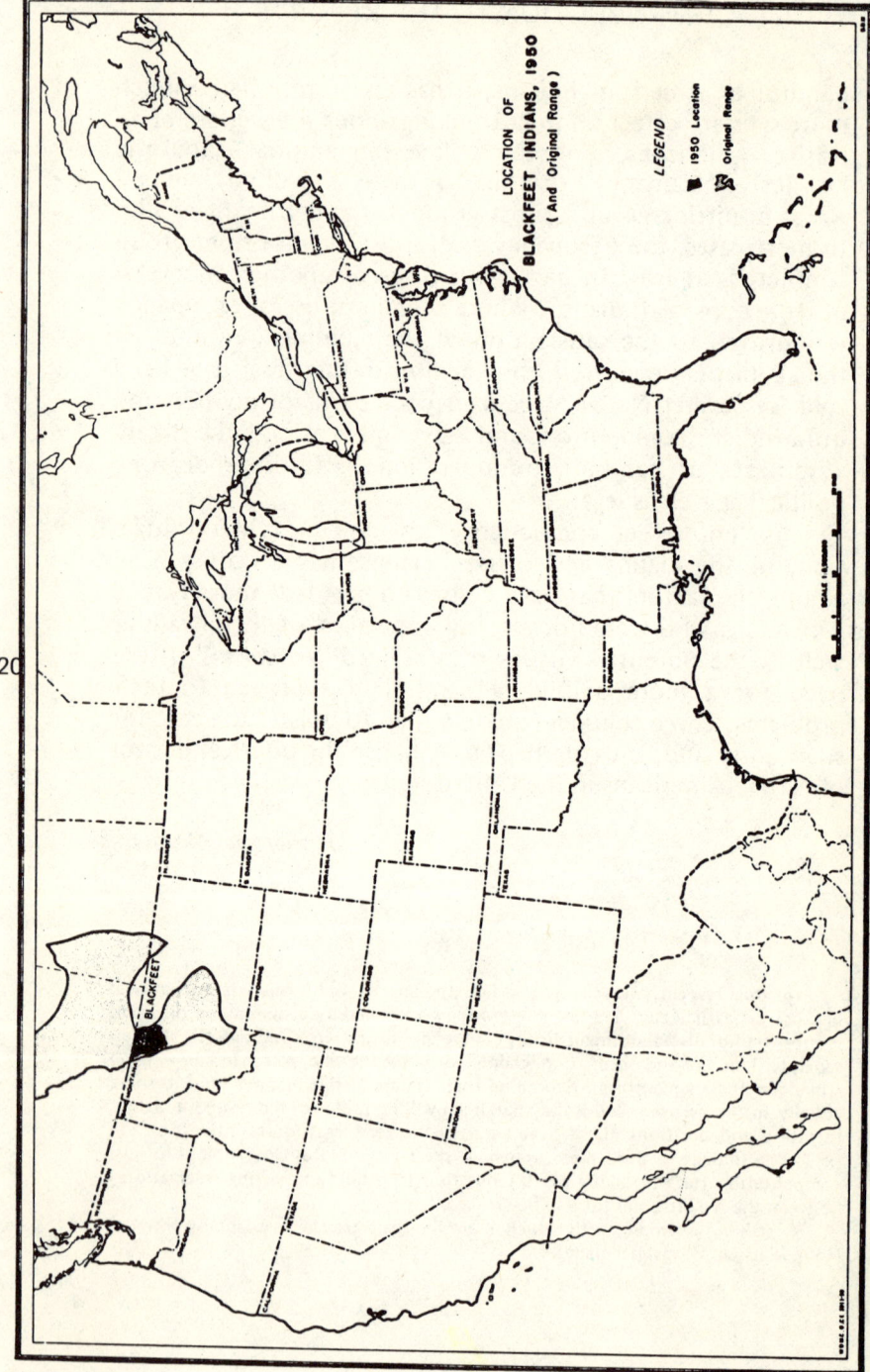

History of the Blackfeet

During the first half of the 19th century the Blackfeet became acquainted with American fur traders but were little affected by the westward movement of American white settlement.

In 1855 a Treaty with the United States recognized the Blackfeet possession of a vast territory in northern Montana. After this treaty many white men began to come into the Blackfeet territories—farmers, gold seekers, cattlemen, traders, soldiers, missionaries, and teachers, in increasing numbers. Various supplies were included in the yearly annuities remitted by the Federal Government such as bread, rice, coffee, gunpowder, shirts, etc.

In 1873-74 Congress moved the boundary of the Blackfeet country northward 200 miles and the lands south of this border were opened to settlement by whites. The destruction of the buffalo about this time completely revolutionized the economic life of the Blackfeet. In 1888 the lands north of the Missouri were broken up into three Indian reservations, Blackfeet, Fort Peck and Fort Belknap. For a while during this period the Blackfeet barely managed to subsist by the aid of Government rations. In 1912 allotments began to be made and in 1918 the first trust patents and fee patents were issued. In 1935 the Blackfeet adopted a Tribal Constitution under the Wheeler-Howard Act.

Blackfeet Population

"The name Blackfeet (or Siksika) is applied both to a single tribe and to a confederacy made up of these and the Kainah or Bloods, and Piegans. The Blackfeet proper and the Kainah are now mostly Piegan, although generally known as Blackfeet. The tribes of the Blackfeet Confederacy formerly ranged over a large area in Montana, Alberta, and Saskatchewan, east of the Rocky Mountains. For some 60 years the Piegan and Blackfeet south of the Canadian Boundary have been largely concentrated in the Blackfeet Reservation in Glacier County, Montana. The number enumerated in 1930 was 3,145, of whom 3,033 were in Montana. In 1910 the corresponding figures were 2,367 and 2,254, indicating a large increase in population. The reports of the Indian Office are in close agreement with the census as to the population of this tribe. The enumeration of 1932 showed an Indian population of 3,242 on the Blackfeet Reservation, of whom 2,955 were Blackfeet and 283 of mixed Blackfeet and other tribal origin."

Source: *The Indian Population of the United States and Alaska*, 1930, p. 37

SELECTED REFERENCES AS OF 1952

(Including the Blackfeet proper or Siksika, the Blood, and the Piegan)

Campbell, F. C. House to House Survey of Blackfeet Reservation. 6 vols. mss. 1922. (Bureau of Indian Affairs).

Disposition of surplus lands of Blackfeet Indian reservation, Mont. Hearings before a subcommittee of the Committee on Indian affairs of the

House of representatives, on H. R. 14732. (July 12, 1916.) Washington, Govt. Print. Off., 1916.
Fox, Charles E. Some Observations on the Blackfeet Reservation. Mss. (Bureau of Indian Affairs).
Krzywicki, Ludwik. Primitive Society and its Vital Statistics. London. 1934. Blackfeet pp. 541–2, Piegan pp. 466–7.
McBride, Freal H. Blackfeet Ten Year Program Report. 1944. 97 pp. (Bureau of Indian Affairs).
McClintock, W. The Old North Trail. London, 1910.
McCullough, H. D. Summary of the Blackfeet Ten Year Program Report. 1944. 21 pp. (Bureau of Indian Affairs).
Murdock, Geo. P. Ethnographic Bibliography of North America. 1941. p. 70.
Rodnick, David. Report on the Blackfeet Indians of Montana. 1936. 11 pp. (Bureau of Indian Affairs).
Surplus Lands. Blackfeet Reservation, Mont. Hearings. Senate, 74th Cong., 1st Sess., on S. 793. Washington, 1916.
United States General Accounting Office. Report on the Blackfeet et al Claims Case E-427, forwarded to the Department of Justice March 28, 1929. 1 vol. 737 pp. mss.
Wissler, C. Material Culture of the Blackfoot Indians. Anthropological Papers of the American Museum of Natural History. N. Y., Vol. V, pp. 1–; 75, 1910.
Wissler, C. The Social Life of the Blackfoot Indians. Anthropological Papers of the American Museum of Natural History. N. Y., Vol. VII, pp. 1–64, 1912.

ETHNOLOGICAL REPORT ON

THE BLACKFEET AND GROS VENTRE TRIBES
OF INDIANS
LANDS IN NORTHERN MONTANA

DOCKET NO. 279-A, INDIAN CLAIMS COMMISSION

MAY 1, 1888

Prepared by
John C. Ewers

TABLE OF CONTENTS

INTRODUCTION	- 1
Factors Influencing Tribal Locations and Movements	- 1
The Area of Occupancy	- 1
Tribes Occupying this Area	- 2
The Factor of Environment	- 5
The Buffalo - The Indians' Staff of Life	- 9
The Factor of Tribal Organization	- 11
The Factor of Political Leadership	- 14
The Factor of Seasonal Movements	- 16
The Factor of Intertribal Relationships	- 20
The Factor of White Contacts	- 23
Indian Occupancy of the Missouri-Saskatchewan Region in 1650, Dr. John R. Swanton's Theoretical Reconstruction.	- 25
HISTORY OF INDIAN OCCUPANCY OF THIS REGION	- 28
I. The Canadian Period (ca. 1730-1810)	- 28
The Blackfeet and Gros Ventre on the Saskatchewan	- 28
The Shoshoni in Present Montana and Alberta ante 1810	- 37
The Flathead East of the Rockies ante 1810	- 44
The Pend d'Oreille East of the Rockies before 1810	- 48
The Kutenai on the Montana and Alberta Plains ante 1810	- 49
The Crow in Northern Montana ante 1810	- 51
Assiniboin Movement Westward into this Region ante 1810	- 51

II.	The Lewis and Clark Interlude (1805-1806)	- 55
III.	Period of American Fur Trade on the Missouri (1806-1850)	- 64
IV.	Period of the First Treaty (1850-1862)	- 77
V.	North Blackfeet, Blood and North Piegan Withdrawal into Canada (1862-1877).	-106
VI.	Period of the Extermination of the Buffalo and the South Piegan Land Agreements. (1878-1900).	-123
VII.	The Gros Ventre and their Allies in the Milk River Country. (1862-1890).	-138

CONCLUSIONS — -158

BIBLIOGRAPHY — -166

INTRODUCTION

Factors Influencing Tribal Locations and Movements.

The Area of Occupancy: The history of Indian occupancy of that portion of the present State of Montana east of the Rocky Mountains claimed by those tribes which, at the time of their first treaty with the United States a century ago, comprised The Blackfoot Nation, cannot be meaningfully presented or clearly comprehended in terms of the history of that area alone. Throughout an extended period of their known history these tribes, as well as their neighbors, were nomadic peoples who knew neither National, State nor Reservation boundaries.

Study of the problems of Indian occupancy in Montana east of the Rockies inevitably leads to consideration of Indian occupancy of that neighboring portion of the northwestern Great Plains which lies within the present Canadian Provinces of Alberta and Saskatchewan. Not only were the tribes of the so-called Blackfoot Nation first seen and described by literate white men within the portion of this vast area granted to the Hudson's Bay Company by King Charles II of England in 1670, and commonly referred to by American writers prior to 1869 as "the British Possessions", but some of these tribes continued to live primarily within that area to the present day. Since the year 1877 three of the five reservations upon which descendants of the tribes of The Blackfoot Nation have resided have been located within the Province of Alberta in the Dominion of Canada.

Tribes Occupying This Area: Within the period of recorded history of this area at least sixteen different Indian tribes have occupied it or portions of it for longer or shorter periods. They are:

The tribes of the so-called Blackfoot Nation.

The term "The Blackfoot Nation" was employed at the time of the first treaty negotiated between the four tribes of the Blackfeet, Blood, Piegan and Gros Ventre with the United States at the mouth of the Judith River in 1855. It was an expedient designation to cover these four tribes which, at that time, were allies. Actually it was a misnomer. They were not a nation in the sense of their recognizing any common, central governmental authority. Even their alliance did not last for more than six years after their leaders signed that treaty.

While the Blackfeet, Blood and Piegan were recognized as separate tribes by Mathew Cocking as early as 1772, they speak a common language and believe themselves to have had a common origin. They have no such feeling about the Gros Ventre. Although the Gros Ventre also speak a dialect of the Algonkian language family, it is most closely related to Arapaho speech. The Gros Ventre and Blackfoot languages are so different that members of one tribe cannot understand speakers of the other unless they have made a special effort to learn their dialect. On the other hand, the close similarity between the Gros Ventre and Arapaho dialects, coupled with surviving traditions in both tribes of their separation has led ethnologists to conclude that they were once one people. The date of this separation has been estimated at no more recently than 1700. (Flannery, 1953, p. 1). The name Gros Ventre is a French corruption of the Blackfeet term for these people, Atsina ("gut people"). In the records of the fur trade in the British Possessions prior to 1800 they were commonly called "The Fall (or Waterfall) Indians. Lewis and Clark referred to them as "Minnetarees of Fort de Prairie". They have been commonly confused with the Siouan-speaking Hidatsa, known also as the Gros Ventre of the Missouri. (Swanton, 1952, p. 389).

Considerable confusion has resulted from the fact that the same name, Blackfoot or Blackfeet, has been used to identify all or a part of the tribes of the so-called Blackfoot Nation in four ways (1) to identify the three Blackfeet tribes plus the Gros Ventre, (2) to identify the three Blackfeet tribes, (3) to identify the tribe now living on the Blackfoot Reserve in Alberta, and (4) to identify the tribe now living on the Blackfeet Reservation in Montana. The word is used in its most accurate sense in identifying a specific tribe, the Blackfoot of Canada. They are sometimes spoken of as the North Blackfeet to distinguish them from the other Blackfeet tribes. The Indians living on the Blackfeet Reservation in Montana are more precisely Piegan, and still more accurately they are South Piegan, which distinguishes them from the North Piegan residing on the reserve of that name in Alberta.

The North Piegan certainly were recognized as a division

of the Piegan before the 1855 treaty. Thaddeus Culbertson listed the "North Piedgans" in 1850 (T. Culbertson, 1952, p. 137). Their distinction from the South Piegan bands on the basis of land occupancy became increasingly important to the time they became established on their Canadian reserve in 1877.

There is no confusion over the Blood tribe. Even though these Indians have preferred their native name of Kainah (Many Chiefs) that name is rarely used in the literature.

Of the other tribes who occupied lands claimed by the tribes of the so-called Blackfoot Nation it may be well to list them in three groups:

(1) Those who lived in the area before the 1855 treaty but not at the time of the treaty: Shoshoni (or Snake).

(2) Those who lived in the area both before and after the 1855 treaty: Assiniboin
　　　　　　　　　　　　　　　　Flathead
　　　　　　　　　　　　　　　　Pend d'Oreille
　　　　　　　　　　　　　　　　Kutenai

(3) Those who entered the area after the 1855 treaty but before the breakup of the large Blackfeet Reservation in 1888:

　　　　　　　　　River Crow
　　　　　　　　　Yanktonai Sioux
　　　　　　　　　Santee Sioux
　　　　　　　　　Hunkpapa Sioux
　　　　　　　　　Arapaho
　　　　　　　　　Cheyenne
　　　　　　　　　Plains Cree

Discussions of the occupancy of the area by these tribes

will appear in the historical sections of this report.

The Factor of Environment: It is no accident that the history of Indian occupancy of the valley of the Saskatchewan River and of the valley of the Missouri River should be inseparably linked. If one will but look at an accurate, modern physiographic map of the Missouri-Saskatchewan Region, such as Dr. Erwin Raisz' map in W. W. Atwood's Physiographic Provinces of North America (Atwood, 1940), he will recognize that the 49th parallel which now separates Montana from Alberta and Saskatchewan is a man-made boundary. In terms of physiographic characteristics this is one great region with no natural barriers to the movement of people from north to south or south to north. Neither mountains, nor rivers nor lakes separate that portion of the region lying north of the 49th parallel from the portion to the south of it. On the contrary we may note that one of the larger rivers of this region, Milk River, has its source in Montana, flows northward into Alberta and turns southward into Montana where it empties into the Missouri.

Throughout the greater part of their known history the majority of the tribes of The Blackfoot Nation were as much or more at home in the valley of the Saskatchewan and its tributaries as they were in the valley of the Missouri and its affluents.

Rivers were not important to these Indians for travel. They did not use boats or canoes. They traveled overland. But rivers were important natural resources. From them the Indians obtained water for themselves and their dogs and horses. Their tree-bordered banks furnished timber for firewood and for fashioning weapons and household utensils and cottonwood bark for winter horse feed. The river valleys also offered shelter for their winter camps and winter pasture for their horses. The number of rivers and streams in the Missouri-Saskatchewan Region was sufficiently great and their distribution was such that nomadic bands of Indians could travel widely throughout the area with rarely any need for a dry camp.

Rivers were extremely important as points of reference to early white observers in locating the Indian tribes of the region. They also were commonly designated as boundary markers in the treaties of the United States with these tribes and in the Executive Orders defining tribal reservations. Especially useful in defining the locations of tribes and negotiating tribal boundaries in the United States was the Missouri River and its larger tributaries - the Milk, Marias (and its western branches Birch Creek and Cut Bank Creek), Teton and Sun rivers on the north, and the Musselshell on the south. Equally important to these Indian tribes were the North and South Saskatchewan and the latters' affluents the Red Deer, Bow, Oldman and Belly rivers.

After the buffalo were exterminated and their nomadic days were ended these Indians settled down along river valleys and tried to farm until they began to receive cattle following the 1888 Agreements.

Climatically this Missouri-Saskatchewan region is a land of long, cold and often severe winters, where temperatures of 20 or more degrees below zero are not uncommon. Blizzards, deep snows and rapid changes in temperature make winter a hazardous season in this region even today. Summers are relatively short with cool nights and warm, sunny days. A short growing season with both late spring and early fall frosts, and limited rainfall discouraged agriculture on the part of Indian occupants of this region under aboriginal conditions. Repeated failures at dry land farming due to these same climatic factors, plus occasional plagues of grasshoppers, convinced many an early Indian Agent of the futility of making successful farmers of his Indian charges. It is true that winter wheat, potatoes, turnips and rutabagas have done well in the Blackfeet country, but none of these crops were known to the Indians before their introduction by white men.

The relatively uniform distribution of the natural resources exploited by the Indians living in the Missouri-Saskatchewan region was of greater importance than were the minor local differences in the occurrences of particular raw materials. While the primitive Indians employed stone in making weapons, household utensils, and smoking pipes there is no evidence that they exploited the resources of the region in coal, gold, silver, copper or oil before the economic values of these resources were demonstrated to them in the years

33

following the first treaty. In fact the oil resources of the region were not recognized by the whites at the time of the Agreement negotiated in 1895. A great variety of wild plants of this region were employed by these Indians in concocting medicines. The most important edible plants exploited by the Indians were the spring roots of the prairie turnip and the fall berries of the chokecherry, buffaloberry (bullberry), and sarvisberry. They also made use of the roots of bitterroot and camass, found near the mountains, but not characteristic of the area as a whole. All of these plant foods were of secondary importance to the Indians' diet. Undoubtedly, the most important flora of the region throughout the period of its known history has been the short grass which covered the plains and valleys, offering abundant feed for herbivorous wild animals and for domesticated horses, cattle and sheep.

Faunal wild life abounded in this region. Among the animals of economic value to the Indian were antelope, badger, bear (both black and grizzly), beaver, bighorn, buffalo, deer, elk, foxes, mink, mountain sheep, muskrat, otter, rabbit, weasel and wolves. Recently Schaeffer (1950, pp. 37-46) listed some 80 bird species (in some cases families) recognized by the Blackfoot as residents of their territory, including several species of game birds. Although fish were abundant in the streams and lakes, they were rarely eaten by the Blackfeet tribes.

In spite of this faunal richness of the Missouri-Saskatchewan

Region, there were two mammals which far outranked all the others in their economic importance to the Indian occupants of the region in the eighteenth and nineteenth centuries. They were the buffalo and the beaver. The buffalo was the primitive Indian's staff of life. The beaver was the most sought after animal by white fur traders, who furnished our earliest knowledge of the Indian occupation of this region and who influenced the movement of tribes within it.

The Buffalo - The Indians' Staff of Life: It is a truism that the buffalo was the staff of life of the Indians occupying this area in the period prior to 1883. Not only was buffalo their primary food resource, but buffalo hides provided their winter clothing, covers for their lodges, and materials for the construction of nearly 100 other articles useful in the daily and ceremonial lives of these Indians. (Ewers, 1955, pp. 149-151). The existence of vast herds of buffalo in this region, and the habits of this gregarious, wandering animal strongly influenced the customs of the Indian tribes who exploited the buffalo as their primary natural resources. Following the moving buffalo made the tipi a practical dwelling. Hunting this gregarious animal made the division of tribes into bands a practical social and political arrangement.

35

Not only was the Missouri-Saskatchewan area stocked with vast herds of buffalo before and at the time of the first treaty of these Indians with the United States, but it was the last refuge of the great northern buffalo herd until 1883.

The abundance of buffalo in this region was not only sufficient for the support of those tribes living within this area the year round, but it furnished partial support for a number of tribes from west of the Rockies who crossed the mountains to hunt buffalo on the plains, in some years spending the entire winter on the plains. Such tribes were the Flathead, Pend d'Oreille and Kutenai in the nineteenth century.

As the range of the buffalo contracted in the middle and late nineteenth century (see the map showing the progressive shrinkage of the buffalo range in William T. Hornaday's classic study, The Extermination of the American Bison, 1889) the country of the Blackfoot tribes and the Gros Ventre remained well stocked, and other tribes, which had been accustomed to live upon buffalo east or south of this area tended to move into it to continue buffalo hunting after buffalo were exterminated in their own country. This was certainly true of the Yanktonai and Santee Sioux in the 1860s, and to a lesser degree of the Arapaho and Cheyenne in the '70s. By '79 the buffalo were exterminated in Canada, and both Blackfeet and Plains Cree from Canada came south to seek buffalo in the remaining buffalo country, which was within the country of the Blackfeet and Gros Ventre tribes in the United States. According to verbal testimony of elderly Piegan Indians which I received more than 15 years ago, the last wild buffalo killed by members of their tribe were 4 animals shot in 1884 near the Sweetgrass Hills, in the area then claimed by that tribe (South Piegan).

So strong was the attraction of buffalo hunting for the Indian tribes which occupied this region that they continued to subsist primarily upon this animal until the buffalo were exterminated. In spite of their Agents' warnings of the disappearance of this resource in the near future and of Agents' efforts to encourage them to settle down and to till the soil, these Indians, by their own preference, continued to hunt buffalo until they were gone, or as a South Piegan more picturesquely expressed it, until "the tail of the last buffalo disappeared from the prairie."

This extermination came more rapidly than either the Indians or their Agents had anticipated. Consequently it brought suffering, starvation and death to hundreds of Blackfeet and Gros Ventre Indians. Then, with the buffalo gone and unprepared to make a living by any other means than hunting, these Indian people had no alternative but to settle down near their Agencies where they could obtain weekly supplies of government rations. Not until they began to receive cattle under the terms of the Agreements negotiated in the field in 1887, did they begin to spread out over their reservations.

The Factor of Tribal Organization: During the nomadic period, prior to the extermination of the buffalo, the basic residential as well as political group among both the Gros Ventre and the Blackfeet tribes was the hunting band, not the tribe. Each tribe was divided into a number of these hunting bands which usually wintered separately and which gathered in one great circle camp only during summer for the great tribal hunt and the tribal sun dance.

During the nineteenth century, at least, these hunting bands were fluid organizations. Population growth and internal frictions caused the splitting up of bands. Loss of population due to devastating smallpox epidemics and disastrous enemy attacks necessitated the regrouping of bands. Individuals or families dissatisfied with the leadership of their band could and did leave that band to join another. It was not uncommon for poor people to attach themselves to the band whose leader they felt would be most liberal in loaning them horses or dispensing his favors. Certainly all members of a band needed not to be kinsmen, nor was marriage within the band forbidden.

Due to these factors the numbers and sizes of the hunting bands changed. The names of bands also changed with the acquisition of new leaders or for other reasons. Unfortunately no real study of the bands of the Blackfeet tribes was made until after the buffalo disappeared and they had ceased to be of major importance as residential units. Two lists of the bands in the three Blackfeet tribes have been compiled by students of those tribes. Grinnell (1892, pp. 208-211) listed 24 Piegan bands, 13 Blood bands and 8 Northern Blackfeet bands. Wissler (1911, p. 21) listed 23 Piegan bands, 7 Blood bands and 6 Northern Blackfeet bands. However, Wissler acknowledged the inadequacy of his data. It appears quite probable that the Piegan bands listed by both these authorities are in excess of the number of bands in that tribe at any time during the nineteenth century and that the large number listed includes duplicate, or even triplicate listings of some of the same bands under different names. On the other hand, there may be important omissions in their listings of Blood and Northern Blackfeet bands. More reliable as an indication of the number of hunting bands into which each of these tribes was divided was, I believe, the census of bands existing in the summer of 1870, compiled by Gen. Alfred Sully, Supt. of Indian Affairs for Montana Territory on the basis of information obtained from fur traders and missionaries. Sully listed 13 South Piegan bands, 2 North Piegan bands (a Piegan total of 15), 9 Blood bands and 9 Northern Blackfeet bands. These bands varied in size from 10 to 36 lodges and in population from 110 to 432 persons. A median size of 24 lodges and about 288 souls is indicated by his figures. (Sully, 1870). This size provided a camp large enough to offer a stiff resistance to an enemy attack and to impound or surround a herd of buffalo. At the same time it was small enough not to place too great demands upon a limited food supply in severe winters when game was scarce.

  The names of 12 Gros Ventre bands were listed by Flannery (1953, p. 25); ten of which agree with those earlier listed by Kroeber (1908, p. 148). It is possible that these lists also may include some duplications due to the listing of the same band under two names.

The Factor of Political Leadership: In the important political unit of the hunting band men rose to positions of leadership through their individual qualities. Two factors were important in qualifying a man for leadership in the eyes of their fellows (1) a fine war record and (2) sufficient wealth to be able to dispense favors to the less fortunate members of the community. There might be two or more of these recognized headmen or chiefs in a band although one generally was recognized as the principal one. As Wissler (1911, p. 23) has explained, "Such chiefs rarely venture to act without the advice of some head men, as to stand alone would be fatal. In tribal assemblies, the head men of the bands usually look to one of these as spokesman, and speak of him as their chief."

In each of the Blackfeet tribes there was a head chief who was the most powerful band leader in the tribe. Wissler explained his function and that of his council among the Blackfeet tribes. "All the head men of the various tribes came by degrees to unanimity as to who would succeed the living chief, though the matter was rarely discussed in formal council. The main function of the tribal chief was to call councils, he having some discretion as to who would be invited.... Everything of importance was settled in council. While each band was represented there was no fixed membership; yet the head chief usually invited those in excess of one member for each band. There seems to have been no formal legislation and no provisions for voting. In former times the council was rarely convened except in summer." (Ibid., p. 25).

Flannery (1953, pp. 31-34) indicates clearly that the same political organization prevailed among the Gros Ventre.

It is important to keep this rather democratic system of government in mind in considering the official relations of these tribes with the United States government. No one man could make an important decision regarding war or peace or tribal boundaries on his own for the entire tribe. Tribal decisions were made by the head chief in consultation with the chiefs of all the bands. Band decisions were made after consultation with the other head men in the group by their principal chief.

If we keep these facts in mind, some of the statements made by Indians at counsils with representatives of the United States make far more sense than if we do not understand this basic principle of political organization in these tribes. There is evidence that the United States became increasingly cognizant of Blackfeet political democracy when in the land agreements of the 1880s and 1900s it was required that they be signed not alone by the chiefs but by the majority of the adult males of the tribe. This was not the case in the ratified treaty negotiated in 1855 or in the unratified treaties of 1865 and 1868, when chiefs and head men only signed the official documents.

It may be seriously doubted whether, in terms of the Indians' own political system, the North Blackfeet were ever a party to either a treaty or agreement with the United States. Only four, a minority of their chiefs, signed the 1855 treaty, only one signed the 1865 and 1868 treaties, none signed the land agreements of the 1880s and 1890s.

By the same token neither the North Piegan nor Blood tribes were parties to these late nineteenth century agreements. Some individual members of those tribes may have been on the Blackfeet Reservation in Montana at the time these agreements were made and may have signed them. But it is certain that neither the chiefs nor the majority of the adult male members of the Blackfeet tribes then residing on reservations in Canada (ie. the North Blackfeet, Blood, and North Piegan) signed these agreements.

The limited authority of the chiefs restricted their ability to make promises in their treaty negotiations which would be binding upon all the members of their tribes or bands. Thus, in the treaty negotiated in 1855, the Blackfeet tribes and Gros Ventre agreed to intertribal peace with neighboring tribes. Yet in the treaty proceedings Onis-tay-say-nah-que-im, head chief of the Blood tribe, expressed his fear that the chiefs could not prevent their young men from going to war. Actually the provisions of Articles 2 and 6 of this treaty were broken within two weeks of its signing when Blood war parties departed on expeditions against the Crow. (Annual Report Commissioner of Indian Affairs, 1856, p. 75).

The Factor of Seasonal Movements: Although the Blackfeet tribes and the Gros Ventre as well as neighboring tribes dwelling on the plains the year round have been properly considered nomads, we should recognize that their yearly round in buffalo days comprised alternate periods of active and passive nomadism. Factors involved in determining these seasonal movements I have discussed in considerable detail elsewhere. (Ewers, 1955, pp. 123-129). They included the need for shelter in winter, the need to band together for protection in summer when enemy raiders were most active, the requirements of the ceremonial calendar (primarily the holding of the tribal sun dance in late summer), and the need for obtaining winter food supplies in fall.

Since the Blackfeet tribes and the Gros Ventre reckoned years in terms of winters, it may be well to begin with a brief description of their winter camps. It would have been suicidal for these Indians to have remained on the open plains in the treacherous winter season of intense cold, high winds, heavy snows and blizzards. In late October or early November each band sought the shelter of a river valley where they could pitch their lodges among the trees and obtain shelter from the elements. They preferred winter camp sites where high banks afforded protection from winds, and required locations which would provide not only good drinking water but sufficient wood for their campfires and grass to pasture their horses. Not all river valleys met these requirements. Generally, it was only the valleys of the larger tributaries that did. So long as the food supply held out and the necessary timber and grass were available the band could and often did remain in that location all winter. Although the bands generally wintered separately, many of them tended to select the same river valley, the individual bands strung out along the course of that river for many miles at intervals of a few miles or less. Many of the descriptions of the locations of these tribes refer to their positions at this relatively inactive winter season. Generally the Indians spent between five and six months in their winter camps, from late October or early November to late March or early April.

When the winter camps broke up in spring the bands went their separate ways hunting buffalo, and collecting wild roots which offered variety to their limited winter diet of meat and dried vegetables. In June, when buffalo bulls were prime, the scattered hunting bands gathered to form the great tribal encampment. When they were all arrived, which might require several weeks, the tribal summer hunt was inaugurated under the leadership of the head chief of the tribe and strictly regulated by members of the military societies. In August occurred the great tribal religious festival of the sun dance, when the tribe remained in one locality for a period of 8 to 10 days or more.

At the conclusion of the sun dance the hunting bands again separated for the fall hunt, to kill buffalo, pick berries and to prepare dried meat, pemmican and dried fruits for their winter food reserve. The number of moves and the extent of travel by each band during this fall season were dependent upon the availability of buffalo. If a band found game in abundance they needed to make few moves during this period. If game was more scarce they moved much more frequently. The period of the fall hunt ended with the approach of cold weather and the making of winter camp.

It is obvious that if we had a complete record of the location of the winter camp of each band in each of the tribes occupying the area under consideration, plus the direction and movement of each band in its spring and fall hunt, plus the movement of the tribal summer hunt and the location of the tribal sun dance, for each year from about the beginning of the nineteenth century until the extermination of the buffalo in 1883, we sould have a complete and adequate history of Indian land occupancy in this region during that period. How very incomplete our data are may be shown by the fact that we do not even have accurate compilations of the names and numbers of bands in these tribes at various times during this period. Nor is there any possibility that this information can be obtained from the literature and from living Indian informants.

The yearly round of those Indians from west of the Rockies whose use of a common hunting ground south of the Musselshell River was provided for under Article 3 of the 1855 treaty differed from that of those tribes who, like the Blackfeet tribes and the Gros Ventre, spent the entire year on the plains. Taking the Flathead yearly round as the type for the Pend d'Oreille and the Kutenai as well, we find that these people subsisted upon the natural resources of the plains and the region west of the Rockies. During spring, summer and fall the women gathered vegetable foods west of the Rockies (bitter root, wild carrots, camas, berries), while men fished and hunted deer and elk in the same region. However, during the summer the men made a short hunting excursion to the plains to get buffalo hides. In the fall the entire tribe moved to the plains, where they spent the winter hunting buffalo and did not return to the west until early spring. (Turney-High, 1937, pp. 111-122). Another modern student of Flathead cultural history has stated that they left for the plains on their winter hunt in October and did not return until the approach of the gathering season in spring. (Schaeffer, 1937, p. 239). Some definite dating of the time spent on the winter hunts is available in the journal of John Owen, trader among the Flathead in the Bitterrott Valley. On March 8, 1861, he recorded "Passed the Flathead Camp Some twenty Miles below this on their way home after an absence of some Seven Months. They Wintered on the Muscle Shell...They made a fair hunt." (Owen, 1927, Vol. I. p. 234) On April 24, 1862, he wrote, "Victor and his poor ½ famished Weather beaten Village arrived after an absence of Some Nine Months in quest of Buffaloes". (Ibid., Vol. I, p. 253). So it is apparent that at that period the Flathead were accustomed to spend more than half of the year on the plains hunting buffalo.

The Factor of Intertribal Relationships: Of considerable importance to the problem of land occupancy in this region is the fact that from the time of white men's first knowledge of the Indians of this area until the year 1887 (when intertribal horse raiding ended) the region was a theatre of intertribal warfare. The Blackfeet tribes when allied with the Gros Ventre were regarded by early writers as the most warlike (the word "bloodthirsty" was repeatedly used) Indians in the region, feared by neighboring tribes and white traders alike. Documentation will be provided to show that the Blackfeet tribes acquired probably all and certainly nearly all of their lands within present Montana occupied at the time of the 1855 treaty by conquest from other tribes within the preceding period of 75 years.

For the Blackfeet tribes as a whole war with neighboring tribes was the rule, peace the exception. However, before the 1855 treaty, one large Piegan band, the Small Robes, were friendly with the Flathead, and this had an important bearing upon the joint occupancy of that area south of the Musselshell defined as a common hunting ground in that treaty.

47

As a general rule tribal boundaries were considered unimportant between tribes which were at peace. Not only were they unimportant but they were practically non-existent in the minds of the Indians. Tribes at peace with one another intermingled within the same gross area. At various periods bands of two or more of the Blackfeet tribes established their winter camps in the same river valley. At the time of the 1855 treaty the Gros Ventre and the Blackfeet tribes were allies and neither the Indians nor the Commissioners deemed it necessary to define a boundary between the Blackfeet tribes and the Gros Ventre, whereas it was important to distinguish the boundaries between these tribes and the enemies of some or all of them - the Assiniboin, Crow, and the tribes from west of the Rockies whose hunting grounds were restricted to the common hunting ground south of the Musselshell.

In the second half of the 19th century, however, conditions changed. In 1861 the Blackfeet and their old allies the Gros Ventre became enemies. The Gros Ventre had already made their peace with the Assiniboin (still enemies of the Blackfeet tribes) and shared their hunting grounds with the Upper Assiniboin. Shortly thereafter they made peace with the River Crow (still enemies of the Blackfeet tribes) and shared their lands with them also, as well as with migrant Arapaho and Cheyenne hunting bands.

In the history of Indian occupancy of this region prior to the disappearance of the buffalo (after which hunting grounds were of no significance as such) friendly tribes tended to share hunting grounds in common; while hostile tribes tended to winter some distance back from the frontier area.

It is important also to distinguish between a tribe's theatre of warfare and its area of occupancy. Throughout the period of intertribal warfare prior to 1887, Blackfeet and Gros Ventre war parties traveled great distances to make war upon their enemies both

Indian and white. They raided west across the Rockies, south to present Wyoming, and east beyond Fort Union at the mouth of the Yellowstone, and their presence in those areas was noted by whites. In the early decades of the nineteenth century American fur traders fought a number of battles with these Blackfeet and Gros Ventre warriors, some of them within the area designated as a common hunting ground in the 1855 treaty, others still farther south. Some of these battles occurred on lands of alien tribes, others on debatable ground. Occupancy, I should think, would require proof of Indian use of an area for the purpose of making a living - which in terms of the Indian cultures of this region would mean hunting buffalo and/or collecting wild plant foods.

The Factor of White Contacts: White settlement in this region, both north and south of the international boundary came late. Nevertheless, the influence of European civilization upon these Indians was felt even before their first contacts. The horse, acquired sometime between 1730 and 1750, transformed these Indians from plodding footmen into mobile warriors and hunters. Firearms, the first of which may have been acquired at even a slightly earlier date, gave their warriors a distinct advantage over those of tribes to the south and west who hadn't yet acquired them. Possessing both increased mobility and firepower the Blackfeet tribes embarked on a period of territorial expansion and conquest in the latter part of the 18th Century such

49

as they probably had never known before and certainly have not experienced since.

The fact that the fur trade first reached these Indians by way of the Saskatchewan River and that their trading posts prior to 1832, were all in the British Possessions, and primarily on the North Saskatchewan tended to hold the Blackfeet and Gros Ventre in the north during the years prior to that date. Whereas, the establishment of posts on the Missouri in 1832 and thereafter encouraged them to move southward where they could find a ready market for buffalo robes as well as peltries.

The invasion of the Blackfeet and Gros Ventre country by settlers didn't occur until the Montana gold rush of 1862. Then, until 1870, the international line served as a convenient escape hatch for Blackfeet war parties who attacked white settlers and freighters in the United States and fled north across the line. It is significant, also, that prior to 1883 white pressure for the cession of the Indians' land in Northern Montana east of the Rockies involved primarily Blackfeet lands between the Musselshell and Birch Creek, lands not occupied by the Gros Ventre.

Finally the location of the Indian Agencies established by the Government for the Blackfeet and the Gros Ventre came to have an increasingly important influence upon the locations of the Indians as they became more dependent upon the issuance of weekly rations when the buffalo became scarce, then disappeared altogether.

INDIAN OCCUPANCY OF THE MISSOURI-SASKATCHEWAN REGION IN 1650
DR. JOHN R. SWANTON'S THEORETICAL RECONSTRUCTION

No literate human being is known to have lived in or to have visited the Missouri-Saskatchewan Region three hundred years ago. Yet the problem of aboriginal occupancy of this region at that time is not just a matter for idle speculation by the ethnologist. Through weighing such factors as the known relationships of Indian languages, traditions of tribal migrations, the known location of the tribes at the time of their first recorded contacts with whites and consideration of the attractions and pressures causing tribal movements in the early historic period, it is possible for the ethnologist to suggest the probable locations of tribes within this area in 1650.

One theoretical reconstruction which attempts to portray graphically on carefully executed maps the location of tribes in this region is deserving of particular consideration because of the high reputation its compiler has enjoyed for more than a half century as a thorough and exceedingly competent student of the ethnohistory of the Indian tribes of the North American continent. I refer to the maps in Dr. John R. Swanton's *The Indian Tribes of North America*, Bulletin 145, Bureau of American Ethnology, 1952.

Maps numbered 2, 3, and 4 of this study cover the 1650 locations of tribes occupying the Missouri-Saskatchewan region at

51

that time and tribes which later were known to have lived within that area. Reference to these maps shows clearly Dr. Swanton's considered opinion that none of the three Blackfeet tribes nor the Gros Ventre lived in the valley of the Missouri and its tributaries in 1650. Rather he places all these tribes well to the north of the 49th parallel in present Canada and in the valley of the Saskatchewan River. He places the Atsina (Gros Ventre) along the South Saskatchewan just above its junction with the North Saskatchewan within the present Province of Saskatchewan. He places the three tribes of the Siksika (Blackfeet) westward of them on the North Saskatchewan and southward including the northernmost branches of the South Saskatchewan, in the present Canadian Provinces of Saskatchewan and Alberta. On the plains south of these tribes and between them and the 49th parallel he places the Kutenai; while south of the Gros Ventre, and extending into present Montana he places their close relatives the Arapaho. (See Map No. 2 Swanton, 1952).

    South of the 49th parallel, east of the Rockies in the headwaters of the Missouri he places the Salish (Flathead). Eastward of them he places the Kiowa Apache and Kiowa (tribes occupying the plains much farther south in the historic period). In the extreme northeastern portion of present Montana extending northeastward into present Canada he places the Crow Indians. (Maps No. 2 and 4. Swanton, 1952).

It is noteworthy that he places the Assiniboin, who in the nineteenth century occupied the northeastern portion of present Montana, far to the eastward in the vicinity of the Lake of the Woods. (Map No. 3. Swanton, 1952). In this he is supported by contemporary evidence, for Father Alloux in 1656 knew the Assiniboin as occupants of the region around Lake of the Woods and Lake Nipigon. (Thwaites, 1896-1901. Vol. XLIV, p. 249).

Other of Dr. Swanton's 1650 tribal locations are speculative. He recognizes that his placements of the Arapaho, Kiowa and Kiowa Apache are "extremely speculative" (Swanton, 1952, p. 9). The matter of location of the Arapaho and Gros Ventre is pertinent to our problem, whereas the exact locations of the Kiowa and Kiowa Apache in 1650 are not. To my mind the early movement of the Arapaho is one of the greater enigmas of Plains Indian history. "According to the tradition of the Arapaho they were once a sedentary, agricultural people living far to the N.E. of their more recent habitat, apparently about the Red r. valley of N. Minn." (Hodge, 1907, Vol. I, p. 72). I believe it quite possible that they did not migrate westward until after 1650 and that the Gros Ventre did not separate from them until after that date. If so it would have meant that the Gros Ventre in 1650 were part of the Arapaho living well to the eastward of present Montana.

As for Swanton's placement of the Blackfeet tribes in the valley of the Saskatchewan in 1650, I believe that is highly probable, although their westward extension as far as the Rockies is doubtful at that early period.

HISTORY OF INDIAN OCCUPANCY OF THIS REGION

I. The Canadian Period (ca. 1730-1810).

A. The Blackfeet and Gros Ventre on the Saskatchewan.

It was in the British Possessions in the valley of the Saskatchewan River that white men, in the person of fur traders from Montreal and Hudson's Bay first came to know the Blackfeet tribes and the Gros Ventre. Quite possibly French traders from Montreal were the first whites to meet these Indian. That is strongly suggested in name for Frenchmen which has survived in the language of the Blackfeet - "real (or original) white men". However, if the French did meet these Indians prior to 1754 (the year of the first recorded visit to their country), they left no recorded description of the Indians or the country in which they lived.

Nevertheless, David Thompson, an intelligent English trader, renowned as the most able geographer among the early traders on the Saskatchewan, who wintered among the Piegan in 1787, obtained from their old men a brief description of their location in the period of their greatgrandfathers and information on the direction of their subsequent movements - "their old men always point out the North East as the place they came from, and their progress has always been to the south west. Since the Traders came to the Saskatchewan River, this has been their course and progress for the distance of four hundred miles from the Eagle Hills to the Mountains near the Missouri but this rapid advance may be mostly attributed to their being armed with guns and iron weapons." (Thompson, 1916, p. 348). About the year 1730, as nearly as could be determined from the recollections of an aged Cree Indian who had lived since his young manhood among the Piegan, the Piegan, then footmen, were at war with the Shoshoni. The Shoshoni surprised their Piegan enemies with a new secret weapon - horses - on which they "dashed at the Peeagans, and with their stone Pukamoggan (war clubs) knocked them on the head". In this unequal conflict the Piegan footmen "lost several of their best men."

Unable to cope with their enemies' new mobility alone, the Piegan sent messengers to friendly Cree and Assiniboin camps asking for help. These Indians not only sent warriors, but they brought a new secret weapon - 10 guns. In a large scale battle with the Shoshoni soon thereafter the deadly "magic" of these firearms threw the Shoshoni into a panic, and they were routed. (Thompson, 1916, pp. 330-332). Following the Shoshoni retreat the Piegan advanced to the valley of the Red Deer River. (Ibid. p. 336).

Warfare with the Shoshoni continued with the Piegan, always the frontier tribe in the southwestern movement of the Blackfeet tribes bearing the brunt of conflict against them. In 1781 a devastating smallpox epidemic swept the northwestern plains. The Shoshoni suffered heavy losses from this plague, and apparently unaware that the Blackfeet had also been weakened by it, they again retreated southward, leaving all of the Bow River country in present Alberta to the Piegan. (Ibid. p. 338).

It was in the interval between the Piegan conquest of the Red Deer valley in ca. 1730, and their taking over the Bow River valley due to the retreat of the smallpox-ridden Shoshoni a half century later that the Gros Ventre and Blackfeet first met white traders.

By 1748 the French from Montreal had established trading posts on the Saskatchewan. The westernmost of these posts, Fort a la Corne, was some 15 miles east of the forks and only a few days' journey from the Blackfeet country. At that time the Cree Indians referred to the tribes living to the west of them on the plains by the general term "ayatchiyiniw", meaning "foreignor or stranger". As early as 1743 the English on Hudson Bay had learned something of these strangers from a young woman of their number who had been brought to the Bay as a slave. The lands of the strangers were described to them as ones blessed with "great plenty of the best and finest furs." (Isham, 1949, p

Alarmed by the French traders' advance toward the country of the strangers, on land granted to the Hudson's Bay Company by the English king, officials of that company sent Anthony Hendry (or Henda from York Factory southwestward to try to persuade the strangers to being their furs to trade with them on the Bay. Guided by a small group of Cree Indians, Henday left York Factory in June 1754. Hendry reached the South Saskatchewan on August 20, crossed it next day above the present town of Saskatoon. His record of distances traveled overland and both the directions and distances of his movements west of a point south of present Battleford, Saskatchewan (which he reached early in September) have been differently interpreted by scholars. We do know that on October 14 he received a firendly reception at a large camp of 200 lodges of "Archithinue Natives" (his rendering of the Cree term "strangers"). Other bands soon joined this camp and its size grew to 322 lodges. (Hendry 1907, pp. 337-340). The most recent thorough student of Hendry's travels has located this camp about 18 miles southeast of the present town of Red Deer, Alberta. (Mac Gregor, p. 147).

The white trader wintered on the plains. In the spring he started on his long trip back to the bay. On his way down the South Saskatchewan he met and visited four camps of "Archithinue" totaling 327 tents. (Hendry, pp. 350-351). The similarity in number between the lodges of the great camp met in the fall and of the four camps in spring suggest that Hendry met the same people at two seasons of the year, first when they were together in one camp, and second when they were separated into bands for hunting. His failure to identify these Indians by any tribal names leaves their identity in doubt. Dr. Burpee, who edited Hendry's journal, never seemed to have any doubt but what they were "Blackfeet". However, Clark Wissler, a leading Blackfeet scholar believed they were Gros Ventre. (Wissler, 1936, p. 5). I am inclined to agree with Wissler that this first "tribe of "strangers" wintering on the South Saskatchewan and hunting between the two branches of the Saskatchewan, which would have been met by a traveler moving westward in 1754, would probably have been the Gros Ventre rather than one of the Blackfeet tribes.

Hendry's efforts to get these Indians to bring their furs to trade at the Bay were in vain. After France relinquished her possessions in Canada to England in 1763, free traders from Montreal, whom the Hudson's Bay Company men referred to derisively as "pedlars", entered the Saskatchewan field. Alarmed at their progress, the Hudson's Bay Company again sent a man to try to get the "strangers" to bring their furs to Hudson Bay to trade at their posts.

This man, Mathew Cocking, encountered an "Archithinue" band of 28 lodges west of the Eagle Hills south of the North Saskatchewan. Cocking spent two weeks with these Indians in December 1772, while they tried to drive buffalo into a pound. He also failed in his attempt to get them to bring their furs to Hudson Bay. However, he was more observant than had been Hendry. He definitely made it clear that the Indians he met at the pound were "Water-fall Indians". Cocking for

the first time named the other tribes which the Cree identified by
the general term of "strangers" - ie. the Blood, Blackfeet, Piegan,
and Sarsi. (Cocking, 1909, P. 110-111).

There can not be the slightest doubt but what Cocking's
"Water-fall Indians" were the Gros Ventre. Edward Umfreville, who
traded in the area in 1784-88, explained the appelation "Fall Indians"
was a synonym for Gros Ventre. While the Canadian French called
these Indians "gros ventres or big bellies" the Cree and English
traders termed them "Fall Indians....from their inhabiting a country
on the Southern branch of the river (Saskatchewan), where the rapids
are frequent." (Umfreville, 1790, p. 197).

Beginning with the establishment of Buckingham House on the
North Saskatchewan River in 1780, the Blackfeet tribes and Gros Ventre
had ready access to traders' posts in their own country. The subsequent
19 years was one of frequent fort building by both the Hudson's Bay
Company and their rivals the Northwest Company. The Northwest Company
more than held their own in attracting the trade of the Blood, North
Blackfeet and Gros Ventre. But the Hudson's Bay Company held the
lion's share of the Piegan trade until their rivals built Rocky Mountain
House, high up on the North Saskatchewan in 1799.

These forts provided the Blackfeet tribes and Gros Ventre a
ready supply of arms and ammunition for use against their enemies to
the south and west who had not the advantage of firearms. In less

59

than two decades after the smallpox epidemic of 1781 they drove not only the Shoshoni, but also the Kutenai, Flathead and Pend d'Oreille from the plains to seek safety beyong the Rockies. (See sections of this report dealing with these tribes ante 1810).

Alexander Mackenzie described the location of the Blackfeet tribes, the Gros Ventre, and their allies, the small Sarsi tribe, on the Saskatchewan in 1801. However, this description, written by a high official of the Northwest Company, probably refers to their locations in 1789 or 1790.

"At the Southern headwaters of the North Branch dwells a tribe called Sarsees, consisting of about thirty-five tents, or one hundred and twenty men. Opposite to those Eastward, on the headwaters of the South Branch, are the Picaneaux (Piegan), to the number of from twelve to fifteen hundred men. Next to them, on the same water, are the Blood Indians, to the number of about fifty tents, or two hundred and fifty men. From them downwards extend the Black-Feet Indians, of the same nation as the two last tribes; their number may be eight hundred men. Next to them, and who extend to the confluence of the South and North Branch, are the Fall, or Big-bellied Indians, (Gros Ventre), who may amount to about six hundred warriors." (Mackenzie, 1801, p. lxx).

In the next decade the Gros Ventre, easternmost of these tribes were dislodged from their position between the forks of the

Saskatchewan by the westward moving, better armed and much more numerous Cree and Assiniboin. The Gros Ventre were forced to move south.

David Thompson does not define the Gros Ventre area in his description of the lands occupied by the Blackfeet tribes in ca. 1800, but he does give a good picture of the habitat of all three Blackfeet tribes at that time.

"The Peeagans, with the tribes of the Blood, and Blackfeet Indians, who all speak the same language, ...by right of conquest have their west boundary to the foot of the Rocky Mountains, southward to the north branches of the Missourie, eastward for about three hundred miles from the Mountains and northward to the upper part of the Saskatchewan. Other tribes of their allies also at times hunt on part of the above..." (Thompson, 1916, pp. 345-346).

The younger Alexander Henry, who traded with the Blackfeet tribes and the Gros Ventre at Fort Vermilion on the North Saskatchewan in 1809 described their territory at that time as follows:

"The Missourie on the S., the Rocky Mountains on the W., and the North Branch of the Saskatchewan on the N., seem to be the bounds of the foregoing numerous tribes, beyond which all are considered enemies." (Henry and Thompson, Vol. II, p. 532-533). In that year he placed the southern boundary of the land claimed by the three Blackfeet tribes ("the tract of land which they call their own") as

61

"the South Branch of the Saskatchewan". (Ibid., p. 524). Two years later, after he came to know the Piegan better in trading with them at Rocky Mountain House, Henry placed their extension southward "on Bow river, and even as far S. as the Missouri." (Ibid, 724).

The ability of these English traders, who met the Blackfeet tribes and Gros Ventre at their trading posts on the Saskatchewan to define the southern limits of these tribes may be questioned, especially when they employ no more precise terms as "S to the Missouri". What was meant by that? Was it the main stream of the Missouri, or only its northernmost tributaries?

The late Dr. Clark Wissler, a thorough student of the Blackfeet tribes, carefully reviewed the evidence (with the exception of David Thompson's important data which had not been published at the time of Wissler's study) and concluded regarding the southern boundary of the Piegan, southernmost of the three Blackfeet tribes - "All the evidence at hand implies its approximate position before 1800 to have been near the Two Medicine River and eastward, or just below the United States boundary." (Wissler, 1910, p. 12). He concluded that at that time the Gros Ventre territory touched that of the Piegan on the south and east. (Ibid, 1910, p. 12). Wissler believed that the fact that there were no opportunities to trade in the United States at that time "would of itself account for the tendency on the part of these tribes to camp on the Saskatchewan near the posts of Henry." (Ibid., p.

D. D. Mitchell who traded with the Blackfeet on the Missouri in 1833, and for a period of seven years thereafter stated, "From all I could learn, the Blackfeet originally inhabited that region of country watered by the Saskatchewan and its tributaries, never extending their hunting or war parties farther south than the headwaters of the Milk River, a tributary of the Missouri." (Schoolcraft, Vol. V, p. 685).

B. The Shoshoni in Present Montana and Alberta ante 1810: The earliest contemporary evidence that the Shoshoni (or Snake) Indians were on the northwestern plains at no great distance from the Gros Ventre and Blackfeet tribes appears in Mathew Cocking's journal of his trip to the South Saskatchewan in 1772. Under the date of August 24, he mentioned that the Indians who accompanied him saw several horses. "They are all in general afraid, supposing the horses to belong to the Snake Indians with whom they are always at variance." (Cocking, 1908, p. 103). They saw a strange horse again on September 16, and "supposed it to belong to the Snake, their enemies." (Ibid., p. 106). Again Cocking stated that his companions "Showed me a Coat without sleeves six fold leather quilted, used by the Snake tribe to defend them against the arrows of their adversaries. (Ibid., p. 110). And while with the camp Gros Ventre, "three natives of the same tribe" brought word that their people were going to war against the Snake Indians. (Ibid., p. 112).

Although Cocking did not attempt to locate the Shoshoni enemies at that time his remarks certainly indicate that their war parties were not unexpected on the South Saskatchewan in the early '70s. David Thompson was much more specific in his accounts of the progressive advance of the Piegan and withdrawal of the Shoshoni from the Saskatchewan valley after they were weakened by the smallpox plague of 1781 (Thompson, 1916, pp. 336-339). The Shoshoni withdrawal southward must have been rapid thereafter, for when Thompson was among the Piegan in 1787 he accompanied a hunting camp "southward to about eighty miles beyond Bow River" (which may have taken them well south of the 49th parallel). From thence a war party was sent to examine the country for a few days journey south to find out where their enemy the Shoshoni were. They did not encounter a Shoshoni camp for six days. (Thompson, 1916, pp. 341-342). Thus it is possible that the Shoshoni may have retreated as far as the main stream of the Missouri by 1787.

64

The next we hear of them from contemporary sources, these Indians had taken refuge west of the Rockies. When Lewis and Clark met them in 1805 they found: "The Shoshonees with whom we now are amount to about 100 warriors, and three times that number of women and children. Within their own recollection they formerly lived in the plains, but they have been driven into the mountains by the Pawkees (Gros Ventre and/or Blackfeet), or the roving Indians of the

Sasskatchawain, and are now obliged to visit, occasionally and by stealth the country of their ancestors. Their lives are indeed migratory. From the middle of May to the beginning of September they reside on the waters of the Columbia, where they consider themselves perfectly secure from the Pawkees who have never yet found their way to that retreat. During this time they subsist chiefly on salmon and as that fish disappears on the approach of autumn, they are oblied to seek subsistence elsewhere. They then cross the ridge to the waters of the Missouri, down which they proceed slowly and cautiously, till they are joined near the Three Forks by other bands, either of their own nation or of the Flatheads, with whom they associate against the common enemy. Being now strong in numbers, they venture to hunt buffalo in the plains, eastward of the mountains, near which they spend the winter, till the return of the salmon invites them to the Columbia. But sich is their terror of the Pawkees, that as long as they can obtain the scantiest subsistence they do not leave the interior of the mountains; and as soon as they obtain a large stock of dry meat, they again retreat, thus alternately obtaining their food at the hazard of their lives, and hiding themselves to consume it. In this loose and wandering existence they suffer the extremes of want; for two-thirds of the year they are forced to live in the mountains, passing whole weeks without meat, and with nothing to eat but a few fish and roots." (Lewis and Clark, Coues edition, Vol. II, p. 554-5).

In the summer of 1805, the French trader Francois Larocque, while among the Crow Indians (whom he termed "the Rocky Mountain Indians") referred to the Snakes (Shoshoni) living westward of the Crow, who were south of the Yellowstone in present southeastern Montana. Larocque noted, "One of their tribes has been destroyed and the remainder being about 12 tents live with the Rocky Mountain Indians who are at peace with the whole nation... They call themselves Shoshone that tribe that I saw at the Rocky Mountains" (Larocque, 1910, p. 73).

Whether this was indeed a tribe or merely a band of the Shoshoni is questionable. At any rate it was a Shoshoni remnant of a larger group that had been greatly reduced either as a result of the smallpox epidemic of 1781, or enemy action or both, and had taken refuge among friendly Crow Indians. Probably it became absorbed in the Crow tribe and lost its Shoshoni identity.

Memory and traditions of the Shoshoni occupancy of the plains east of the Rockies on land later claimed by the Blackfeet tribes and the Gros Ventre survived long after they were driven from the plains by the aggressive Blackfeet and Gros Ventre. In 1822, Jedidiah Morse reported that the fur trader, Ramsey Crooks had told him that the "Shoshonee or Snake Indians ...." formerly occupied the fine Buffalo country north of the Missouri, along the Rocky Mountains. But the Blackfeet Indians, about 10,000 souls, living east of the Shoshonees, on the waters of Assiniboin river, meeting with the British fur traders, obtained of them firearms. With these they attacked the Shoshonees, who having no other weapons of defense than bows and arrows, were driven into, and even across, the Rocky Mountains." (Morse, 1822, pp. 34-35). In the 1870s Lieut. James Bradley, pioneer Montana historian, obtained information on the history of the Blackfeet from Major Alexander Culbertson, who had known these Indians as a fur trader since 1834. "At the time Maj. Culbertson came to the country these bands still had traditions of having driven the Shoshonees and Crows from much of this country, the former tribe having formerly ranged as far eastward as the Bear Paw Mountains." (Bradley, Original Manuscript, Book A. p. 180).

In 1854, James Doty, in endeavoring to find out about the history of the Blackfeet in the field, wrote .. "from the best information obtained, it would appear that they originally lived in the region of country about the mouth of Saskatchewan River that being driven South by the Crees and Assiniboines of the north they came to the Missouri at the Great Falls. All this country was then occupied by the Snake Indians, and on these the Blackfeet at once commenced a war of extermination. The Blackfeet having guns which they obtained from the Hudson Bay Company possessed greatly the advantage over the Snakes, who were armed only with Bows and Arrows and soon drove them to the mountains. The great body of the Snakes then passed south to the headwaters of the Great Snake River, and when Lewis and Clark passed through their region in 1805 but a few Lodges of the Snakes remained in the mountains bounding the country of their ancestors. These soon disappeared and for Fifty Years the Blackfeet have held undisputed possession of the country." (James Doty to Isaac I. Stevens, Dec. 20, 1854, Indian Office Records, The National Archives). Isaac I. Stevens, while en route westward from Fort Benton to the Rockies on Sun River wrote Sept. 22, 1853, "This whole country was once occupied by the Snakes, and, in later times, by some of the tribes of the Flathead nation." (Stevens, in Pacific. R.R. Reports. Vol. XII. Book I, p. 118).

Ethnologists, working with the Blackfeet, Gros Ventre and tribes west of the Rockies within the present century have found traditions of former Shoshoni occupancy were still recalled by their elderly Indian informants. Wissler found that in the first decade of the present century, "The Piegan have definite consistent traditions that the Snake formerly occupied all the streams flowing toward the Missouri, that they were eventually driven out and their people did not make definite movements toward the Missouri until horses became numerous among them." (Wissler, 1910, pp. 11-12). At a somewhat later date Curtis, working with Blackfeet informants found, "The migration of the Blackfoot confederacy was southward. On Old Man River they encountered Pitsikinai-tapiw, Snake People, the Shoshoni. Piegan, Blackfeet, Bloods and Sarsi were allies in the wars that followed, and the Shoshoni were driven out of the country. This was before the horse era, and the principal weapon was a flint-pointed spear. The Shoshoni at Blackfoot, Idaho, visited by the informant's brother a few years ago, told him that they have the same tradition." (Curtis, 1928, p. 177).

In the early forties I questioned two elderly Indians on the Blackfeet Reservation regarding this matter. In the course of our discussion of the Snake Indians as enemies of the Blackfeet tribes, on Sept. 15, 1942, Weasel Tail, an 84 year old Blood Indian, who proved to be my best informant on the cultrual history of his people said. "This was their land - right here. We drove them out back in the days when we had guns but they didn't. We also had horses. We sure made them run." On January 27, 1943, Richard Sanderville, mixed-blood Piegan, for many years official interpreter for the Blackfeet Reservation in Montana told me that the Shoshoni, he had been told, occupied this region before the Blackfeet had guns. He believed this reservation was about as far north as the Shoshoni lived.

Dr. Regina Flannery, who worked among the Gros Ventre in the 1940s, has reported "the very definite tradition current among the Gros Ventres today that they had to drive the Snake from the territory which they occupied." (Flannery, 1953. p. 6).

James Teit, working with elderly Flathead and Kutenai informants prior to 1910, recorded their traditional information to the effect that the Shoshoni formerly occupied the plains east of the Rockies in present Montana both north and south of the Missouri.

He placed their northern boundary at the Sweetgrass Hills at the 49th parallel stating, "It is not known how long the Shoshoni had been in possession of their country between the Missouri and the Sweet Grass Hills before the advent of the horse, but they are thought to have been there a long time." (Teit, 1930, p. 321). The map prepared by Franz Boas on the basis of Teit's field data which was published in the 41st Annual Report of the Bureau of American Ethnology, entitled "Distribution of Salish Dialects, and of Languages Spoken in the Adjoining Territory, before 1800", places the Shoshoni on the plains east of the Rockies in the Missouri River valley extending northward to Milk River, which forms the boundary between the Shoshoni and the Blackfoot and Gros Ventres to the north.

It is noteworthy also that Peter Pond's map of 1785 (previously referred to) places the Snake Indians on the plains east of the Rockies and northeast of the southern headwaters of the Missouri River. (Innis, 1930, Map).

The evidence of Shoshoni occupancy of a large portion of the area defined as the territory of The Blackfoot Nation in the treaty of 1855, prior to 1800 is based on both contemporary and persistent traditional data. This evidence appears to me to be both abundant and conclusive.

C. <u>The Flathead East of Rockies ante 1810</u>: The pattern of Flathead occupancy of the plains eastward of the Rockies prior to 1810 appears to have been similar to that of the Shoshoni.

David Thompson (who knew both the Blackfeet and the Flathead prior to that date) said that the Saleesh (Flathead) formerly occupied the plains south of the Kutenai and North of the Shoshoni and were driven across the mountains in the aggressive southward push of the Blackfeet. (Thompson, 1916, p. 327-328). In 1833, the fur trader W. A. Ferris, was told by Faro an intelligent Flathead Indian, of this retreat across the mountains "a great many snows ago".. "when I was a child". The Blackfeet, armed with guns, were making life miserable for the Flathead on the plains, and killing many of their warriors, until the Flathead chief, Big Foot, assembled his warriors in council to discuss the situation, and decided to retreat to the mountains to avoid their destroyers. (Ferris, 1940, pp. 91-92). Lewis and Clark met the Flathead in Ross' Hole in the valley of Ross' Fork of Clark's River west of the Rockies on Sept. 4, 1805. They found the tribe then en route to hunt buffalo on the plains. On September 6 the Flathead (whom Lewis and Clark termed the Ootlashoots) set out "to join the different bands who were collecting at the Three Forks of the Missouri". (Lewis and Clark, Coues edition, Vol. II, pp. 581-584). Sergeant Ordway of the expedition also reported that these Indians were "on their way to the Meddison River or Missouri whire they can kill pleanty of buffalow" and that when the expedition parted from them on Sept. 6, the Indians "Struck their Lodges in order to set out for the Missourie". (Ordway, 1916, pp. 281-2).

71

In Lewis and Clark's statistical estimate they described these Ootlashoot (Flathead) as "33 lodges, 400 persons, reside in spring and summer in the Rocky Mountains on Clark's river, in winter and fall on the Missouri and its waters." (Lewis and Clark, Coues edition, Vol. III, p. 1246). Lewis and Clark's account of Shoshoni movements at that time (quoted above) indicates that the Flathead joined them on the plains for their mutual protection against the Blackfeet.

A contemporary of Lewis and Clark, Francois Larocque, while among the Crow in the summer of 1805, was told of the Flathead, who then traded with the Crow, "They come every fall to the fort of the Missouri or thereabout to kill Buffaloes of which there are none across that range of mountains, dress robes, dry meat with which they returned as soon as the Winter set in. (Larocque, 1910, p. 71).

In the fall of 1809, David Thompson crossed the Rockies and traded with the Flathead. For the first time they were able to obtain firearms and ammunition such as the Blackfeet had had for many years. (Thompson, 1916, p. 411). Next summer, armed with guns, the Flathead crossed the Rockies to hunt buffalo, met and defeated a large Piegan war party. (Thompson, 1916, pp. 423-425; Henry and Thompson, 1897, Vol. II, pp. 712-713). As a result of this defeat the Piegan sought to make peace with the Flathead and asked Thompson for his advice in the matter. He advised "Let your answer be that you claim by ancient rights the freedom of hunting the Bison, that you will not make war on any of them but shall always be ready to defend yourselves." (Thompson, 1916, p. 550).

Ross Cox, a trader who knew the Flathead well, referred to this ancient Flathead claim to land east of the Rockies in 1813, "The Black-feet lay claim to all that part of the country immediately at the foot of the mountains, which is most frequented by the buffalo; and allege that the Flat-heads, by resorting thither to hunt, are intruders whom they are bound to oppose on all occasions. The latter, on the contrary, assert that their forefathers had always claimed and exercised the right of hunting on these 'debateable lands'; and that while one of their warriors remained alive the right should not be relinquished." (Cox, 1832, p. 121). Cox tried to induce them to abandon their dangerous expeditions to the plains. He argued that their lands west of the mountains were well supplied with smaller game which could support them. But "they replied, that their fathers had always hunted n the buffalo grounds; that they were accustomed to do the same thing from their infancy; and they would not now abandon a practice which had existed for several generations among their people." (Ibid., p. 122).

Teit's traditional evidence from elderly Flathead informants was to the effect that aboriginally (ante 1800) the Flathead lived entirely east of the Continental Divide, near the mountains in winter and ranging eastward in summer. Their territory included "practically all of present counties of Deerlodge, Silver Bow, Beaverhead, Madison, Gallatin, Jefferson and Broadwater, and parts of Park, Meagher, and Lewis and Clark". (Teit, 1930, pp. 303-304). The map in B.A.E. 41st Annual Report, based on Teit's data shows the Flathead and Plains Salish occupying the plains and southern headwaters of the Missouri east of the Rockies.

Wissler found definite and consistent traditions among the Piegan to the effect that "before the white man dominated their country" the Flathead occupied the Sun River country. (Wissler, 1910, p. 17).

D. <u>The Pend d'Oreille East of the Rockies before 1810</u>: At the treaty negotiations of 1855 with The Blackfoot Nation, Alexander, Head Chief of the Upper Pend d'Oreille, vigorously championed the right of his people to hunt on the plains north of the common-hunting ground, within the area described by the Commissioners as reserved for the Blackfeet. He based his argument upon the traditional use of this northern area by his people, saying, "A long time ago our people, our ancestors belonged in this country. The country around the Three Buttes. We had many people on this side of the mountains...A long time ago our people used to hunt about the Three Buttes and the Blackfeet lived far north. When my Father was living he told me that was an old road for our people." (Partoll, 1937, p. 7). The proceedings of the council do not indicate that any of the chiefs of The Blackfoot Nation questioned Alexander's statement.

In 1811, David Thompson obtained information from an aged Kalispell (Pend d'Oreille) Indian telling of his people's flight to the mountains to escape the aggressive Piegan, and of his happiness that the acquisition of firearms by the Pend d'Oreille (since 1809) had made it possible for his people to "have regained much of our country, hunt the Bisons for food and clothing, and have good leather tents." (Thompson, 1916, p. 463).

In that same year Alexander Henry stated that the Kullyspell (Pend d'Oreille) were abundantly provided with horses and "frequently accompany the Saleeish to the plains to procure buffalo meat. (Henry and Thompson, 1897, Vol. II, p. 711).

E. The Kutenai on the Montana and Alberta Plains ante 1810:

David Thompson also mentioned the Kutenai as one of the tribes driven across the mountains by the aggressive Blackfeet in the latter part of the eighteenth century. They were formerly in full possession of the plains north of the Salish peoples. (Thompson, 1916, pp. 327-328). In 1811, Alexander Henry noted that empty Kutenai lodges were still standing near Rocky Mountain House, mute reminders of that tribe's former occupancy of the area. (Henry and Thompson, 1897, II, 707).

Wissler's Piegan informants possessed a tradition that the Kutenai formerly lived in the vicinity of the present Blood Reserve in Alberta. (Wissler, 1910, p. 17).

Teit's informants west of the Rockies told him of the former Kutenai occupancy of the plains as far eastward as the Sweetgrass Hills, including the area of the present Blackfeet Reservation in Montana as well as the Blood Reserve in Canada. They claimed that the main seat of the tribe was near present Browning, Montana, and that the old tipi circles and fireplaces found on the Blackfeet Reservation were the former camp sites of the Kutenai Tunaxe. (Teit, 1930, pp. 307, 311). Boas' map interpreting Teit's data shows the Plains Kutenai south and west of the Blackfeet on the plains of present Alberta and Montana. (Map in 41st Annual Report, BAE).

Dr. Turney-High (1941, p. 10), the most recent student of the Kutenai, has stated that "the best information boils down to not only an eastern provenience for the Kutenai but even a trans-Rocky mountain one." He believed that the term tunaxa referred to an extinct social group, a part of the Kutenai who lived on the plains, who were reduced to a small remnant by an epidemic, and that the remaining members took refuge among the other Kutenai, the Pend d'Oreille and Flathead. (Ibid., pp. 11-14). Perhaps they were decimated by the smallpox plague of 1781, as were the Shoshoni remnant who were met among the Crow by Larocque in 1805.

F. The Crow in Northern Montana ante 1810: Although there are no contemporary references to the location of the Crow Indians in present Montana north of the Missouri in the late eighteenth century, the Blackfeet have had rather persistent traditions of driving the Crow south at the same time they drove the Shoshoni southwestward. Curtis (1928, p. 177) was told that at the time the Shoshoni were on the northern plains "The Crows then ranged along Milk River. The Blackfoot confederacy drove them south." Yet when the Crow country was first described by a white trader who traveled with them, in 1805, they were living south of the Yellowstone. While at the Crow camp on an island in the Yellowstone River a few miles east of present Billings, Montana, September 14, 1805, Larocque recorded the earliest known definition of Crow territory. "They told me that in winter they were always to be found at a Park by the foot of the Mountain a few miles from this or thereabouts. In spring and fall they are upon this River and in summer upon the Tongue and Horses River." (Larocque, 1910, p. 45). "Horses River" is present Pryor Creek.

G. Assiniboin Movement Westward into this Region ante 1810: According to tradition the Assiniboin separated from the Yanktonai Sioux, probably in the region around the headwaters of the Mississippi River before 1640. They were recognized by the Jesuits as a distinct tribe as early as 1640, and were living in the vicinity of Lake Nipigon or Rainy Lake in 1658. (Hodge, 1907, Pt. I, p. 102). In September 1679, the French explorer, Duluth, met the "Assenipoulaks" at "the extremity of Lake Superior" and arranged a peace between them and the Sioux in the hope of diverting their trade from the newly established English posts of the Hudson's Bay Company on Hudson Bay. (Kellogg, 1917, pp. 330-331). However, the French were unsuccessful in their competition with the English. In 1700 the French trader, Le Sueur, explained the influence of this trade upon the Assiniboin alliance with the Cree in opposition to their old Sioux allies. "The Assinipoils speak the Scioux language, and are really of that nation; and it is only within a few years that they have been at enmity with that people. The origin of that war was this: The Christinaux (Cree) having obtained the use of firearms before the Scioux did, by means of the English of Hudson's Bay, continually waged war against the Assinipoils, who were their nearest neighbors. The latter finding themselves weak asked for peace; and to render it more firm, allied themselves to the Christinaux, taking their women to wife." (Le Sueur, 1902, p. 190).

The Assiniboin-Cree alliance was a long and profitable one during which the Assiniboin moved northward and westward. In 1729 the French trader, La Verendrye, noted that the Assiniboin were living in the buffalo country west of Winnipeg River. (La Verendrye, pp. 59-60).

Eight years later an Assiniboin chief, whom he met at the mouth of the Assiniboin River told him that location was "their own proper territory". (Ibid., p. 251). As early as 1734 La Verendrye learned that the Assiniboin were making excursions southward to the villages of the horticultural Mandan on the Missouri (in present North Dakota) to trade for corn. (Ibid. 153), and in the winter of 1738-39 he accompanied them on one of these trading expeditions. (Ibid., pp. 318 ff.). In 1754 Anthony Hendry located the Eagle Indians, an Assiniboin band as far west as the present Province of Saskatchewan. (Hendry, 1907, p. 351).

The allied Cree and Assiniboin continued to move westward spreading out over the plains and putting pressure upon the eastern flank of the Gros Ventre and Blackfeet. In February 1776 an Assiniboin chief described the territory occupied by his tribe to the English trader, Alexander Henry the elder. "With regard to the country of Osinipoilles, he said, that it lay between the head of the Pasquayah, or Saskatchiwaine, and the country of the Sioux, or Nadowessies, who inhabit the heads of the Missisipi. On the west, near the mountains, were the Snake Indians and Black-feet, troublesome neighbors, by whose hands numbers of his warriors fell." (Henry, 1809, pp. 297-298).

In 1794 Assiniboin bands were trading at Fort George on the North Saskatchewan River above the mouth of Moose Creek, within the present Province of Alberta. This was the same post at which the

three Blackfeet tribes and the Gros Ventre then traded.
(M'Gillivray, 1929, p. 30-31).

Meanwhile the Assiniboin continued to expand their territory to the southwest. In 1808, Alexander Henry the Younger, who had known the Assiniboin well as a fur trader of the North West Country for several years, defined their territory thus:

"Their lands may be said to commence at the Hair Hills, near Red river, thence running W. along the Assiniboine, from that to the junction of the North and South branches of the Saskatchewan, and up the former branch to Fort Vermilion; then due south to Battle River, then S.E. to the Missourie, down that river nearly to the Mandane villages, and finally N.E. to the Hair hills again. All this space of open country may be called the lands of the Assiniboines." (Henry and Thompson, Vol. II, p. 516).

Actually Henry's knowledge of the range of the Assiniboin south of the 49th parallel was more precise and exact than was his information regarding the southern range of the Blackfeet. He had been south to the Mandan villages himself in 1806. His testimony regarding Assiniboin on the Missouri was corroborated by that of the American explorers, Lewis and Clark, as indicated in the following section of this report.

II. The Lewis and Clark Interlude (1805-1806).

While they were in winter quarters at the Mandan villages below the mouth of Knife River in present North Dakota during the winter of 1804-1805, the two leaders of the Lewis and Clark expedition questioned fur traders and Indians regarding the Indian tribes they might encounter on their overland route westward, up the Missouri toward the Pacific Ocean.

Of the tribes they might encounter on the Missouri and east of the Rockies they found information most available on those Indians who lived nearest to the Mandan, and less precise on the tribes living at a greater distance from them. The Assiniboin, traded with the Mandan and Hidatsa for corn and were known to the traders as well as the Indians in the vicinity of their winter quarters. However, the Gros Ventre and Blackfeet did not trade there, were not known to the white traders in the vicinity from any personal contacts, and were known to the Indians only as enemies.

As early as November 1804 the American explorers met an Assiniboin chief of "one of 3 bands of Assiniboins who rove between the Missouri & Assiniboin river." (Lewis and Clark, Thwaites, Ed. Vol. I, p. 104). In their brief summaries of the various tribes, compiled on the basis of their winter's research, Lewis and Clark listed these three bands as follows:

Canoe Band - "rove on the Mouse River and the branches of River Assinaboin North of the Mandans, those people do not cultivate the ground".

Girl's Band - "Rove on the heads of Mouse river and River Capell (or that Calls) and on a N. West Branch of the Missouri called White earth River."

Big Devils Band - "rove on the plains in Different parties between the Missouris and the Saskatchewan rivers above the Yallow Stone River & heads of the Ossiniboins River." (Ibid., Vol. I, pp. 104-105).

They noted of these Assiniboin bands - "These bands are entirely independent of each other, although they claim a national affinity and never make war on each other." (Ibid., Vol. I, p. 105).

The above description places only one of these three Assiniboin bands, the Big Devils, definitely within the boundaries of the present State of Montana. (Royce Area 565).

The Lewis and Clark summaries referred to the Gros Ventre under the name of Fall Indians, who "rove between the Missouries and Askaw or Bad River a fork of the Saskatchewan, a tribe of Menetaries but little known, they rove as far as the Rock (Rocky) mountains." (Ibid., Vol. I, p. 106).

They were even less certain of the location of the Blackfeet. "Blackfots rove near the Rock mountains on the East Side on the waters of the Missouries. but little known. Those nations (including Flat heads) being little known, the information is from the Menetarres." (Ibid., Vol. I, p. 111).

On their journey up the Missouri to the Rockies the following spring, Lewis and Clark were fearful of meeting the agressive and hostile "Minnetaress of Fort de Prairie" (Gros Ventre). Yet on their way up the Missouri they did not encounter a single Indian, although they found a number of deserted lodges and encampments along the banks of the Missouri. Their numerous references to Indian lodges of sticks and bark seen in timbered localities along the Missouri between the mouth of the Musselshell River to the Great Falls, were not references to tipis, the everyday homes of Indians, but to specialized structures known as "war lodges", built as temporary shelters by war parties. These lodges were used by all of the northwestern plains tribes. They were not distinctive of any tribe. It isn't possible to determine which tribe or tribes built the ones seen by Lewis and Clark. (Ewers, 1944, pp. 182 ff).

However, the explorers did find the remains of at least four encampments which, from their descriptions, sound like they must have been the camps of hunting bands rather than of war parties. On May 29, just above the mouth of the Judith Lewis saw the "fires of 126 Indian lodges which appeared to be of very recent date perhaps 12 or 15 days. Capt. Clark also saw a large encampment just above the entrance of this river on the Star[d] side of reather older date, probably they were the same Indians." (Lewis and Clark, Thwaites Ed., Vol. II, p. 92).

83

Sacagawea examined some moccasins found in the first camp, found them to be of neither Hidatsa nor Shoshoni pattern, and believed them to belong to Indians from the north.

Next day Lewis reported that "we passed several old encampments of Indians, from the apparent dates of which we conceived that they were the several encampments of about 100 lodges who were progressing slowly up the river; the most recent appeared to have been evacuated about 5 weeks since; these we supposed to be the Minetarees or black foot Indians who inhabit the country watered by the Suskashawan and who resort to the establishment of Fort de Prarie. No part of the Missouri from the Minetarees to this place furnishes a permanent residence for any nation yet there is no part of it but what exhibits appearances of being occasionally visited by some nation on hunting excursions. The Minnetarees of the Missoury we know extend their excursions on the S. side as high as the Yellowstone river; the Assiniboins still higher on the N. side most probably as high as about Porcupine river, and from thence upwards most probably as far as the mountains by the Minetares of Fort de Prarie and the Black Foot Indians who inhabit the S. Fork of the Saskatchewan." (Ibid., Vol. 2, p. 98).

84

Farther up the Missouri west of White Bear Island, near the Great Falls of the Missouri, on July 13, Lewis saw the frame of a very large lodge of cottonwood poles, each about 50 feet long, and "about the place the marks of about 80 leather lodges". (Ibid., Vol. 2, p. 227). And on July 16, near the mouth of the Dearborn River, Clark saw a very similar large lodge, 60 feet in diameter, which "appeared to have been built last fall; there were the remains of about 80 leather lodges near the place of the same apparent date." (Ibid., Vol. 2, p. 241). The explorers did not attempt to name the tribe or tribes which might have constructed these lodges, although Lewis seemed certain that they were not dwellings but were used for council lodges or ceremonial ones. (Ibid., Vol. 2, p. 227). To me these huge tipis appear to answer the general description of the Blackfeet sun dance lodge of the earliest known form. However, the Crow Indians also used this type of sun dance structure and it is possible that other tribes may have used a large ceremonial structure of this type at that time. The structure was not distinctive of the Blackfeet alone.

On their return from the Pacific in 1806, the Lewis and Clark party divided into two groups for further exploration of the plains in present Montana. Clark led one party down the Yellowstone. Lewis, with nine men followed a more northerly course down the Missouri. In mid-July Captain Lewis with 3 enlisted men left the rest of his party on the Missouri and headed northward to try to determine the sources of the Marias river which he believed marked the northwestern boundary of the Louisiana Purchase and hence the northwestern limit of the United States at that time.

On the Teton River they saw signs of freshly killed buffalo, but no Indians. They continued northward to Cut Bank Creek, northern tributary of the Marias. There Lewis tried to take observations, but with little success due to cloudy and rainy weather. By July 25, he was convinced that the sources of the Marias were to the westward rather than farther north. Fearing further delay would unnecessarily slow the eastward progress of his party, he turned south. Besides, two of his men returned with the disturbing news that they had seen a great number of Indian camp sites near the forks of the Marias which appeared to have been occupied scarcely six weeks before. Lewis frankly recorded in his journal: "We consider ourselves extremely fortunate not having met with these people." (Lewis and Clark, Thwaites Ed., Vol. V, p. 216).

But their luck was too good to last. Next day while about four miles east of the forks of Two Medicine River and Badger Creek, on the present Blackfeet Reservation, they met a party of eight Indians, and Lewis felt obliged to spend the night with them. That evening, through signs, Lewis and the Indians exchanged diplomatic misinformation. Lewis told the Indians he had come in search of them to get them to make peace with their neighbors and to engage in trade with the Americans (which he had not) and the Indians readily assented to Lewis' apparent insistence that they were Gros Ventre (which they were not). They claimed there were three chiefs among them (which was very unlikely) and that they desired to make peace with the Flathead (also improbable). Early next morning the Indians tried to steal the soldiers' guns, provoking a skirmish in which one of the Indians was killed and another wounded. After the Indians rode away, leaving their dead comrade on the field, Lewis' little party beat a hasty retreat southward, fearing their late adversaries might soon return with reinforcements. Next day they met the rest of their little party at the mouth of the Marias, took to their boats and paddled downstream toward civilization. They were lucky to meet no more Indians on their way down the Missouri to the mouth of the Yellowstone. (Ibid. 218-228).

87

Of the many noteworthy accomplishments of the Lewis and Clark expedition their identification of the Indian occupants of the area north of the Missouri was not one. There can be little doubt that the only Indians they met in this region, the eight with whom they fought on the upper Marias, were Piegan not Gros Ventre. Not only did David Thompson, their Canadian contemporary learn as much (Thompson, 1916, p. 375), but Alexander Culbertson, who knew the Piegan well as an American trader after 1833, was told of the killing of one of their number by Clark's party by the Piegan.

(Bradley, Vol. 8, 1917, p. 135). Later George Bird Grinnell obtained an account of the skirmish from an aged Piegan who claimed to have been a member of the Indian party. (Wheeler, Vol. II, pp. 311-312). Wissler obtained Piegan accounts of it in the first decade of the present century. He concluded: "We feel sure that anyone who has heard the detailed narratives of the Piegan, giving the names of the killed and injured, as handed down to the present generation and in turn compares them with the account of Lewis, will at once agree that the Gros Ventre had no part in the fight." (Wissler, 1910, p. 11).

It is apparent that Lewis expected the Indians he might encounter on the upper Marias would be Gros Ventre. He therefore had an exaggerated opinion of the territory occupied by the Gros Ventre at that time as compared with the territory of the more numerous Blackfeet tribes.

The two encampments with large ceremonial lodges seen by Lewis and Clark on the Missouri in the summer of 1805, may have been Blackfeet, but we cannot be certain of the identification. If they were Blackfeet it would be proof that these Indians did occupy land as far south as the main Missouri at that time, and not just as far south as the upper tributaries of the Marias as Wissler believed.

The remains of encampments Lewis and Clark found farther east on the Missouri in late May 1805, most probably were Gros Ventre as Lewis believed them to be. There is good evidence that the Gros Ventre were still farther south in September of that same year.

Francois Larocque, while among the Crow Indians south of the Yellowstone at that time, mentioned visits by Big Bellys of Fort de Prairie to the Crow seeking to trade for horses with their Crow enemies. Larocque wrote that "The B.B. are encamped on the large Horn River (Big Horn River)...and are come on peaceable terms. They are 275 or 300 Lodges". (Larocque, 1910, p. 44). In questioning them this trader learned that they had traded with John Mc Donald of Garth at the mouth of Red Deer River on the South Saskatchewan the previous winter. (Ibid., p. 44).

    This evidence of a very wide range for the Gros Ventre in the year 1805 - from the Red Deer River in present Alberta to below the Yellowstone in present southeastern Montana surely defines an area considerably larger than the normal habitat of the Gros Ventre. The fact that they wanted to trade for horses from the Crow probably induced the Gros Ventre to visit far to the south of the area in which they were accustomed to hunt buffalo and make a living - their area of occupancy at the time. It appears to me entirely probable that their area of occupancy did extend as far south as the main stem of the Missouri in 1805, as Meriwether Lewis believed.

    Lewis' placement of the Assiniboin range in present northeastern Montana, north of the Missouri as far west as Porcupine Creek near the mouth of Milk River, appears to me to be reasonable in the light of the fact that the traders, with whom Lewis and Clark had consulted the previous winter had first hand knowledge of the Assiniboin.

III. Period of American Fur Trade on the Missouri. (1806-1850).

David Thompson, on the Saskatchewan, profited by Lewis' skirmish with the Piegan. He wrote, "The murder of two Peeagan Indians by Captain Lewis of the U.S. drew the Peeagans to the Missouri to avenge their deaths; and thus gave me an opportunity to cross the mountains by the defiles of the Saskatchewan River which led to the headwaters of the Columbia River." (Thompson, 1916, p. 375).

In the next few years, while Thompson was arming the tribes west of the Rockies and enabling them to reassert more strongly their right to hunt buffalo on the plains east of the Rockies, the vengeful Piegan and their allies were making life miserable for the American trappers who began to try to exploit the rich beaver country around the headwaters of the Missouri.

For a quarter of a century after Lewis' little scrap with the Piegan, "Blackfeet" war parties hounded the American trappers who approached the country around the Three Forks via the Yellowstone River and the country of friendly Crow Indians, enemies of the Blackfeet and Gros Ventre. Twice, in 1811 and again in 1821, the "Blackfeet" drove the trappers out of this country. The details of these conflicts are not important to the problem of Indian land occupancy in this region. (They can be found in Hiram M. Chittenden's The American Fur Trade of the Far West, Two Vols. New York, 1935).

More important is the fact that the American trappers of the period prior to 1831, knew the Blackfeet and Gros Ventre only as enemies. They never became well enough acquainted with them to be able to identify them by tribe. To them all these Indian raiders, whether Piegan, Blood or Gros Ventre were simply "Blackfeet". So there is doubt as to which tribes were actually involved in most of these fights with the trappers. In the winter of 1810-11 Alexander Henry, at Rocky Mountain House on the Saskatchewan learned of both Blood and Gros Ventre attacks on the Americans in preceding months because they brought their booty to Rocky Mountain House. (Henry and Thompson, Vol. II, pp. 735-736).

The Americans of the period were trappers who exploited the fur resources of the Indian lands. They were not Indian traders. Throughout this period the Blackfeet tribes and the Gros Ventre continued to trade with the whites on the Saskatchewan. And it is possible that those traders, who supplied the hostile Indians with their guns and ammunition, may have encouraged the attacks on the Americans to avail themselves of the booty in valuable beaver pelts the Indians brought north after successful depredations upon the Americans.

How little the American trappers really knew of the Blackfeet is illustrated by Jedediah Morse's report on the fur trade to the Secretary of War in 1822. "Blackfoot Indians - These with the Crows aforementioned, and other roving tribes not already named, of whom we know but very little, who inhabit in the Indian manner, the head waters of the Missouri, within the extensive limits of the Missouri Territory, have been conjecturally estimated, exclusively of the Crows, at 20,000 souls. This probably is too low an estimate. The names of some of these tribes are scarcely known; still less their numbers." (Morse, 1822, p. 252).

Three years later (1825) General Atkinson ascended the Missouri to make treaties of peace with the Indians, but he did not get as far as the warlike Blackfeet. Of them he wrote, "The Blackfeet Indians, who, as before mentioned, we did not see, inhabit, it is believed, all the district of country from the Falls of the Missouri back into the Rocky Mountains, and around Northwardly to the head of Maria's River. They carry their war excursions to the South as far as the Big Horn. The intermediate country between the upper part of the Yellow Stone and the three forks of the Missouri is considered as neutral ground, both the Crows and themselves being afraid to visit it, only with war parties, owing to the deadly hostility existing between them. The Blackfeet hunting ground is, therefore, confined to the country embracing the three forks of the Missouri, West into the Mountains, and below, Northeastwardly, to the head of Maria's River, and more Northwards on the head waters of the Katchewina (Saskatchewan), beyond our boundaries. It is understood of latter years, they rarely come below the Falls of the Missouri." (Atkinson, 1826 p. 11).

Yet, whether the Blackfeet actually hunted in the southern headwaters of the Missouri prior to the 1830s is questionable. I have found no contemporary description of a Blackfeet hunting camp in this area prior to the 1830s. F. V. Hayden, who obtained much of his data from experienced fur traders, wrote in 1862, "Previous to the opening of the trade with these Indians on the Upper Missouri, they sold all their skins to the Hudson's Bay Company, seldom visiting the headwaters of the Missouri, except for marauding purposes." (Hayden, 1862, p. 249).

Peter Koch, in his historical sketch of the Gallatin Valley, which was published in 1896, stated, "The Gallatin valley itself has not been the permanent abode of any tribe of Indians since the beginning of this century. It has been debatable ground, claimed by the Blackfeet...but really a common fighting ground for all the surrounding tribes. Hunting and fighting parties of the Crows, the Blackfeet, the Bannacks, the Nez Perces, the Flatheads, the Snakes, traversed it constantly on their way to the hunting grounds of the Yellowstone or the trapping grounds of the Snake river plains; but none of the tribes made their home here, since white men have been in the country." (Koch, 1896, pp. 127-128).

In view of the facts that they traded on the Saskatchewan and that there was no dearth of buffalo on the plains south of that river it does not sound reasonable that the Blackfeet tribes would have chosen to hunt around the region of the Three Forks and southward in this dangerous, debatable land, prior to 1830. Why should they have subjected their women and children to threats of enemy attacks in this "common fighting ground" when there was no necessity whatever for their doing so?

This situation changed markedly with the inauguration of peaceful American trade with the Blackfeet on the Missouri in 1831. The Blackfeet were not opposed to trading with the whites in the United States. What they had opposed vigorously for a quarter of a century was the action of white trappers in exploiting the fur resources of the Indian country, an activity from which the Indians derived no profit.

It was in the fall or early winter of 1830 that Kenneth Mc Kenzie, in charge of the American Fur Company post of Fort Union at the mouth of the Yellowstone, made a daring and successful bid for the Blackfeet trade. He sent Jacob Berger, who had worked for the Hudson's Bay Company and knew both the Blackfeet language and many of their prominent men, westward to open peaceful relations with these Indians. On Badger Creek, on the present Blackfeet Reservation, within a very few miles of the spot where Captain Lewis fought the Piegan in 1806, Berger's little party met some Piegan who took them to their winter camp (on Sun River or Belly River - it is not clear which), where they passed the rest of the winter. In spring Berger led a large Piegan party to Fort Union to trade. And Kenneth Mc Kenzie promised them he would establish a trading post in their country. (Bradley, 1900, pp. 202-203; Stuart, 1876, pp. 84-85).

The following fall Kenneth Mc Kenzie sent James Kipp to establish the first American trading post in the Blackfeet country, Fort Piegan at the mouth of the Marias River. In his first year at this post Kipp won the trade of both Piegan and Blood Indians by his liberal gifts of liquor and his acceptance of buffalo robes in trade. Buffalo robes were a common commodity among the Blackfeet but the traders in the British Possessions could not afford to accept them. They were too heavy and bulky in proportion to their value. The American traders had the advantage of a ready road to market via the Missouri River down which they could transport thousands of buffalo robes by flatboat. The Hudson's Bay men were limited to lighter loads of the more valuable furs which could be portaged from river to river en route to market.

After Kipp and his men returned down river with their profitable trade in the spring of 1832, the Indians (Blood or Assiniboin) burned Fort Piegan. But David Mitchell built a larger post six miles above the mouth of the Marias on the Missouri that fall, and continued to woo the Blackfeet trade away from the Hudson's Bay Company.

95

Undoubtedly, the establishment of a trading post on the Missouri must have had the effect of encouraging the Piegan, probably the Blood, and possibly the North Blackfeet to move southward especially during the winter and spring trading season when robes and peltries were prime. This also enabled the American traders to get to know the Blackfeet tribes, their numbers, locations and customs.

In the summer of 1833 the noted German scientist-explorer, Maximilian Prince of Wied, visited the posts of the American Fur Company as high up the Missouri as Fort Mc Kenzie in the Blackfeet country. Maximilian's journal contains information on the locations of the Indian tribes in present Montana, which he obtained from the fur traders.

He described the territory of the Assiniboin in 1833, as follows:

96

"They live in 3,000 tents; the territory which they claim as theirs, is between the Missouri and the Saskatchewan, bounded by lake Winipick on the north, extending, on the east, to Assiniboin River, and on the west, to Milk River." (Maximilian, Vol. XXII, p. 387).

On his trip up the Missouri, upon reaching the mouth of Milk River July 19, 1833, he noted, "This river comes down in many windings, and constitutes the western frontier of the territory of the Assiniboins. (Ibid, Vol. XXIII, p. 46).

It is noteworthy that his findings on the southern and western limits of Assiniboin hunting grounds are almost identical to those of Lewis and Clark nearly three decades earlier.

Farther west on the Missouri, at the mouth of Arrow River, he met 260 lodges, apparently the entire tribe of the Gros Ventre. (Ibid., Vol. XXIII, pp. 71-76). Although this was well within the Gros Ventre range described by Lewis and Clark, much had happened to this tribe in the interval. They had attacked and pillaged trading posts in the British Possessions, fled far southward to join their Arapaho kinsmen on the Arkansas, suffered from a smallpox epidemic, quarreled with the Arapaho, moved north in 1832, fought a stiff battle with American trappers (the Battle of Pierre's Hole) in western Wyoming, suffered a defeat at the hands of the Crow, and returned to occupy their old territory between the Assiniboin and Blackfeet tribes. (Flannery, 1953, pp. 12-16). Flannery, reviewing the evidence on this remarkable Gros Ventre movement, concluded that it is improbable that the entire Gros Ventre tribe was absent from their old territory for a period of years, and suggests that only a fraction of the tribe made the trip south. (Ibid., 1953, pp. 16-17). Her reasoning appears to be sound.

On approaching Fort Mc Kenzie, July 29, Maximilian learned that there were 150 lodges of Piegan near the fort and "the remainder of this tribe were scattered about Maria River." (Maximilian, Vol. XXIII, p. 61).

While at Fort Mc Kenzie (August 9 - September 14, 1833) Maximilian noted that all three of the Blackfeet tribes had come in to trade, and that a North Blackfeet chief had given Mitchell the scarlet uniform with blue facings and yellow lace which he had received from the British traders as a symbol of his preference for the Americans. (Ibid., Vol. XXXIII, p. 124).

Maximilian described the country of the Blackfeet thus:

"The Blackfeet move about in the prairies near the Rocky Mountains and partly live among these mountains, but especially they dwell between the three forks of the Missouri, of which Jefferson River is the most northerly; the Madison River, the western or central; and the Gallatin the most southerly or easterly. They live, however, especially the Piekanns, as far down as Maria River, in the prairies of which they move about, and where all the three tribes sometimes meet to trade with the American Fur Company. They likewise trade with the Hudson's Bay Company.." (Ibid., Vol. XXIII, p. 96).

Much more detailed, and probably more accurate as a description of the location of the Blackfeet tribes in the middle '30s is Alexander Culbertson's recollection, recorded by Lieut. James Bradley some forty years later:

"The Piegans usually summered about the Three Forks of the Missouri and occasionally wintered there, but their usual wintering place was Sun River. They ranged over the intervening country, Prickley

Pear Valley being a frequent resort.

The Bloods and Blackfeet usually wintered near each other, on Belly River, and summered on the Saskatchewan, ranging over the intervening country. The same region was also the abiding place of the Surcies (Sarsi)." (Bradley, Vol. VIII, pp. 153-4).

The southward shift following the establishment of American traders on the Marias appears to have effected the Piegan primarily. Perhaps the readiness with which the Piegan shifted their allegiance to the traders on the Missouri was a cause of friction between them and the Blood and North Blackfeet, who continued to trade on the Saskatchewan as well as in the United States. Possibly the Piegan were jealous of the fact that the other two tribes traded on the Missouri at all. When Maximilian asked the Piegan chief, Middle Bull, whether he would encounter much danger on a trip he contemplated (but didn't make) westward to the Rockies, the chief replied that "The Piekanns might, perhaps, rob us, but would not probably treat us as enemies; but the Kahna and the Siksekai were fools, and we must be on our guard against them." (Maximilian, Vol. XXIII, p. 164-165). [99]

It is certain that during the '30s we find the first definite proof of occupancy of the area around the headwaters of the Missouri (Royce Area 398) by any of the Blackfeet Indians - the first evidence that this was a hunting ground as well as a fighting one. The occupants were not an entire tribe but a large band of the Piegan, the Small Robes or Little Robes.

Bradley (Vol. IX, p. 281) wrote of the Small Robes: "At the time the whites first became acquainted with the Piegans (1831), though avowedly a part of the Piegan tribe they lived wholly by themselves, seldom meeting with the remainder of the tribe and showing so marked a line of separation that by one or two writers they were classed as a separate tribe." George Catlin, who depended upon the fur traders for his information, listed the Small Robes as distinct from the Piegan. He estimated their numbers at 250 lodges, some 15% of the total population of the Blackfeet tribes. (Catlin, 1841, Vol. I, p. 52). Father De Smet, who became acquainted with the Little Robes in 1840 or 1841, also considered them to be a distinct tribe. (Chittenden and Richardson, 1905, Vol. III, p. 949).

There can be little doubt that this band lived farther south near the Rockies than the other Piegan bands in the 1830s. In the summer of 1837 Jim Bridger visited the village of the then chief of the band, Little Robe, on the headwaters of the Missouri and learned that they were suffering from the smallpox. (Victor, 1877, p. 231). Probably the numbers of band members was greatly reduced by this plague which wrecked havoc among all the Blackfeet tribes.

The Small Robes made peace with the Flathead tribe which crossed the Rockies to hunt buffalo around the headwaters of the

Missouri. When Father De Smet established a Catholic mission among the Flathead in 1840, the Small Robes visited it and came under his influence, offering their children for baptism. (Ewers, 1946, p. 398).

In the year 1845, the Small Robes suffered a severe defeat at the hands of the Crows. De Smet at first believed all of their men were killed in the action. But it developed that a small remnant remained. A dozen lodges of them joined the Flathead in their fall buffalo hunt in 1846, during which this allied force met and defeated the Crow. (Ibid., p. 398).

It is my belief that the strongest claim the Blackfeet had to the area around the headwaters of the Missouri, rested upon occupancy by the Small Robes band of the Piegan in the decades of the 1830s and 1840s. But it is clear the Small Robes were not the sole occupants; that they shared the resources of the region in buffalo with their Flathead friends. This region thus became something of a common hunting ground before it was declared such by the terms of the 1855 treaty.

During the period between the smallpox epidemic of 1837 and the treaty of 1855 there also appeared to be a growing tendency for the Northern Blackfeet to remain north of the international boundary in the British Possessions. This appears to be indicated in the description of the territory of the three Blackfeet tribes during the 1840s as written by William T. Hamilton, an American trader who knew them at that time.

"Three tribes, Blackfeet, Bloods, and Piegans, make up what has been known as the Blackfoot nation. The Piegan and Blood Indians claimed and occupied the country from the British line, 49 degrees north latitude, to the Musselshell River on the south; and west along the summit of the Rockies to a range enclosing what is now known as Prickly Pear Valley, where Helena Montana, is now....The third branch of the Blackfeet resided in and claimed the country from the British line to Fort Edmonton on the Saskatchewan River. (Hamilton, 1905, p. 125).

IV. Period of the First Treaty (1850-1862)

In the middle of the nineteenth century there were no white settlers in or travelers through the country of the Blackfeet tribes and the Gros Ventre. The only whites in this region were fur traders. These Indians, with the exception of a few who had traveled far beyond the area occupied by these tribes, had never seen a white woman. Certainly they had never seen one in their own country.

The great overland emigrant road to Oregon, California and Utah, the Oregon Trail, was located far to the south of the country of these tribes. Its use was increasing annually in the late '40s, and the growing numbers of emigrants passing over this trail were killing buffalo and disturbing their movements, causing increasing alarm to the Indians.

In the fall of 1849, David D. Mitchell, Superintendent of Indian Affairs in St. Louis, recommended that the government should call a great council with all the plains tribes living between the Missouri River and Texas to make formal arrangements to indemnify the Indians for their losses and to define tribal boundaries. He pointed out, "The boundaries dividing the different tribes have never been settled or defined; this is the fruitful source of many of their bloody strifes; and can only be removed by mutual concessions, sanctioned by the Government of the United States." (D. D. Mitchell to Commissioner of Indian Affairs, Oct. 13, 1949. Indian Office Records, The National Archives).

On May 26, 1851, the Commissioner of Indian Affairs authorized Mitchell to hold a council and to treat with the "Indian tribes of the Prairies". The names and numbers of tribes to be invited to this counsil, the choice of council site and details of the proceedings were left to Mitchell's discretion. (Commissioner Lea to D. D. Mitchell, May 26, 1851, Indian Office Letter Book, No. 44, The National Archives).

Alexander Culbertson of the American Fur Company, a former colleague of Mitchell's in the fur trade, was chosen to collect delegations from the Upper Missouri tribes and to conduct them to Fort Laramie, the location Mitchell had chosen for the council. According to Lieut. James Bradley, early Montana historian, word of the proposed council at Fort Laramie reached Culbertson too late to permit him to obtain delegations from the Blackfeet tribes and the Gros Ventre. (Bradley, Vol. III, p. 266). Bradley knew Culbertson well in later years, so it is probable he obtained this information from him.

But Culbertson did collect a small delegation from the Assiniboin and other tribes farther down the Missouri and accompany them to Fort Laramie. Although the Blackfeet and Gros Ventre were not a party to this treaty, a portion of their lands were defined in the treaty, because the Commissioners decided to include within the area described in the treaty all lands in present Montana south and east of the Missouri.

Of great assistance in explaining the tribal boundaries defined in this treaty and in obtaining the agreement of the several Indian delegations present to these boundaries was a map drawn by Father De Smet, who had traveled widely in the area, showing tribal boundaries. De Smet, himself wrote of this map some six years later (July 1, 1857):

"When I was at the council ground in 1851, on the Platte River, at the mouth of the Horse creek, I was requested by Colonel Mitchell to make a map of the whole Indian country, relating particularly to the upper Missouri, the waters of the Columbia and its tributaries west of these mountains. In compliance with this request I drew up the map from scraps then in my possession. The map, so prepared, was seemingly approved and made use of by the gentlemen assembled in council, and subsequently sent on to Washington together with the treaty then made with the Indians." (Chittenden and Richardson, 1905, Vol. 4, p. 1498).

When, on November 11, 1851, D. D. Mitchell, Senior Commissioner, transmitted the Treaty of Fort Laramie to the Commissioner of Indian Affairs he sent this map with it, explaining that the tribal boundaries were clearly marked and defined in the presence of the Indians and were fully approved by them. (Mitchell to Commissioner of Indian Affairs, Nov. 11, 1851, Indian Office Records, The National Archives).

This original map is in the Map Division of the Library of Congress. It is noteworthy that this first official attempt to locate the tribes of the Missouri Valley above the mouth of the Yellowstone does not concern itself with the lands <u>north</u> or <u>west</u> of the Missouri's main stem. It is noteworthy also that neither the map nor the descriptions of boundaries in this region provides any marginal areas - there are no common hunting grounds, no debatable lands, no unoccupied areas along the frontiers between hostile tribes. To the extent that the map and descriptions of tribal lands arrived at in this treaty failed to portray these marginal areas, they failed to present true pictures of Indian occupancy at that time.

We are interested primarily in two areas portrayed in the map and described in the treaty:

106

1. <u>The Blackfoot Territory</u>: This is described primarily in terms of river boundaries - it follows the Missouri river upward from the mouth of the "Muscle-Shell" to its source, thence south along the main range of the Rockies to the northern source of the Yellowstone, down that river to the mouth of Twenty five Yard Creek, - thence across to the headwaters of the "Muscle-shell" and down that river to its mouth. De Smet's map attempts to interpret that description on the basis of the geographical knowledge available to him.

D. D. Mitchell, in describing the territory of the Blackfeet on Jan. 24, 1854, stated: "For a more definite description of their territory I refer you to a map accompanying the Fort Laramie Treaty. This partition of country, as there laid down, was agreed upon by the various tribes assembled on that occasion." (Mitchell in Schoolcraft, Vol. V, p. 686).

Actually this agreement on the part of the tribes participating in the treaty involved no boundary concessions by any of them save the Crow and Assiniboin. The Flathead and other tribes from west of the Rockies who hunted buffalo in the area identified as "Blackfoot" by the Fort Laramie Treaty, were not parties to that treaty and made no concessions.

Note also that the treaty made no attempt to define "Blackfoot" territory north or west of the Missouri. The area described as "Blackfoot" territory in the treaty is not the same as Royce Area No. 398, which extends beyond the Missouri main stem to the Rocky Mountains.

2. *The Assiniboin Territory*: The territory of the Assiniboin described in the Fort Laramie Treaty refers only to that portion of the Assiniboin territory lying south of the Missouri. Its boundaries were described as the Missouri River from the mouth of the Yellowstone to the mouth of the "Muscle-shell", thence southeasterly to the headwaters of Big Dry Creek, thence down that creek to its entrance into the Yellowstone, nearly opposite the

mouth of Powder River, thence down the Yellowstone to the Missouri. (This is Royce Area 300).

However, Edwin T. Denig, who, as a fur trader at Fort Union, married to two Assiniboin women, had known the tribe for nearly two decades, and who is recognized by ethnologists as the leading authority on that tribe, pointed out in a report to Governor Isaac I. Stevens in 1854, dealing with the Assiniboin. "Formerly they inhabited a portion of country on the south side of the Missouri River along the Yellowstone River, but of late years, having met with great losses by Blackfeet, Sioux, and Crow war parties, they have been obliged to abandon this region and now they never go there." (Denig, 1930, p. 397). In another description of the Assiniboin, written by Denig no more than a year or two later he stated, "At this time the entire south side of the Missouri as high up as the Musselshell and as low down as the confluence of the Little Missouri of the Big Bend, extending for 100 miles into the interior, is unoccupied by any Indians...Neither the Crows nor Assiniboines can be induced to remain here. Both have made the attempt and both have been obliged to leave on account of the numerous Blackfoot and Sioux war parties who consider this their favorite range. But the Sioux are numerous and could defend themselves in this region while the Assiniboines, being the weaker party, would be driven northward to their ancient home." (Denig, 1952, pp. 147-148). The Fort Laramie Treaty appears to have been in error in defining this debatable ground, which the Assiniboin did not and could not occupy, as Assiniboin territory.

The Gros Ventre: No mention of the Gros Ventre is made in the descriptions of territory south of the Missouri in present Montana, in the Fort Laramie Treaty. This suggests that the Indians party to that treaty, particularly the Assiniboin and Crow neighbors of the Gros Ventre and the knowledgeable whites who took part in the treaty negotiations recognized no specific Gros Ventre occupancy of land south of the Missouri. It is possible, of course, that they did not distinguish the Gros Ventre from the Blackfeet and considered that the land defined as Blackfeet was also available to their Gros Ventre allies.

Prior to 1851, the Gros Ventre had been allies of the Blackfeet in their wars against the Assiniboin. But in 1851, shortly after the Fort Laramie Treaty, the Gros Ventre made peace with the Assiniboin. Denig, in 1855 or 1856 wrote, "During the four years this peace has lasted the number of horses given to the Assiniboines by the Gros Ventres of the Prairie cannot fall short of four or five hundred. Some of these were bought by the former people but the greater part were bestowed for the purpose of promoting friendly relations." (Denig, 1952, p. 146).

When Isaac I. Stevens' exploring party reached present Montana in the summer of 1853, he found that "a feud had lately broken out between the Gros Ventres and Blackfeet". A Gros Ventre man had been killed by Blackfeet, and the murdered man's tribe was on the verge of sending a war party against their old allies to revenge their loss. (Stevens, 1860, Vol. XII, p. 92-93). It seems that following the Gros Ventre peace with the Assiniboin their alliance with the Blackfeet was weakened and friendship between these long-time allies became increasingly strained until they became avowed enemies in 1861.

Gov. Stevens, desiring to hold a council with the Piegan, sent the artist of his expedition, John Mix Stanley accompanied by the Piegan chief, Little Dog, to bring Indian leaders in to Fort Benton. Stanley found the great camp of the Piegan, their tribal summer encampment, north of the international boundary, in the vicinity of the Cypress Hills. On the basis of information obtained on this trip he described the country of the Blackfeet tribes thus: "The Piegan and Blood bands hunt, trade, and winter on American soil while the Blackfeet extend their hunts as far north as the Saskatchewan river, and trade as frequently with the British as with the American posts." (Stanley, 1855, pp. 448-449).

At the council at Fort Benton, September 21, 1853, Stevens exacted the promise of the Indians who were present not to make war upon the Flathead and Nez Perce, but the chiefs frankly told him "they could not speak for those of their tribes who were not present."

(Annual Report Comm. Indian Affairs, 1854, pp. 202-203).

When Governor Stevens started westward from Fort Benton to continue his explorations for a possible railroad route to the Pacific, he left behind his intelligent, energetic assistant, James Doty. Doty was not only to make meteorological observations and examinations of the country which would be of value to the railroad survey, he was also to collect information about and take a census of the Blackfeet Indians, and to impress on the Indians the benefits they would derive from a proposed peace council with the western Indians.

In December 1853, Doty visited the winter camps of a considerable number of the Blackfeet bands. He found "a large number of the Piegans" encamped on the Marias near the point where the trail from Fort Benton to the Three Buttes (Sweetgrass Hills) crossed the Marias. Moving up river he found "nearly the whole of the Blood, Blackfeet and North Piegan Bands" encamped near Armell's Houses on the Marias. He learned that "a portion of the Blood Indians were in camp five days march to the north and intending to go to the British Posts to trade." (Doty to Stevens, Dec. 29, 1853, The National Archives).

At that time it was no longer necessary for the Blackfeet to bring their furs and buffalo robes in to Fort Benton during winter. The traders built winter posts in the river valleys where the Indians preferred to winter for direct trade with them. Such a location was "Armell's Houses", operated by August in Hamell on the Marias about 10 or 20 miles below Birch Creek. (Montana Historical Society Contribs. Vol. 10, p. 262). In the winter of 1854-5 the American Fur Company built similar houses on Milk River for trade with the Gros Ventre. (Ibid. p. 4). The Fort Benton Journal for that winter makes frequent mention of dispatching and receiving wagons used in hauling trade goods to and robes from these winter posts on the Marias and Milk rivers. (Ibid., pp. 4 ff). Yet in February bands of Piegan, Blood, Northern Blackfeet and Gros Ventre came in to Fort Benton itself to trade their robes. (Ibid., pp. 63 ff). There seems to be no evidence in either Doty's writings or the Fort Benton Journal for the same year that any of the bands of the Blackfeet tribes were wintering south of the Missouri with the exception of the Small Robes. They wintered near Fort Benton and made repeated visits to it. Under date of January 26, 1856, the keeper of the Fort Benton Journal wrote: "Some Little Robes paid us another loafing visit for the 100th time" (Ibid., p. 61).

On December 20, 1854, James Doty submitted to Gov. Stevens his report on the "Blackfoot Nation" based upon his field studies of nearly a year in the country of those Indians.

He describes their locations and numbers.

"The Boundaries of the Blackfoot Country are described as follows:

By a line beginning on the north where the 50th Parallel crosses the Rocky Mountains, thence East on said Parallel to the 106th degree of Longitude, thence South to the head waters of Milk River, down said River to the Missouri, up the Missouri to the mouth of the Judith thence up the Judith to its source, thence west to the Rocky Mountains, thence along the base of the mountains to place of beginning.

The country between the headwaters of the Missouri and the Yellowstone is not permanently occupied by any tribe, but seems to be a common hunting ground for the Crows, Flat Heads and Pend Oreilles." (Doty to Stevens, December 20, 1854, p. 1. Indian Office Records. The National Archives).

113

When we compare this description with the description of the Blackfeet country south and east of the Missouri in the Fort Laramie Treaty we find a very noticeable discrepancy. Doty's description includes only a small part of that area assigned to the Blackfeet on Father De Smet's map - the portion west and north of the headwaters of the Judith River. I believe Doty's is the more realistic presentation of the area occupied by the Blackfeet tribes at the time (1854).

Doty went on to break down the subdivision of the area he described among the "four bands" (actually three tribes, including two subdivisions of the Piegan) as follows:

"1st The Blood Indians No. 270 Lodges 2430 Souls and 810 warriors. These Indians occupy the extreme northern portion of the Blackfeet country, bordering on the south branch of the Saskatchewan and extending south to the headwaters of Marias and Milk Rivers and East to the 106th degree of Longitude, they confine themselves closely to these limits and are seldom found beyond them, at least on the south; Their great trade is in Buffalo Robes and is made at a winter Post of the Am. Fur Co. at the forks of the Marias River, and in the summer a small party usually go to the Hudson Bay Cos Post on the Saskatchewan to trade such small peltries - Ermine, Martin, Beaver etc - as may have been collected by them.

2nd. The Blackfeet proper, No. 290 lodges 2610 Souls and 870 warriors. This band occupy the same country as the Blood Indians, and join them generally in hunting the Buffalo and occasionally for mutual defense against their hereditary enemies the Crees and North Assiniboins.

3rd. The North Piegan No. 90 Lodges 810 Souls and 270 warriors. This is merely a subdivision of the great Piegan Band and differ only from the South Piegan in the fact that in the Summer season they join the Bloods and Blackfeet and go to the North, but it is invariably their custom to consort with the South Piegan during the winter and spring and to trade at Fort Benton or Fort Campbell.

4th. The South Piegan No. 200 lodges, 1800 Souls and 600 Warriors. The Band occupies the country between Milk River and the Missouri and upon the west side of the Missouri as far down as the Judith, they do not usually go lower down the Missouri than the Bear Paw Mountain." (Ibid., pp. 1-2).

Of the Gros Ventre Doty reported:

"There is another tribe known as the Gros Ventres of the Prairies, occupying the country bordering Milk River from its mouth to the territory of the Piegans, and which is generally considered a portion of the Blackfoot nation. But as the Gros Ventres have been formed totally different from the Blackfeet in language, custom and disposition." (Ibid., p. 3).

Doty reported that the Gros Ventres "No. 360 Lodges 2880 Souls and 1080 warriors. They are located upon Milk River from its mouth to the Bear Paw Mountains, and upon the Missouri from the mouth of Milk River to Eagle Creek, a small stream rising in the Bear Paw Mountains and emptying into the Missouri 30 miles below Fort Benton. This tribe has heretofore been considered a component part of the Blackfeet Nation. But as they differ in language, disposition and customs, I shall consider them a distinct nation, and would recommend that, in the event of holding a treaty with them they be regarded as such." (Ibid., p. 8).

Doty found that "the Blackfeet do not consider the Gros Ventres a portion of their nation. They do not hold Councils together neither do they associate in hunting or war parties." (Ibid., p. 9).

In the same year Edwin T. Denig supplied Gov. Stevens with a report on the Assiniboin. Denig distinguished between the Northern Assiniboin and the Southern Assiniboin.

"The Northern Assiniboin 250 or 300 lodges, rove the country from the west banks of the Saskatchewan, Assiniboin, and Red Rivers in a westward direction to the Woody Mountains north and west among small spurs of the Rocky Mountains east of the Missouri, and among chains of small lakes through this immense region. Occasionally making peace with some of the northern bands of Blackfeet enables them to come a little farther west and deal with those Indians, but, these "Peaces" being of short duration, they are for the most part limited to the prairies east and north of the Blackfeet range. The rest of the Assiniboin, say 500 to 520 lodges (who may be called the Southern Assiniboin), occupy the following district, viz., commencing at the mouth of the White Earth River on the east, extending up that river to its head, thence northwest along the Couteau de Prairie, or Divide, as far as the Cyprus Mountains on the North Fork of the Milk River, thence down Milk River to its junction with the Missouri River, thence down the Missouri River to the mouth of White Earth River, or the starting point." (Denig, 1930, p. 397).

Doty and Denig certainly agree on their definition of the Milk River as the boundary between the Assiniboin and Gros Ventre in the year prior to the negotiation of the first treaty with The Blackfoot Nation.

As the time for the council approached, the Commissioners (Gov. Stevens and A. Cumming) sent James Doty to "go north to confer with Tribes and Bands of the Blackfoot Nation and make the necessary arrangements to secure their presence at the approaching council." Doty's report of his mission to the North Camps Aug. 31 to September 15, 1815, throws considerable light upon the movements of the Blackfeet tribes in summer at that period as well as upon the proportions of the several tribes which actually participated in the treaty negotiations. (This report is part of the proceedings of the treaty council in The National Archives.)

To find the Blackfeet and arrange for them to come in to negotiate their first treaty with the United States, Doty had to travel north, across the international boundary into Canada. At that season the buffalo were north of the line, and the Indian hunting bands had followed them north. Doty learned that all four Blackfeet groups and the Gros Ventre had been in the vicinity of the Cypress Mountains (Hills) in July. On going north he did not see buffalo until he had crossed the line and reached Lake Pakowki in present southern Alberta. He found the South Piegan (some 200 lodges, virtually the entire group) encamped on Belly River. There were also about 80 lodges of North Piegan and Blackfeet. The majority of the Blood Indians, some 200 lodges, he was told agreed to meet Lame Bull, the head chief of the South Piegan at "Writing on Stone" on the north side of Milk River (in the British Possessions) to move south to the council together. Doty had to travel north as far as Bow River to find 50 lodges of Blackfeet, 70 of North Piegan and 90 of Blood Indians. Of these 210 lodges, only 110 agreed to come south to the council, the others preferring to stay in the north. He learned there were 170 more lodges of North Blackfeet on Elk (Red Deer) River still farther north. Doty reported (p. 8 of his report): "It appearing to me clearly that these are British Indians, who neither hunt nor trade on American soil, I did not, in view of my instructions, deem it my duty to endeavour to bring them to the Council, and therefore did not proceed to Elk river."

Doty also reported that the 70 lodges of North Piegan on Bow River were among the 100 in that vicinity that did not wish to come south to participate in the treaty with the United States.

Comparing the numbers of lodges of the several Blackfeet groups in Doty's estimates of their total populations, with the number of lodges he indicated came south to participate in the treaty negotiations we find:

Probably 200 lodges, or the entire population of the South Piegan participated.

More than 200 lodges, the great majority of the total of 270 Blood lodges, participated.

At least 170 lodges, and probably considerably more of the North Blackfeet did not participate. This was a majority of the 290 lodges of the tribe.

Some 70 of the 90 North Piegan lodges, an overwhelming majority of that group, did not participate.

In the light of the Indian concept that chiefs could not make decisions for other portions of their tribe without consultation, it is very doubtful whether either the North Blackfeet or the North Piegan people at that time considered that as tribes they had concluded a treaty with the United States. Both were too poorly represented at the treaty council.

No land was ceded in this first treaty of 1855. According to Commissioner of Indian Affairs, George W. Mannypenny's instructions to the treaty Commissioners, "The principal objects to be attained by the proposed negotiations are, the establishment of well defined and permanent relations of amity with all the most numerous and warlike tribes in that remote region of country, both between the Indians and the United States and between the tribes as among themselves." (Mannypenny to Commissioners, May 3, 1855. In House Exec. Docs. 1st Sess., 34th Congress, Document No. 105, 1856, p. 530).

As had been done at the Fort Laramie Treaty, the Commissioners prepared a map which was shown to the Indians displaying the tribal boundaries under consideration and to which agreement was desired. (Stevens, 1860, Vol. XII, Book I). The map employed at the Blackfoot Treaty Council is in The National Archives.

The only serious controversy arising out of the Commissioners' proposed boundaries arose out of their proposal to make that portion of the country east of the Rockies, south of a line from Hellgate Pass to the headwaters of the Musselshell River, including the southern headwaters of the Missouri, (Royce Area 398) a common hunting ground for the tribes west of the Rockies who came over the mountains to hunt buffalo and the Blackfeet tribes; while restricting the plains north of that line to the Blackfeet. It is noteworthy that the Blackfeet had no objections to this proposal. It is very doubtful if they hunted in that area in the mid-1850s anyway.

But the Pend d'Oreille objected strenuously to this proposal as shown by the official proceedings of the council. Alexander the Pend d'Oreille head chief, protested, "It is a very small place you give us for a hunting ground. A long time ago our people used to hunt about the Three Buttes and the Blackfeet lived far north. When my Father was living he told me that was an old road for our people... Now you point us out a little piece of land to hunt our game on. When we were enemies, I always crossed over there, and why should I not now, when we are friends?" (Partoll, 1937, p. 7).

Alexander then pointed to the Blackfeet and said, "Which of these chiefs says we are not to go there? Which is the one?" And Little Dog, Piegan in reply stated, "We are friendly. But the North Blackfeet are bad, it might produce a quarrel if you hunted near them." He then went on to explain, "I went to the North with Mr. Doty. These Indians would not come to the treaty. I do not know what they intend to do." (Partoll, 1937, p. 7).

So it is apparent from this interchange between Alexander and Little Dog at the council that (1) the Pend d'Oreille were not in favor of the boundaries as drawn, since they prevented them from hunting in the area north of the common hunting ground where they claimed traditional rights. None of the Blackfeet chiefs at the council denied these rights. In fact, Little Dog stated, "Since he (Alexander) speaks so much of it, we will give him liberty to come out in the North". (Ibid., p. 7). It was not the Blackfeet but the Commissioners who objected to this plan. They did not deny Alexander's traditional right to hunt on land north of the common hunting ground but pointed that the new boundaries were proposed, as Commissioner Cumming said, "to preserve their hungtin grounds distinctly apart...The

Whites make these lines to show where each must hunt so that there shall be no quarrels." (Ibid., p. 8).

It is also apparent that (2) neither the western tribes nor the Piegan considered that the North Blackfeet were sufficiently well represented at this council to be regarded as a party to the decisions made there. As Little Dog stated, "I do not know what they intend to do."

Another insight into the prevailing attitudes of the Indians toward the boundaries can be gained from the short speech of Big Canoe, a prominent Pend d'Oreille chief. ..."I thought our roads would be over all this country. Now you tell us different. Supposing that we <u>do</u> stick together, and <u>do</u> make a peace. That is the way we talk on the other side. Now you tell me not to step over that way. I had a mind to go there." (Ibid., p. 8). This is an expression of the Indian feeling that boundaries between friendly tribes were unnecessary, that if the Pend d'Oreille and Blackfeet tribes made peace there would be no more necessity for a boundary between them than for a boundary between the Piegan and Blood tribes.

The council proceedings of the first day were concluded without reaching an agreement on the Pend d'Oreille objection to their exclusion from the area reserved for the exclusive use of the Blackfeet tribes. When the council reconvened the next day Commissioner Stevens offered a compromise. "We will give to the Western Indians the liberty to hunt on the trail down the Muscle Shell to the Yellowstone. Thus the Blackfeet give to you the right to hunt in their country down the Muscle Shell." (Ibid., p. 8). The boundaries were then explained to the Indians, with the aid of the map and a rough sketch of the country drawn on a buffalo skin. The proceedings state, "The Indians appearing fully to comprehend and assent, no objections being made." (Ibid., p. 9).

The Commissioners then went on to explain other articles of the treaty. After all the articles were explained, there was discussion of the major objective of the council, major in terms of both Commissioner Mannypenny's instructions to the Commissioners and to the minds of the Indians. Onis-tay-say-nah-que-im, Head Chief of the Bloods, pointed out a common problem in the tribal government of these tribes. "I wish to say that as far as we old men are concerned we want peace and to cease going to war; but I am afraid we cannot stop our young men." (Ibid., p. 10). No satisfactory solution to this problem was proposed.

123

The treaty was signed by the Commissioners and by 15 Piegan chiefs (only one of which, Mountain Chief, may have been a prominent North Piegan chief), 8 Blood chiefs (probably representing a majority of the Blood bands at that time), 4 North Blackfeet chiefs (certainly representing a minority of the bands of their tribe), 8 Gros Ventre chiefs (probably a majority of the bands being represented). It was also signed by 12 Nez Perce chiefs, and 15 chiefs of the "Flathead Nation", which included both Flathead and Pend d'Oreille.

The area described as the territory of the Blackfoot Nation in this treaty included Royce Areas 399, 574, and area 565 as far east as a line drawn directly north from the mouth of Milk River to the international boundary. No effort was made to distinguish the territories of the three Blackfeet tribes from one another or to distinguish their territories from that of the Gros Ventre. However, the Assiniboin were granted "the right of hunting in common with the Blackfeet, in the country lying between the aforesaid eastern boundary line, running from the mouth of Milk River to the forty-ninth parallel, and a line drawn from the left bank of the Missouri River, opposite Round Butte, north to the forty-ninth parallel." This concession to the Assiniboin actually was made by the Gros Ventre alone, since the Blackfeet tribes did not hunt in that area. It reflects the Gros Ventre acknowledgement of Assiniboin right to hunt in the valley of the Milk River as well as their friendly relations with the Assiniboin since 1851.

It is my belief that the reason the Blackfeet tribes made no objection at the council to the area set aside for their exclusive use was that this area, plus the large area over which they hunted in the British Possessions was much more than was adequate for the support of Doty's estimated total of 850 lodges or 7,650 souls for the North Blackfeet, Blood, North Piegan and South Piegan Indians.

It was considerably larger than the area actually occupied by these tribes as Doty described it in 1854 and as his field investigations in the winter of 1853 and the late summer of 1855 revealed. It appears most probable that at that time the great majority of the bands of the three Blackfeet tribes wintered on the Marias River and northward, while on their summer hunts they moved northward into the British Possessions where Doty found them in the summer of 1855, and where Stanley had found the Piegan two summers before.

They did come south to trade at Fort Benton in late winter, but there seems to be no positive evidence that they made much use of their territory south of the Marias for hunting or collecting at any season of the year. The Small Robes band appears to have been an exception. They definitely wintered near Fort Benton in 1854-5. On July 24, 1860, Lt. John Mullins met this band near the Judith Mountains south of the Missouri River. He reported:

"They proved to be the 'little Robes', a band of the Blackfeet Indians. They were delighted to meet me, and I accompanied them to their village, half a mile distance, where, to my surprise, I saw waving from the top of the chief's tent the Star-Spangled banner. I counted 54 lodges, and estimated the number of the Indians to be about 150 or 200 ... I was enabled to talk with them through my guide and interpreter, James Bridger, who spoke the Flathead language and was readily understood as there were several members of the band who were Flatheads and could interpret to the rest." (Raynolds, 1868, pp. 163-4).

125

Possibly the continued friendship with the Flathead caused the Small Robes to summer south of the Missouri where they could visit with the Flathead when they came over the Rockies to hunt buffalo along the Musselshell. It is possible some of the 54 lodges seen by Lt. Mullins were occupied by Flathead visitors. Agent Vaughan estimated the Piegan (both North and South) at 460 lodges. (Annual Report Comm. Ind. Aff., 1860, p. 308). The 54 lodges in the Small Robes camp that summer must have comprised less than 10% of the total Piegan population.

It appears probable that the Commissioners of the 1855 Treaty with the Blackfoot Nation extended the boundary of these people south-eastward to meet and conform with the northwestern boundary of the Crow territory as defined in the Fort Laramie Treaty of 1851. (See Royce Area 517). If so this boundary was located by precedent rather than on the basis of Indian occupancy at the time of the 1855 treaty.

As an instrument of intertribal peace the 1855 treaty with the Blackfoot was unsuccessful. Agent Hatch reported that Blood Indians war parties started for the Crow camps within ten days of the signing of the treaty and that many others followed. The haughty Blood warriors passed through Piegan and Gros Ventre camps and ridiculed them for listening to the advice of the whites. (Annual Report Comm. Ind. Affairs, 1856, pp. 75-76). That same winter the Blackfeet were fighting the Assiniboin on their eastern front. (Montana Hist. Soc. Contribs., Vol. X, p. 157). Peace with the tribes west of the Rockies lasted but little longer. John Owen, trader among the Flathead wrote on June 30, 1860, "Since the treaty of /55 the Blackfeet have made frequent predatory Excursions to the different Camps from (on) this side and have run off Many horses. (Owen, Vol. 2, p. 215).

Nor did the treaty prevent the tribes north of the Flathead on the west side of the Rockies from exercising what they continued to regard as their traditional right to hunt buffalo on the plains in the region set aside for the exclusive occupancy of the Blackfeet Nation. Alexander, head chief of the Pend d'Oreille, even though he had signed the treaty, continued to lead his tribe across the Rockies to hunt in the designated Blackfeet country. In 1860 he led his winter hunt across the Blackfeet territory as far as Milk River, where the Pend d'Oreille camp was attacked by Cree and Assiniboin, 20 of his people were killed and 25 wounded, and 290 of his horses were stolen. John Owen, who recorded this disaster, met Alexander and his footsore, defeated people on their return from their 400 mile retreat across the plains and mountains. The spunky old chief was thirsting for revenge. (John Owen, Vol. 2, pp. 234-235). As late as the fall of 1875, the Blackfeet agent reported a visit of 20 lodges of Pend d'Oreille who had crossed the Rockies to hunt north of the Marias River in Blackfeet territory. (Agent Wood's Letter Book, Oct. 8, 1875. The Museum of the Plains Indian, Browning, Montana.)

Likewise, the Kutenai, north of the Pend d'Oreille continued to exercise what they believed to be their aboriginal right of hunting buffalo on the plains. William T. Hamilton described in detail a series of fights between the Kutenai and North Blackfeet in late October, 1858, in which he had participated. One Blackfeet attack occurred near St. Mary's Lake and others while the Kutenai were attempting to cross the Rockies to their lands on the west side. (Hamilton, 1900, pp. 79-96).

Three descriptions of the territory occupied by the Blackfeet and their neighbors to the eastward in Royce Area 565 are available for the period immediately following the 1855 treaty. Agent Vaughan's description in 1858, follows Doty's 1854 description closely for the territory of the Blackfoot Nation, but describes the areas of the individual tribes differently:

"The portion of country claimed and occupied by the Blackfeet nation is generally conceded to be bounded as follows: by a line beginning on the north where the 50th parallel crosses the Rocky mountains; thence east on said parallel to the 106th meridian; thence south to the headwaters of the Milk River, down said river to the Missouri, up the Missouri to the mouth of the Judith; thence up the Judith to its source to the Rocky Mountains, and north along their base to the place of beginning.

Of this region the Bloods and Blackfeet occupy the country upon the source of the Marias and Milk rivers to the 50th parallel of latitude; the Piegans between Milk and Marias rivers, upon the

Marias and the Teton, and between the Teton and the Missouri; and the Gros-ventres that portion bordering the Milk river, from its mouth to the territory of the Piegans." (Annual Report Comm. Ind. Affairs, 1858, pp. 431).

Notice that Vaughan did not extend the area of Piegan occupancy south of the Missouri. Apparently he neglected to include the movements of the Small Robes band south of that river in his computation. Nor did he make a distinction between the North and South Piegan.

F. V. Hayden, who obtained much of his information from well-informed fur traders, published descriptions of the locations of all the tribes of the so-called Blackfoot Nation in 1862, although his data probably refer to their locations in the last half of the previous decade (ca. 1855-1860):

"The Blood Indians range through the district along Maria, Teton, and Belly Rivers, inclining west and northwest far into the interior.

The Blackfeet inhabit a portion of country farther north than the Bloods, extending to the banks of the Saskatchewan along which they often reside. They have never altogether abandoned their English friends, and more frequently dispose of their furs to them than to the American traders on the head branches of the Missouri.

The Piegans roam through the Rocky Mountains on the south side of Maria River, on both banks of the Missouri. ... They also hunt as far down the Missouri as the Musselshell River, and up that stream to the borders of the Crow country." (Hayden, 1862, p. 249).

Of the Gros Ventre he wrote: "At present and for many years past, they range along the Milk River, on the east side of the Missouri, extending as far as the Cypress Mountains. From this line to the Marias River stretches a beautiful level country well covered with grass and adapted to pasturage of buffalo. Here the Indians under consideration may be found at all seasons - in the winter along the banks of the Milk River where wood may be obtained and in summer on the plains where fuel is not so necessary." (Ibid., p. 101).

Hayden's description differs from Vaughan's in placing the North Blackfeet farthest north, the Blood in the center and the Piegan farthest south. The attachment of the Blackfeet to the north was borne out in their light representation at the 1855 treaty. Hayden's extension of the Blood as far south as the Teton appears questionable. His mention of the Piegan south of the Missouri must refer primarily to the small Small Robes band.

Denig's account of the Assiniboin, written very shortly after the 1855 Blackfoot Treaty, recognizes six bands of the Southern Assiniboin with a total population of 520 lodges or (allowing 4 persons to a lodge) 2,080 souls. The western most of these, the Gens du Gauche, lived "along the Woody Mountains on the west side in summer, often moving westward to the heads of the Riviere aux Tremble (poplar River), and towards fall place their camp at or above Big Muddy River or along the first named stream." The easternmost of these bands, the Gens des Canots "Are commonly found along the White Earth River, extend their travels in the summer season as far north as the heads of La Riviere aux Souris, Grand Coulee and Pambinar River. Indeed the entire extent of country east of Fort Union as far down as the Great Bend is hunted by them at different times. But owing to the absence of wood on this great plain they are obliged to place their camp on or near the Missouri in the winter season. They are usually found at that time either on White Earth River or above that point where trading houses are established... "The remaining bands mentioned are scattered over the intervening region between the locations of the two already spoken of, move about near the divide in warm weather, approaching the Missouri in the fall and stationing themselves on its banks or low down on some of its tributaries. These bands commonly make their winter hunt near the Riviere aux Tremble (Poplar River) and along that stream, but when traveling over the unwooded plains permits, proceed as far north as the Cypress Mountains. Some of them, especially those called Les Gens du Nord, go still farther and make their trade either at some of the Hudson's Bay Company's posts on Assiniboine River or with the Red River half-breeds." (Denig, 1952, pp. 136-138).

There is no indication in this description of Assiniboin

occupancy of lands west of Milk River, in fact all landmarks mentioned lie to the eastward of Milk River.

At the close of this period (1850-1862) all the area under discussion was still Indian country. There was no white settlement within it. Nor was the country of the tribes of the so-called Blackfeet nation crossed by any emigrant route. The Indians' locations were still determined primarily by their own needs for subsistence and for protection from the elements in winter, plus their desire to obtain sufficient surplus from the natural resources of their region to enable them to trade with the whites for useful weapons, ammunition, tools, utensils, liquor and other attractive luxuries.

132

V. <u>North Blackfeet, Blood and North Piegan Withdrawal into Canada.</u>
(1862-1877)

The decade of the '60s was a particularly difficult one for the Blackfeet, beginning with the Montana Gold Rush, which in the summer of 1862 brought a host of white settlers through the Blackfeet country to the mines at the eastern base of the Rockies.

One of the first effects of this white invasion of Blackfeet territory upon the Indians was the abandonment of his little farm on Sun River by Little Dog, head chief of the Piegan, the only Indian to have shown any interest in the white men's program for getting the

Indians to give up buffalo hunting and turn to growing crops. Feeling insecure so near the trail from Fort Benton to the mines, Little Dog left his farm and returned to the nomadic camps of his people. (Annual Report Comm. Ind. Affairs, 1863, p. 180).

In 1864 the Territory of Montana was created, and its new Governor Edgerton, in his first speech to the new Territorial Legislature voiced a popular hope among the white settlers, that "the Government will, at an early date, take steps for the extinguishment of Indian title in this territory, in order that our lands may be brought into market." (Montana Historical Society Contribs., Vol. 3, p. 344).

In 1865 Blackfeet Agent Gad E. Upson was instructed by the Commissioner of Indian Affairs to negotiate a treaty with the Blackfeet tribes and the Gros Ventre under which they would agree to cede their land south of the Missouri and south of a line from the 48th parallel on the Rocky Mountains to the Teton River and down the Teton and Marias to the Missouri in return for annual payments to the value of $50,000 for a period of 20 years. (Annual Report Comm. Indian Affairs, 1865, 250-252).

At Fort Benton on Nov. 16, 1865, Commissioners Upson and Thomas F. Meagher, Acting Governor and ex officio Supt. of Indian Affairs for Montana Territory, concluded the treaty which was signed by 16 Piegan chiefs, 9 Blood ones, and 14 Gros Ventre chiefs, as well as by a single chief of the North Blackfeet. (This treaty is in the Office of Indian Affairs Records, The National Archives).

Meagher wrote that "The Blackfoot Nation was fully represented on the occasion, although the Blackfoot tribe appeared in the person of one Chief only, and all the hostile Bloods were absent." (He explained that the hostile Bloods were those involved in the massacre of 11 whites on the Marias the previous spring.) "These two bands retired some time ago, beyond our line into the British Possessions and have been living there ever since."

Meagher went on to state, "It strikes me forcibly that Indian tribes who voluntarily abandon their lands, seeking shelter and protection in a foreign country, cease to be essential parties to any treaty which the United States, previous to their emigration, might have held it necessary to conclude with them." (Meagher to Comm. Ind. Aff. Dec. 14, 1865). Indian Office Records, The National Archives).

There were no official proceedings kept of this treaty council However, the trader William T. Hamilton, who knew the Blackfeet well and who had been Sergeant at Arms at the council, explained 42 years later:

"The Small Robes band of Piegans claimed the land on the south side of the Missouri River as far as Musselshell River. They ceded in the treaty all their rights to this territory. Other Piegans and the Blood Indians claimed territory along the summit of the Rocky

Mountains south to the Little Blackfoot River and thence southeast to the Missouri River. In the treaty they ceded all the territory from the mouth of the Marias River up the Marias to the Teton River, following the middle of the stream to its source, for a stipulated sum to be given them for twenty years. The Gros Ventres had no land to cede. The Blackfeet also had no land to cede, and according to the views of many they had no business in this treaty because they lived in, and claimed to belong to, what they called Red Coat Land, namely that belonging to King George. Some of them wore King George's medals, and showed that they felt proud of them." (Hamilton, 1907, p.649).

Hamilton's statement appears to me a sensible one. It bears out the evidence from other sources in the previous decade to the effect that the little Small Robes band was the only Piegan band living south of the Missouri, and points out again that the North Blackfeet were really British Indians through their own choice. The Gros Ventre, of course, ceded no land under the terms of this treaty because none of the land ceded was occupied by them.

This treaty was never ratified because Commissioner of Indian Affairs Cooley, upon hearing of Indian depredations upon white settlers during the winter following the signing, refused to recommend it for ratification. On April 12, 1866, he wrote James Harlan, Secretary of the Interior, "In view of the facts, which appear to be well established, that the other bands of the Blackfeet nation have violated the treaty - obligatory upon them from the time it was made - I cannot recommend its ratification, but submit the papers for your consideration and for such directions as you may see fit to give in the premises." (D. N. Cooley to James Harlan, April 12, 1866. Indian Office Records. The National Archives).

Three years later Commissioner of Indian Affairs N. G. Taylor stated that this unratified treaty was still on file in his office. "I think that better arrangements can be made with the Blackfeet than this treaty proposes, and do not therefore recommend that it be ratified." (Annual Report Comm. Ind. Affairs, 1868, p. 223).

Although the Indians did not understand ratification, and certainly didn't know this treaty would not be ratified, their withdrawal to lands north of the Teton following the treaty was due more to hostile relations with white settlers than to their desire to comply with the stipulations of the treaty. On July 25, 1866, Acting Agent Hiram D. Upham reported from the Agency at Fort Benton:

"Bloods, Blackfeet and most of the North Piegans are at open war with the whites as well as with other tribes of Indians. They live for the most part in the British possessions, and only come here to receive their annuity goods or to commit some depredations. Many of them have never been here at all."

He also stated that 350 or 400 lodges of Lower Piegans live on the headwaters of Milk River and the Marias. They were led by two head chiefs Little Dog and Big Lake. (Annual Report Comm. Ind. Aff., 1866, p. 203).

Two months later the new Blackfeet Agent, George B. Wright reported that 375 lodges of the Lower (South) Piegan were on Marias River, along with some 40 lodges of Blood Indians. "The balance of the Blood Indians are with the Upper Piegans, in the British Possessions." Of the North Blackfeet he wrote, .. "they are still, as they have been for some time past, in the British possessions. They trade at Fort Edmonton...The treaty of last year they do not consider as binding upon them, for they were, numerically, poorly represented at that treaty by their chiefs and head men." (Annual Report Comm. Ind. Affairs, 1866, p. 204).

In 1868 W. J. Cullen was commissioned to make another treaty with the Blackfeet, under which they would cede the same area south of the Teton as specified in the 1865 unratified treaty. The other terms of this treaty were nearly identical with that earlier one, including the payments of $50,000 annually after ratification. The treaty was signed by large delegations of Piegan and Blood leaders, but again by only one North Blackfeet chief. (The treaty is on file in Indian Office Records, The National Archives).

But this treaty suffered the same fate as its predecessor of 1865. It was not ratified. And for the same reason Blackfeet depredations against the white settlers in violation of promises of peace at the treaty.

In 1868 Agent Wright reported, "The Blood and Blackfeet tribes roam mostly along the Saskatchewan river, and would try to be honest if left alone, but are encouraged by the trading post at Fort Edmonton to steal horses in this Territory and run them over on British soil for trading purposes." (Annual Report Comm. Ind. Aff., 1868, p. 205). Although Wright's statement regarding the location of these tribes was undoubtedly correct, his accusation against the Hudson's Bay Company traders was not proven.

During the next year (1869) the Blackfeet Indian Agency was moved from Fort Benton, where it had never been a popular location with the Indians because of the hostility of many of the townspeople toward the Indians, to a new site on the Teton River about 75 miles northwest of Fort Benton and some 5 miles north of present Choteau, Montana. The following winter the so-called "Blackfeet War", never more than a guerilla operation, was abruptly ended with the massacre of a camp of friendly Piegan on the Marias River by U. S. Cavalry commanded by Col. E. M. Baker (Jan. 23, 1870).

The following summer Gen. Alfred Sully described the lands occupied by the Blackfeet tribes thus:

"...while the Blackfeet nation claims in common, as their lands, the country both north and south of the British line, yet it is only the Piegans who generally inhabit the country south of the line. The Bloods occupy the country about the line, and the Blackfeet proper, all the country north as far as the Saskatchewan." (Sully to Comm. Ind. Affairs, July 10, 1870, Indian Office Records, The National Archives).

During the early seventies the South Piegan found the new Agency on the Teton much to their liking, and, though efforts to get them to settle down and raise crops in that locality were largely futile, many bands of that group wintered on the Teton not far from the Agency, while they hunted buffalo in warmer weather farther north. The Blackfeet and the majority of Blood Indians, living primarily in Canada, rarely if ever visited the Agency. The Agents' reports of the period 1871-74 are evidence of these facts.

In 1871 Agent Armitage reported: "The Blackfoot and Bloods are much together, traveling and hunting through about the same range of country, and during the summer months frequently go as far north as the Hudson Bay trading-post on the Elk (Red Deer) River, in the British possessions, a distance of between two hundred and two hundred and fifty miles from this point. The Piegans, more attached to their home, as they are learning to term the agency, do not extend their hunting excursions so far, but remain nearer, so that bands of them are coming and going to and from the agency and their main encampment constantly." (Annual Report Comm. Ind. Aff. 1871, pp. 427-428).

In 1873 Agent Ensign reported: ... "Piegans are the only Indians who, as a tribe, come to the agency for supplies. One band of the Bloods, under the chief Running Rabbit, also come regularly for their rations, but every effort on my part to induce the Blackfeet and the main camp of Bloods to visit the agency has thus far proved abortive. These tribes range north of the British line, from two hundred and fifty to four hundred miles from the agency, and are kept from coming in by illicit traders, who stop at nothing to accomplish the purpose, thus securing the very profitable trade of the Indians." (Annual Report Comm. Ind. Aff., 1873, p. 252).

On January 22, 1874, Agent May reported that the majority of the Piegan were in winter camp on the Teton River about 25 miles from the Agency. There were Blood Indians about 40 miles to the northwest on the forks of the Teton. While the Blackfeet tribe was wintering 50 to 100 miles north of the Agency. (R. F. May to Commissioner of Indian Affairs, Jan. 22, 1874. Indian Office Records, The National Archives).

Less than two months later May wrote:

"The Blackfeet Indians rarely if ever visit this reservation... They are nearly if not all, across the line, in the British Possessions. I have not seen more than 20 to 25 Blood Indians - they are, I understand, on and about Belly River which I believe is in the British Possessions.

About 60 to 65 miles north of this reservation, Cut Hand, a Piegan chief, is camped and he has with him some 10 to 12 lodges of Blood Indians, which I think comprises nearly a majority of the Bloods upon this Reservation.

The Piegans are encamped at various points upon this Reservation, and have had great success during the winter in killing buffalo." (May to Commissioner of Indian Affairs, March 6, 1874. Indian Office Records, The National Archives).

In early fall May wrote:

"For several years the ...Blackfeet and Bloods... have ranged across the line, none of the Blackfeet coming here, occasionally a few of the Bloods."

"The Piegans are in frequent intercourse with the Agency". (Annual Report Comm. Ind. Affairs, 1874, p. 259).

It is not surprising that none of the Blackfeet tribes were upset when the Executive Order of July 5, 1873, restricted their land to the area north of the Missouri and its western tributary Sun River. The Piegan, southernmost of the Blackfeet tribes, had not lived south of Sun River for at least 8 years. And for some time prior to that the only Piegan hunting band occupying the area south of the Missouri was the Small Robes. The loss of Royce Area 399, was no handicap to the Blackfeet tribes in making a living in the year 1873.

But when the Piegan heard that the Government was contemplating the further restriction of their area, the movement of their southern boundary north to the Marias and its southern tributary of Birch Creek, that was a different matter. Cession of land north of the Teton meant giving up land on which they were currently dwelling and from which they were making a living.

On March 24, 1874, Agent May wrote to Commissioner of Indian Affairs Edward P. Smith:

"Sir: Yesterday the Piegan Chief, Little Plume accompanied by several of his tribe, visited the Agency - and made known that a rumor had reached him and his people to the effect that it was in contemplation to remove the line of the Blackfoot Reservation to the Marias River. Little Plume says his people will never voluntarily consent to this change of line, for the reason it would confine them to too narrow strip of territory and deprive them of a large and desirable portion of their hunting ground.

I have conversed with a number of Piegans, and they are all decidedly opposed to the change, if contemplated. I wish to add, as my impression that the change would be unjust to the Indians, and cause great dissatisfaction.

Respectfully, R. F. May."

(May to Edward P. Smith, March 24, 1874, Indian Office Records, The National Archives.)

Agent May's letter to the Commissioner angered Martin Maginnis, Montana Territorial Delegate to Congress, who had introduced into Congress the bill to move the reservation boundary northward. On May 8, he wrote a letter to the Helena Weekly Independent stating in part, ... the bill which I introduced to move the Blackfoot Reservation back to the line of the Marias and Birch Creek has become a law. The present

Agency will be moved back on the Reservation and the Teton Valley thrown open to settlement. The remonstrances of the present Agent against this bill were received at the Department before its passage, but it was passed and signed notwithstanding, and that too with the approval of the Department." (Helena Weekly Independent, May 22, 1874).

May then wrote Maginnis, "I am sure I do not overstate the case when I say the Indians residing upon this reservation are unanimous in their opposition to the change of line - that is the removal beyond the Teton - south of the Teton they do not care for...I could have sent to you for presentation to Congress a 'remonstrance' bearing more than two thousand Indian signatures, but I contented myself by sending to the Hon. Commissioner the substance of the words spoken by the Chief Little Plume, and I know, and knew then that he spoke the sentiments of his Tribe." (May to Martin Maginnis, May 25, 1874. Martin Maginnis Papers, The Montana Historical Society).

The Executive Order was issued April 15, 1874, moving the southern boundary of the reservation northward from the Missouri River- Sun River boundary to the Marias River-Birch Creek line, thus freeing for white settlement Royce Area 574.

In his Annual Report Agent May again showed his indignation at this treatment of his Indians. "To take from peaceable, friendly Indians a very large portion of their best hunting and pasture land without consultation or remuneration, is a violation of the wise and

Christian policy of the Government." (Annual Report Comm. Indian Affairs, 1874, p. 260). Agent May took no steps to comply with the Executive Order and he was removed from his office.

His successor, John S. Wood entered on duty January 24, 1875. On February 15, he wrote the Commissioner: "The Indians would be satisfied if the South Bank of the Teton was made the line of the reservation." (Wood to Comm. Ind. Affairs, Feb. 15, 1875. Indian Office Records, The National Archives).

In The National Archives, Indian Office Records, there is a report from Andrew Dusold, Detective for the Blackfeet Agency to Agent Wood dated February 12, 1875, explaining the importance of the area between the Teton and Birch Creek to the Indians. The Indians had used and in fact were at that time using the valley of the Teton for winter camps. He stated, "Piegans and Blackfeet are camped on this stream in different camps for a distance of 55 miles from the Agency." The Teton offered the Indians an abundance of firewood, whereas none of the smaller streams between the Teton and Birch Creek afforded sufficient firewood for their winter camps. He pointed out that very few Indians encamped on the forks of the Marias in winter, but camped on the Teton and the main Marias where the buffalo ranged; that most of the timber along the Marias was on the south side of the river, which would be outside the boundaries of the new reservation; that there was no problem in summer "as the Indians will move to the Mountains and will camp along the described Forks of the Marias, hunting for small game, or will make their camp in the vicinity of the "Three Buttes" or "Sweet Grass Hills". He explained that "The Indians will and must follow the range of the Buffalo in winter:- In the beginning of Winter when the Buffalo appear from the North, their Range is away from the Mountains, crossing the Marias below its forks, ranging South-East, crossing the Teton about 30 miles below the Agency, and then crossing the Missouri River about 20 miles below Fort Shaw." Dusold also stated "The Piegans, Bloods and Blackfeet range to the line of Longitude 111 degrees". This would place the eastern limit of the Blackfeet tribes' range in the United States at that time in the neighborhood of the East Butte of the Sweet Grass Hills, and a little west of the big bend of the Marias.

It was on the basis of these practical considerations - the known winter range of the buffalo and the Indians' requirements for winter firewood - that Dusold recommended revision of the south boundary of the Reservation so as to include the Teton River within it. (Andrew Dusold, to John Wood February 12, 1875, Indian Office Records, The National Archives).

In the light of Dusold's explanation the Indian opposition to movement of the boundary north to Birch Creek makes much sense.

It was not based upon mere whim or obstinancy on their part. It was based upon their current needs for making a living in their country.

Meanwhile white settlers were applying pressure to make the Indians move north of the newly established boundary. The Agency on the Teton was becoming untenable. On February 2, 1875, Agent Wood reported that "partys here have preempted and filed claims covering the farm and stockade of this Agency and it makes matters here very unpleasant for an Agent." He found that the Indians "have a great love for this portion of the Country as their forefathers lived here and are buried here." He found that Agent May had led the Indians to believe that he would get the land back for them, which complicated his task. Yet he reported, "I have the consent of the greater portion of them to go to the new reservation and am told that there is plenty of wood, water and grass and the most of the buffalo is in that section of the country." (Wood to Comm. Ind. Affairs, Feb. 2, 1875. Indian Office Records. The National Archives.)

On May 14, Wood reported that within the past six weeks Indians visiting the Agency had between 75 and 100 horses stolen from them by whites, so that the Indians didn't want to return to the Agency on the Teton. (Wood to Commissioner of Indian Affairs, May 14, 1875. Indian Office Records, The National Archives). In the same letter Wood explained that he had selected a site for a new Agency on Badger Creek about 10 miles from the mountains.

The new Agency was constructed on the site now known as Running Crane's property, and early in November 1876, 19 months after the Executive Order of April 15, 1874, the headquarters of the Blackfeet Agency was moved north within the boundaries of the reservation established by that order.

Further proof of the withdrawal of the Blood and North Blackfeet into Canada is available in the action of the Indians on the Blackfeet Reservation in Montana, under the guidance and at the instigation of Agent Wood, of organizing and adapting a code of laws for their conduct in April 1875. A council was called of the headmen (chiefs) of bands to elect a head chief and two subordinate chiefs and to draft a code of laws to be administered by those chiefs in cooperation with the Agent. Of the fifteen chiefs of bands who took part in this council, I recognize the name of only one, "One-who-pulls-the-sun-down (or "Brings Down the Sun") a North Piegan Chief, who was not of the South Piegan division. Certainly the head chief they elected, Little Plume, and the two subordinate chiefs, Generous Woman and White Calf, were all chiefs of well known South Piegan bands. My field data indicate that Little Plume was chief of the Worm Band; Generous Woman chief of the Fat Roasters (or Grease Melters); and White Calf chief of the Skunks band. (The original of this document including the code of laws adopted April 23, 1875, is in the Indian Office Records, The National Archives).

Two years later the withdrawal of the North Blackfeet, Blood and North Piegan Indians from the United States culminated in their negotiation of a treaty with the Dominion of Canada. At Blackfoot Crossing on Bow River, September 22, 1877, these Indians along with the Sarcees and the Stonies (the northwestern division of the Assiniboin) signed Treaty No. 7 under which they agreed to behave and conduct themselves as good and loyal subjects of Her Majesty the Queen (Victoria). Under the conditions of this treaty they surrendered to the crown all their lands, comprising some 50,000 square miles lying westward of the Cypress Hills, northward of the international boundary and east of the Rocky Mountains. In return the Canadian Government agreed to permit the Indians to continue to hunt throughout this vast tract and assigned reserves to each tribe within the area of sufficient size to permit the Indians to allow 1 square mile for each family of five. (Morris, contains the complete text and proceedings of this treaty).

The Blackfeet, Bloods and Sarcees first took a reservation in common on both sides of Bow River above and below Blackfoot Crossing. But they did not get on well together and in the next year the Bloods were transferred to a new location on the Belly River and the Sarcees to the Elbow above Calgary. The Blackfeet remained near Blackfoot Crossing. The North Piegan located on a reservation in the Porcupine Hills on Oldman River above Fort Macleod. All of these reservations are in the Canadian Province of Alberta.

Since that time these organized tribes have been recognized subjects of the British Empire. They have had no official relations with the United States Government.

VI. <u>Period of the Extermination of the Buffalo and the South Piegan Land Agreements</u> (1878-1900).

In 1878, the year after Treaty No. 7, Agent Young reported from the Blackfeet Agency in Montana that the Indians were "now calling themselves by the general name Piegan". (Annual Report Comm. Ind. Affairs, 1878, p. 82). It would have been strange indeed if they didn't, for those hunting bands organized under the code of laws and then properly wards of the United States were Piegan Indians. They were more properly South Piegan, since the North Piegan, along with the Blood and North Blackfeet had chosen to become subjects of the Canadian Government rather than wards of the United States.

At that time the South Piegan were under the leadership of White Calf, chief of the Skunks band, who had been elected head chief of the tribe in October 1877, following the death of Little Plume. The South Piegan were divided into eleven hunting bands as indicated by Agent Young's description of the distribution of annuities in the spring of 1879. "In the afternoon distributed the annuities to Big Nose Band, and Three Suns occupied in giving the annuities to the other ten bands viz., White Calf, Running Crane, Fast Buffalo Horse, Horse Head, No Runner, Red Paint, Tearing Lodge, Four Bears, The Horn, The General, Big Lake and Lodge Pole Chief." (Agent Young's Letter Book, May 8, 1879, Blackfeet Agency Archives, Museum of the Plains Indian, Browning, Montana). Big Nose (also known as Three Suns) probably was second chief of the South Piegan at the time. Some of the bands must then have had more than one chief, since the number of names exceeds eleven.

Ever since the 1855 treaty Blackfeet Agents had been trying to interest their Indian charges in planting crops and tilling the soil, but without rousing any great interest among the Indian buffalo hunters. In 1878 Young reported that "there are still a large number who will only pursue the chase for a living, and until the game becomes too scarce to afford it, are not likely to give up their roving mode of life." (Annual Report Comm. Indian Affairs, 1878, p.84).

In the winter of 1878-1879 Agent Young reported that one large camp of his Indians, under White Calf made a successful hunt near the Bearpaw Mountains. (Agent Young's Letter Book, Feb. 1, 1879. Blackfeet Agency Archives). That summer the main camp was also hunting near the Bearpaw Mountains. (Ibid., Aug. 1, 1879).

But by the winter of 1879-1880 the buffalo had been nearly exterminated in the Blackfeet country in Canada. To minimize the starvation among his wards the Canadian Indian Commissioner Edgar B. Dewdney gave his Indians some provisions and advised them to cross the line to hunt buffalo in Montana. He later claimed that this action had saved the Canadian Government "at least $100,000." (Sharp, 1955, p. 155, quotes the Dewdney correspondence on this subject).

From then on the South Piegan were forced to hunt buffalo where they could find them, on or off the reservation. They were in competition for the dwindling game supply not only with other Indians in Montana, but with the Blackfeet, Cree and Assiniboin who came down from Canada after the buffalo had disappeared in their own country. In the winter of 1879-1880 they went far south to the Judith Basin. White men, disturbed by this great influx of red men onto their lands, protested that the Indians were killing cattle and had the South Piegan escorted back north to their reservation by the army. Agent Young later learned that cattle had been killed by young men of Running Rabbit's North Piegan that winter on land south of the reservation. (Agent Young Letter Book, Jan. 6, 1882. Blackfeet Agency Archives).

From then on the number of Indians encamped near the Agency on Badger Creek (then moved a few miles down stream from the Running Crane site to the location still known as "Old Agency"), in winter increased as the number of buffalo decreased. The South Piegan remained buffalo hunters to the end. And the bitter end came in 1883 and 1884 when upward of 400 of them starved to death after the buffalo were gone.

In the fall of 1883, shortly after the buffalo were gone a Subcommittee of the Special Committee of the United States Senate, appointed to visit the Indian tribes of Montana, composed of Senator Vest of Missouri and Delegate Maginnis of Montana, met with the chiefs of the South Piegan at the Blackfeet Agency. They found the starving Indians quite willing to offer some of their gameless land in exchange for those things which would help them to make a living now that the buffalo were gone. In council on September 15, 1883, Chief Little Dog described the land that might be retained for their reservation and the land that might be given up. "I want a reservation with the Birch Creek on the south, as now. We like the land near the mountains. On the east you can draw a line from the western end of the Sweet Grass Hills to the Marias River. That would touch the river near Willow Sound. The country between that and the mountains we would like to have. From that line down to the Bear Paw we have no use for the country. There is no game there. We don't want to go there. We would rather stay here where there are streams and good land, and where our homes lie. The reason I put the line so far east is that I want the people to have a good living; plenty of range for horses and stock. We want the Government to help us." (Report of the Subcommittee to visit the Indian Tribes of Montana, pp. 242-243).

Head Chief White Calf, Little White Cow, Big Nose and Running Crane all spoke in support of Little Dog's proposal as to the lands to be ceded. (Ibid., pp. 243-244). This description throws considerable light upon tribal land claims upon the great northern reservation (Royce Area 565). The South Piegan regarded the land as far eastward as the Bearpaw Mountains as theirs, and of this they were willing to cede that part which was of least value to them now that the buffalo were gone - ie. that part from the western end of the Sweet Grass Hills (ie. West Butte) eastward. The landmark "Willow Sound" in the text must be a misprint for "Willow Round" which was a former camping place of the Piegan on the Marias less than five miles east of its forks. (See the map in Ewers, 1955, Plate 7).

The Subcommittee recommended "the appointment of a commission to treat with the tribes for part of their lands". (Report of Subcommittee etc., p. 234). But apparently Mr. Maginnis decided not to wait for the action of such a commission. On February 25, 1884, he introduced into the House of Representatives a bill "To provide permanent reservations for the Indians in Northern Montana, and for other purposes", which provided for a reservation for the "Piegan, Blood and Blackfeet Indians belonging to the Blackfeet Agency" in the western portion of the existing large reservation, west of "a line drawn due south from the national boundary, at the western extremity of the Sweet Grass Hills to the Maria's River". (H.R. 5427, 48th Congress, 1st Session). A similar bill (S. 1710) was introduced in the Senate by Senator Vest on March 4, 1884. However, the Commissioner of Indian Affairs, expressed his disapproval of the Bill, although he seemed to have no specific objection to that portion of it dealing with the Blackfeet Reservation and its establishment. (Commissioner of Indian Affairs, to The Secretary of the Interior, April 3, 1884. The National Archives, Record Group 233).

By Act of May 15, 1886, The Northwest Commission was appointed to negotiate with the Indians in the great reservation north of the Missouri (Royce Area 565). On February 8, 1887, the members of this Commission (John V. Wright, J. W. Daniels, and C. F. Larrabee) arrived at the Blackfeet Agency after taking 16 days to make the last 100 miles of their journey northward from Sun River under abominable weather conditions, with as much as 2 feet of snow and temperatures as low as 50 degrees below zero. No minutes of their council with the Blackfeet (South Piegan) were taken, but the Commissioners' Report of Negotiations, dated Blackfeet Agency February 11, 1887, is in The National Archives. (Indian Office Records, Special Case 144). This report is sufficient to show that the Indians originally demanded $3,000,000 for the relinquishment of their interest in the surplus lands of the reservation and stubbornly refused to accept the Commissioners' offer of $125,000 per annum. "Finally, however, after long and patient reasoning with them they agreed to accept $150,000 per annum for the period mentioned".

The Commissioners reported that the Indians' demands for a proportionately greater sum for their land cessions than was agreed upon by the Indians of Fort Peck and Fort Belknap Agencies were based upon two arguments. Both of them appear to me to have been spurious.

The First argument was based on population - that there "are more than 2,000 Indians at present attached to the Agency, and there are from 500 to 1,000 on the other side of the international line, who properly belong to the agency, and are likely to return sooner or later." This argument took advantage of the ignorance of the Commissioners. My elderly Indian informants on the Blackfeet Reservation in the early 1940s recalled that it was a favorite Indian device among the Blackfeet tribes on both sides of the line at that period to play both ends against the middle and receive annuities from both countries, and that they were able to get away with it in view of the poor records of individual Indians then kept at the Agencies. If we will refer to the Appendix on Indian Populations accompanying this report we will see that the populations of the Blackfeet Reservation in 1887 was officially listed as 1,927 and that it did not exceed 2,293 in any year from that time until 1900. There is no sharp rise of from 500 to 1,000 souls such as this argument promised.

The second argument was based upon longer occupancy - that "these Indians, no doubt have the most ancient claim upon the ceded territory - as far eastward as the mouth of Milk River.

They occupied it as far back as their history is known, and they naturally feel that they have a stronger claim to it than any of the other Indians." As brought out in the earlier sections of this report, the Piegan were not aboriginal occupants of this area (Royce Area 565). Like the Gros Ventre they entered it after the smallpox epidemic of 1781. They did not occupy the region north of the Missouri as far as the mouth of Milk River. That was Gros Ventre territroy.

The reduction of the lands of the South Piegan and their establishment on the Blackfeet Reservation in Montana was approved and became law by Act of Congress May 1, 1888. The reservation is Royce Area 695.

None of the land ceded by the South Piegan under this Agreement was occupied by them at the time. At the time of the cession the Blackfeet owned some 30 head of cattle. They were living within a limited area on the southwestern part of their reservation within a radious of less than 15 miles of their Agency, where they received weekly rations from the Government. The Agents' Annual Report in the summer of 1888 stated that they then cultivated 340 acres of land, and estimated that 83% of their subsistence was obtained from Government rations, 12% from labor in civilized pursuits and 5% from hunting, fishing, root gathering etc. (Annual Report Comm. Indian Affairs, 1888, p. 419, 436).

In the summer of 1951 Dr. Claude Schaeffer, Curator of the Museum of the Plains Indian and I went over the Badger Creek area both east and west of Old Agency with Adam White Man, an elderly Piegan and Louis Bear Child, a Piegan Interpreter, and they pointed out and explained to us just where the Piegan bands lived in the period after the buffalo disappeared (1884-1887). Proceeding down stream from west to east these people resided in the following localities:

The Black Door Band was settled on Badger Creek from the crossing of the present road from Browning to Heart Butte community and Swims Under School eastward. They were the westernmost band on Badger Creek.

Below them around the site of the first Badger Creek Agency and downstream to the end of Albert Mad Plume's property was the Lone Eater's Band.

On the north side of Badger Creek opposite the present Mad Plume School was a mixed group, families from different bands, under the leadership of Big Plume.

Below this group were the Grease Melters, under Big Nose (Three Suns). In 1881 this band had moved north to Two Medicine River and built some cabins. But a series of horse raids by Cree Indians forced them to abandon their little settlement and return to Badger

Creek in 1883.

Below them lived the greater part of the Black Patched Moccasins Band under Little Dog.

Below them in the area of the crossing of the present highway from Great Falls to Browning lived the Piegan's "white brother-in-laws", the squaw men with their Indian wives and mixed-blood children.

Below them was the Old Agency and near it about 100 cabins built to house the old people when Old Agency was first built (1879).

The Small Robes lived near Old Agency but the band was in process of breaking up as a residential unit, and its members were going to live with other bands.

About a mile east of Old Agency on the flat south of Badger Creek was the trading post operated by Joe Kipp.

Just east of the trading post the Buffalo Dung Band was settled.

Below them were some of the older people of the Black Patched Moccasins Band. On the flat south of this group was the site of the first medicine lodge in which cattle tongues were employed as sacred food the summer after the buffalo disappeared.

Below this locality lived another group of the Buffalo Dung Band under Shorty White Grass.

Below them lived the easternmost band on Badger Creek, a small group, constituting all that was left of the Bugs Band after the starvation winter.

In addition to these groups on Badger Creek, Adam White Man stated that the following bands, the remainder of the tribe, lived on the next stream southward, Birch Creek:

    The Blood Band, under Chief Fast Buffalo Horse.
    The All Chiefs, under Chief Horn.
    The Skunks, under Head Chief White Calf.

This accounts for the location of the 11 bands of the South Piegan in that period. Adam White Man stated that it was not until after the land Agreement negotiated in 1887 that the Indians began to move north and establish permanent homes north of Badger Creek.

This information appears to be confirmed by Agent Baldwin's Annual Report of August 22, 1888, in which he states:

"Heretofore their farm work was confined to Birch and Badger Creek bottoms. This season about 150 acres on Two Medicine Creek were plowed and sown with potatoes, oats and barley. On Cut Bank Creek about 70 acres were broken and planted with like seed, and on both sides of the White Tail Creeks a number of patches of ground have been plowed and planted, all of which promises a fair return for their labor." (Annual Report Comm. Ind. Aff. 1888, p. 151).

Undoubtedly this northern movement over the reservation reflected the hope of the Indians for better times ahead with the assistance they were about to receive from the Government under the

159

terms of the Agreement. They had traded land for an opportunity to make a living. In 1890 some 1,000 heifers and 25 bulls were issued to these Indians and additional issues of cattle were made in subsequent years. In 1893 Agent George Steel stated: "The Indians are now well scattered out over the reservation on ranches which they have selected, instead of being bunched up in bands as formerly." (Annual Report Commissioner of Indian Affairs, 1893, p. 172). By scattered, he of course meant scattered along the river valleys, where, like their ancestors of buffalo days, the Indians' homes were sheltered from the elements in winter, and ready access to firewood and drinking water.

The South Piegan were prospering under the new Agreement. By 1896 there were more than 500 different cattle brands on the reservation stock book. (Annual Report of the Commissioner of Indian Affairs, 1896, p. 176). The building of the Great Northern Railway across the reservation in the early '90s, the opening of the new boarding school on Willow Creek in 1892 and the movement of the Blackfeet Agency to present Browning, north of the railroad in March 1895, further encouraged the development of the northern portion of the reservation. This movement of settlement was from north to south on the plains, not westward into the mountainous area of the reservation.

In his annual Report for the year 1893 Agent George Steell,

who had known the South Piegan for some 40 years, wrote:

"The western border of this reservation is the summit of the Rocky Mountains. Eastward from the summit for an average distance of 20 miles the country is very mountainous and broken, and totally unfit for grazing or agriculture. It is of no use to the Indians, as they do not even hunt the game it contains. This section is said to contain considerable mineral, and I am constantly having trouble with the whites, who are persistently prospecting it. A police force many times larger than I have would hardly be able to patrol it, and the Indians are continually worrying, saying the whites are stealing their gold, and that when the Government gets ready to buy it the mineral will have been carried off and they will get little or nothing. I suggest that a strip of the western border of the reservation, at least 20 miles in width, be sold and the proceeds be placed to the credit of the Indians as an additional fund for their support and maintenance." (Annual Report Comm. Ind. Aff., 1893, p. 172-173).

In September 1895, another Commission met with the South Piegan on the Blackfeet Reservation to negotiate for the cession of this troublesome western area of the reservation. (The Proceedings of the Commissioners are Doc. No. 51,494, 1895, in the Indian Office Records, The National Archives). The Commissioners visited the western portion of the reservation with the aim of determining where a line could be drawn which would separate the mineral bearing land from the grazing lands and as much of the timber lands as possible.

In the council with the Indians which followed they again asked $3,000,000 for the area to be ceded. This was more than the Commissioners believed they were authorized to agree to. At the conclusion of the session on Sept. 23, there appeared no possibility of an agreement being reached. But when the council convened again on Sept. 25, after the Indian leaders had conferred with Agent Steell, Joe Kipp the old trader, and Joe Cook the butcher, Head Chief White Calf offered to cede the mountainous strip from Birch Creek to the international boundary, with all grazing land excluded and retaining the Indians' right to hunt, fish and obtain timber in the mountain area for one and one-half million dollars. The Agreement was concluded on this basis on Sept. 26, 1895, and signed by the Commissioners and 306 of the total adult male population of the Blackfeet Reservation of 381.

This agreement extended for another 10 years the assistance which the Government had inaugurated with the conclusion of the previous land agreement in the '80s.

It is impossible to assess the value of this assistance in terms of money alone. It provided the South Piegan, weakened by short rations after the buffalo suddenly disappeared, with no knowledge or experience in making a living in a world in which there were no buffalo, and with no resources other than an abundance of land, an opportunity to exchange their surplus land for the means of making a living, to obtain an education for their children, and to gain experience in the white man's civilization of which they must henceforth be a part.

One has but to compare the figures from the Annual Reports of the Blackfeet Agents for the years 1886 (before the assistance offered under the first Land Agreement became available) with those for the year 1900 (with seven more years of aid ahead under the provisions of the second Land Agreement) to realize how much this assistance meant to the South Piegan in the short period of 14 years.

	1886	1900
Number of Indians who can read	18	900
Number who wear citizens dress	40	2,085 (all)
Horses and mules owned by Indians	1,205	22,004
Cattle owned by Indians	None	12,000
Acres cultivated by Indians	12	500
Oats, barley, rye harvested	30 bu.	700 bu.
Vegetables harvested	100 bu.	3,700 bu.
Hay cut	170 tons	6,000 tons

As a serious student of Blackfeet cultural history for more than 15 years it is my opinion that in no other period of comparable duration have the South Piegan made such progress. It is my further belief that this progress would not have been possible without the annual expenditures for their benefit under the terms of the land agreements.

At the same time it should be pointed out that the South Piegan ceded none of their occupied lands under these agreements, and that they retained a far higher ratio of land to population than was granted to their relatives in Canada, the North Piegan, Blood and North Blackfeet.

If the South Piegan's land seems small today in comparison to their population it is due to two factors (1) the relinquishment of ownership to land by individual Indians since the period these agreements expired and (2) the phenomenal growth of the South Piegan population since that time. As recently as 1910 their population was 2,268, and the Bureau of the Census commented, "Since 1885 there has been little change in numbers". (Indian Population in the United States and Alaska, 1910. Washington, 1915, p. 75). No one at that time or prior to it would have predicted that their numbers would have nearly tripled in the next thirty years (ie. 5,914 in 1950).

VII. The Gros Ventre and their Allies in the Milk River Country. (1862-1890).

Basic to an understanding of the problems of Gros Ventre land occupancy in this period is some understanding of their inter-tribal relations during this period. Although some Government officials continued to regard them as a part of the so-called "Blackfoot Nation" for years after the 1855 treaty they definitely were not. In 1862 they not only were not allies of the Blackfeet tribes - they were enemies and throughout the remainder of buffalo days they remained apart from and generally hostile to the Blackfeet.

Yet the Gros Ventre were numerically a small tribe. In 1860 Agent Vaughan estimated their population at 265 lodges, with a total population of 2,100, of which only 400 were men. (Annual Report Comm. Indian Affairs, 1858, p. 308). By contrast, the Blackfeet tribes were estimated by Vaughan at 910 lodges and 1,660 men. (Ibid., p. 308). The Piegan alone had 900 men, roughly twice the manpower of the Gros Ventre. (Ibid., p. 308).

To protect themselves against the powerful and warlike Blackfeet tribes, as well as against the powerful Sioux who were pressing westward from present North Dakota as the buffalo became scarce in their former hunting ground, it was necessary for the Gros Ventre to ally themselves with and to share their hunting grounds with segments of other tribes which were enemies of the Blackfeet tribes and had been displaced by the aggressive Sioux from their own territories. These allies were primarily the River Crow, the northern segment of the Crow Indians, and the Upper Assiniboin, the southwestern segment of the Assiniboin.

So from the early '60s until the extermination of the buffalo the Gros Ventre could not claim sole occupancy of their hunting grounds. During this period also Gros Ventre population declined due to war losses, a serious smallpox epidemic in 1869-70, and starvation as the buffalo became extinct as a wild species in their country.

Piegan-Gros Ventre relations were strained at the time of the 1855 treaty. In the fall of 1861 a Pend d'Oreille war party stole horses from the Gros Ventre camp on the Missouri about 35 to 40 miles below Fort Benton, and to throw their pursuers off their track as they headed homeward the clever horse thieves left some of the stolen horses near a Piegan camp on the Marias some 12 miles from Fort Benton. The Gros Ventre, recognizing their horses and believing the Piegan had taken them, attacked the Piegan camp and killed an old chief. (Bradley, Vol. 9, p. 313-314).

Thus warfare between these old allies was inaugurated. In the following winter the fur trader, Charles Larpenteur, found that because of their war with the Piegan the Gros Ventre were afraid to take their robes to Fort Benton to trade. (Larpenteur, Vol. 2, p. 335). And Father De Smet, who traveled up the Missouri to Fort Benton by steamboat in the summer of 1862, commented, "A war between the Gros Ventres and other Blackfeet bands rendered traveling in the country somewhat unsafe." (Chittenden and Richardson, Vol. 4, p. 1512).

When the unratified treaty of 1865 was made with "The Blackfoot Nation" at Fort Benton in the fall of 1865, the Commissioners had difficulty getting the Gros Ventre leaders to come in to take part in the negotiations. When they did come the Gros Ventre camped apart at the other end of the bottom land from the Blackfeet tribes, and the whites had considerable difficulty in preventing the Blackfeet from attacking the Gros Ventre camp after the negotiations were ended. (Hamilton, 1907, pp. 648-649). Hamilton explained, "for the last four years they had been at war and there was the bitterest hatred between them." (Ibid., p. 648).

Undoubtedly their warfare with the stronger Blackfeet tribes caused the Gros Ventre to withdraw to the southeast. Agent Upson reported in 1864 that the Gros Ventre "occupy the extreme eastern portion of the Blackfeet lands, in the vicinity of Milk River, near its mouth." He estimated their number at 233 lodges or 1,864 souls, a reduction from Vaughan's estimate of four years earlier. (Annual Report Comm. Ind. Affairs, 1864, p. 296). At the same time the River Crow were "at or about the mouth of the Muscle Shell river, having been driven by the Sioux from their country on the Yellowstone river." (Ibid., p. 263). [167] These two tribes, both harrassed by more powerful neighbors, joined forces and hunted northward in Gros Ventre territory.

On February 2, 1866, Acting Agent Upham wrote, "The Gros Ventres and Crows are camped near together." He reported that Gros Ventre chiefs complained, "Why do the whites sit still and let the Piegans and Bloods steal their horses and kill them like dogs?" (Annual Report Comm. Ind. Aff. 1866, p. 199). The following summer the allied Gros Ventre-Crow attacked a large Piegan camp consisting of nearly all the bands of that tribe near the Cypress Hills. The

Piegan rallied and routed these enemies inflicting upon the Gros Ventre the most severe defeat in their history. (A detailed, dramatic account of this battle appears in Grinnell, 1895, pp. 134-142).

The Gros Ventre were afraid to show up at Fort Benton that fall for distribution of goods by their Agent. He explained "The Gros Ventre tribe could not receive theirs owing to their fears of meeting with the Piegans at Fort Benton, who had but recently fought and badly whipped them near the Cypress Mountains, killing some three hundred, capturing some three of their squaws and two children, besides taking from them nearly all their horses." (Annual Report Comm. of Indian Affairs, 1867, p. 258).

When a treaty was made with the Blackfeet tribes in 1868, the Government found it necessary to treat with the Gros Ventre separately, because of the impossibility of getting the Gros Ventre and Blackfeet together. While the Blackfeet negotiated at Fort Benton, the Gros Ventre did so at Fort Hawley on July 13, 1868. (See copy of this treaty in Indian Office Records, The National Archives).

Although the Government continued to support the fiction that the Gros Ventre were a part of "The Blackfoot Nation" (a fiction which Doty had recognized as such even before the 1855 treaty), the Commissioner of Indian Affairs recognized that they did not associate with the Blackfeet tribes but with the River Crow, and that they should be treated with on that basis.

"Although the Gros Ventres are a part of the Blackfeet Nation, yet they are not on friendly terms with the other tribes composing that nation, live away from them, and, it is understood, speak a different language. These, in my judgment, should be treated with separately, and as they are friendly toward, and associate with, the River Crows, no doubt the best disposition that could be made would be to place them upon a reservation with that tribe." So wrote N. G. Taylor, Commissioner of Indian Affairs to the Secretary of the Interior on April 18, 1868. (Annual Report Comm. Ind. Affairs, 1868, p. 224).

Although the Gros Ventre participated in both the 1865 and 1868 treaties with the "Blackfeet Nation" the lands described for cession in these unratified treaties had not been ones occupied by that tribe. Anything they might have gained from such cessions would have been pure gain without any compensating loss of land. Nevertheless, they like the Blackfeet tribes were disappointed when no annuities were received due to failure of these treaties to be ratified.

By 1869 the Gros Ventre on Milk River were shifting their preference from the River Crow to the Upper Assiniboin, their neighbors to the east. During the summer of 1868 the Gros Ventre married about 100 of the Assiniboin women which the Agent wrote "will have a tendency to cement these two tribes together". However, these Assiniboin and the River Crow were not friendly, and the Agent recommended that the River Crow, estimated at 2,000 souls, should either be sent south to the Crow Reservation or go on a reservation by themselves. (Annual Report Comm. Ind. Aff., 1869, pp. 200-201; 291; 299-300). At the same time he recommended that the Assiniboin and Gros Ventre be placed on the same reservation. (Ibid., p. 201).

In that same year Gen. Alfred Sully, Superintendent of Indian Affairs for Montana Territory, wrote of the Gros Ventre, "There are about two thousand souls in the tribe - this is as near as I can learn - and are located on a reservation on Milk River." (Ibid., p. 292) At the same time he wrote of the Assiniboin. "Those who occupy our country permanently muster about two thousand souls.... I believe it would be well to remove these Indians to the agency lately built on Milk River for the Gros Ventres and River Crows provided the latter tribe should move and join their people, Montana Crows, on the reservation south of the Yellowstone, for they are not firendly with these Indians, while they are with the Gros Ventres." (Ibid., p. 289).

The Agency mentioned was the Milk River Agency, built on the Milk River about 70 miles due north from the Missouri, for the Gros Ventre and River Crow in 1868. The River Crow considered the Milk River country a buffalo hunter's paradise and so were reluctant to leave it. Yet they did so temporarily when the Gros Ventre contracted smallpox in the winter of 1869-70. The Gros Ventre suffered terrible losses from the plague. General Sully reported that 741 of them died, leaving "only about 1200 of this nation alive." (Sully to Comm. Ind. Affairs, Jan. 31, 1870, Indian Office Records, The National Archives).

The majority of the River Crow fled southward across the Missouri to the Judith Basin, and they suffered only 30 deaths. In the winter of 1869-70 all of the Gros Ventre, 60 lodges of Assiniboin and 12 lodges of Arapaho (who had come north in the previous fall to visit their Gros Ventre kinsmen) were camped near the Milk River Agency. In the early part of the winter the Crows camped but 40 miles distant. (Sully to Comm. of Indian Affairs, Feb. 26, 1870, Indian Office Records, The National Archives).

While the Gros Ventre were weakened by the smallpox, the Sioux approached from the eastward and attacked the Agency. General Phillip H. Sheridan, while passing down the Missouri in the spring of 1870, learned that, "the Gros Ventres of the Prairie...have been driven into Bear Paw Mountains by a war band of Yanktons from Fort Randall, assisted by Santee Sioux from Lake Winnipeg, who now hold the Milk River country." (Sheridan to Adjt. General of the Army, July 1, 1870, Indian Office Records, The National Archives).

Sheridan passed a band of River Crow on the Missouri and recommended that they "should be placed on a good reservation at some point along the Missouri, or a little South of it, at the Judith Mountains, and well fed." (Ibid.). From the Crow Agent,

E. M. Camp we learn that 40 lodges of the River Crow joined the Mountain Crow in May, 1870, and went on the summer hunt with them. The rest of the River Crow, 60 lodges later joined them. He expressed the desire to make the meeting of the two Crow divisions permanent. (Annual Report Comm. Indian Affairs, 1870, p. 198).

In early July 1870 the Santee and Yanctonai Sioux again attacked Milk River Agency, but the Gros Ventre had already fled westward to escape the Sioux. General Sully wrote, "I believe it to be the intention of these Sioux to take forceable possession of this Country, driving off from it the Indians who now occupy it, who are much weaker in number than they are." (Sully to Comm. of Indian Affairs, July 20, 1870, Indian Office Records, The National Archives).

From 1870 on these hostile Sioux were a factor of importance in the Indian occupation of the Milk River country and eastward in present Montana. Next summer Special Agent Simmons reported that large bands of the "Yankton, Santee, and other Sioux have attached themselves to the Milk River country declaring their intent to stay there." (Annual Report Comm. Ind. Affairs, 1871, p. 412). Simmons estimated their numbers at about 2500 Santee, and about 4,300 Yankton, Yanktonai and Cutheads. In the face of this invasion the weaker Assiniboin, Gros Ventre and River Crow were forced westward. The Gros Ventre and their friends the Upper Assiniboin and River Crow hunted farther west between the Bearpaw Mountains and the Little Rockies, and with them were their friends the Northern Arapaho and Cheyenne. Frequently the Gros Ventre joined the River Crow to hunt in the Judith Basin and south of the Missouri. (Annual Report Comm. Ind. Affairs, 1871, pp. 430-431).

In 1872 the Cowan Commission was sent west to investigate conditions. Upon their recommendation the Milk River Agency was abandoned and two new Agencies established - Fort Belknap farther west on Milk River (near present Chinook) and the first Fort Peck Agency, on the Missouri, just above the mouth of Milk River. In the same year that these Agencies were built the large northern reservation was established comprising all of Montana north of the Missouri and its western tributary, the Sun River, by the Executive Order of July 5, 1873. This area was designated as a "reservation for the Gros Ventre, Piegan, Blood, Blackfeet, River Crow, and other Indians of the Territory of Montana." (Kappler, 1904, pp. 855-856). (Royce Area 565).

The land ceded by the Indians as a result of this Order did not include any of the area then occupied by the Gros Ventre north of the Missouri River, nor did the land ceded by the Executive Order of April 15, 1874, (Royce Area 574).

In 1874 the Gros Ventre numbered 960, and the Upper

Assiniboin (also assigned to Fort Belknap Agency) totaled almost twice that number (1,700). In addition "bands of Lower Assiniboines and of Northern Assiniboines and of Northern Crees from British America, to the number of 1,000 are often camped with the Indians of this agency." (Annual Report Comm. Ind. Affairs, 1874, p. 50). At that time game was abundant in the region and the Indians had undertaken no farming operations. (Ibid., p. 50). The River Crow, named in the Executive Order of July 5, 1873, preferred to join their kinsmen the Mountain Crow on the Crow Reservation farther south. Actually the majority of the River Crow (50 of some 90) lodges were living in the south when the Executive Order was issued. (Annual Report Comm. Ind. Aff., 1873, p. 248). So the joint occupancy of land north of the Missouri by the Gros Ventre and Crow lasted for just about a decade, or from 1864 to 1874.

In 1874 the Gros Ventre and Assiniboin were sandwiched between two of the most powerful and warlike peoples on the Great Plains - the Sioux on the east and the Blackfeet on the west. Their retreat from the Sioux had taken them closer to the Blackfeet. Blackfeet Agent May reported a battle between the Piegan under Black Eagle against an Assiniboin and Gros Ventre force in which four Piegan were killed. The fight took place on January 20, 1874, between the Milk River and Bearpaw Mountains. (May to Comm. Indian Affairs, Jan. 24, 1874, Indian Office Records, The National Archives). On May 16 of that year the Piegan signed separate treaties of peace with the Gros Ventre and Assiniboin at Fort Benton. (The signed treaties are in The National Archives, Indian Office Records). However, like virtually all peace negotiations between Blackfeet chiefs and the chiefs of neighboring tribes, they were of little practical value, because the ambitious young men refused to abide by them. The Gros Ventre - Piegan peace lasted less than eight months. In early December 1874, a Piegan war party killed a Gros Ventre in sight of Fort Benton. (Bradley, Vol. 9, p. 314). Several of my own elderly Piegan and Blood Indian informants of the early 1940s, who took active part in the intertribal warfare of the late 1870s and early 1880s told me of their exploits against the Gros Ventre and Assiniboin. The Blackfeet tribes did not become really friendly with the Gros Ventre and Assiniboin until after 1885.

The number of the Assiniboin sharing the western portion of the former Gros Ventre country with the Gros Ventre varied from year to year as large groups or families moved back and forth between the Upper and Lower Assiniboin. In 1875 as many as 3,500 Upper Assiniboin were reported. (Annual Report Comm. Ind. Affairs, 1875, p. 307). When, in 1876, the Government attempted to consolidate the Fort Peck Agency for the Gros Ventre, Assiniboin and neighboring Sioux, Fort Belknap Agency was discontinued. The Upper Assiniboin consented to move to Wolf Point, but the Gros Ventre refused to go there because of their fear of the Sioux. (Annual Report Comm. Ind. Affairs, 1876, p. 93). That summer the Indians of Fort Peck Agency (which would include the Gros Ventres in the west) were described as hunting as far west as the Little Rockies and Bearpaw Mountains. (Idem. p. 91). Again in 1877 the Gros Ventre refused to go to Fort Peck to receive supplies. (Annual Report Commissioner of Indian Affairs, 1877, p. 137).

Next year it became necessary to again establish two Agencies, one for the Lower Assiniboin and Sioux at new Fort Peck (on Poplar River), and the other at Fort Belknap for the Gros Ventre and Upper Assiniboin. The new Agent at Fort Belknap found his Indians "in a very demoralized state, and very much scattered, some of them on the Marias River, and some of them across the Missouri River. A part of the Gros Ventres and other Indians were camped near the fort. (Annual Report Commissioner of Indian Affairs, 1879, p. 89). The buffalo were becoming less numerous and it became necessary for the Indians to travel more widely to obtain food. But the Gros Ventre and Upper Assiniboin were prevented from hunting on the Lower Milk River by the Sioux. "My Indians have started several times to go to the Lower Milk River Country in pursuit of buffalo, but have invariably been frightened back by hostile Sioux." (Ibid., p. 89). To add to the Gros Ventre difficulties there were at least 2,000 British Indians, both Assiniboin and Cree coming south to hunt buffalo, no longer found north of the line. Part of the River Crow came north during the winter and in spring 35 lodges of them again, but they became frightened of the Sioux and retreated south of the Missouri. (Ibid., pp. 98-100).

In 1881 the same Agent made a realistic appraisal of the large area covered by his reservation - some 2,500 square miles (even excluding the large Fort Assiniboine military Reservation established in 1879), between the international line on the north, the Missouri River on the south, the 109th parallel on the east and the Marias River on the west - and concluded it was much larger than the wants of his 2,000 Indians required. They numbered at that time some 1,100 Gros Ventre and 900 Assiniboin. (Annual Report Comm. of Indian Affairs, 1881, p. 117-118).

When the Subcommittee of the Special Committee of the United States Senate appointed to visit the Indian Tribes in Northern Montana visited Fort Assiniboine on September 19, 1883, they met the Gros Ventre chief Jerry and Assiniboin chief Little Chief, in council. They were fully aware of the fact that the buffalo were nearly gone and willing to give up part of their land in exchange for such more useful items as farming implements, seed etc. Jerry expressed his desire to retain the land from the military reservation on Milk River east to the mouth of Beaver Creek from Milk River on the north to the Missouri River on the south. He was willing to give up the land north of Milk River and "towards the Sweet Grass Hills". When it was suggested that he might take land farther east from the west line of the Little Rockies eastward beyond Beaver Creek, he replied, "I been raised here, and do not want to go further east. I know this to be good country, and would like to keep it." (Report of the Subcommittee etc., p. 245). The Assiniboin Little Chief, however, said that his people wanted to live with the Gros Ventre but, "Assinaboines want reservation to extend east to mouth of Milk River." (Ibid., p. 248).

In conversations with Gros Ventre and Assiniboin delegations informally after the council there appeared to be agreement that a reservation from the mouth of Clear Creek to the Three Buttes then along the summit of the Little Rockies and down Beaver Creek to Milk River would be large enough, although the Assiniboin appeared to be still desirous of a reservation on the lower Milk River farther east than the Little Rocky Mountain. (Ibid., p. 248).

Martin Maginnis' Bill to provide permanent reservations for the Indian in Northern Montana, and for other purposes, H.R. 5427, 48th Congress, 1st Session described a reservation "for the various bands of Assinaboine and Gros Ventre Indians belonging to Fort Belknap Agency" as follows:

"Inside a line beginning at Milk River at the mouth of Clear Creek, and running thence east of south below the foot-hills of the Bear Paw Paw Mountains to the Three Buttes; from these to the western extremity of the Little Rocky Mountains; thence easterly along the dividing ridge of this range to the head of Beaver Creek; thence down the channel of Beaver Creek to Milk River, and thence up the channel of Milk River to the point of beginning."

In his letter to the Secretary of the Interior of April 3, 1884, Commissioner of Indian Affairs Price objected to the definition of the limits of the proposed Fort Belknap Reservation on the ground that "the Indians would have very serious objections to the reduction of the reservation to the extent proposed in the bill." He proposed instead a reservation recommended by Agent Lincoln which would include "all the country which lies between the Milk River on the north, and the Missouri River on the south, and between the Bull Hook or Buckman's creek on the west, and the confluence of the Milk and Missouri Rivers on the east."

He enclosed a map marked to contrast the area described in the bill with the one represented as desired by the Indians. (See map of Montana Territory, No. 879, Record Group No. 75, Cartographic Records Section, The National Archives).

He proposed that a commission be appointed to negotiate with the Indians in the field. Early in 1887 the Northwest Commission negotiated an Agreement with the Indians of Fort Belknap Agency. No minutes of the council with the Indians were kept but the Report of the Negotiations of the Commissioners, dated Blackfeet Agency, Montana, Feb. 11, 1887, is in The National Archives, Special Case 144).

The Fort Belknap Reservation established, on the basis of these negotiations, by Act of Congress May 1, 1888, is Royce Area 694, described as:

"Beginning at a point in the middle of the main channel of the Milk River, opposite the mouth of Snake Creek; thence due south to a point due west of the western extremity of the Little Rocky Mountains; thence due east to the crest of said mountains at their western extremity; and thence following the southern crest of said mountains to the eastern extremity thereof; thence in a northerly direction in a direct line to a point in the middle of the main channel of Milk River opposite the mouth of People's creek; thence up Milk river, in the middle of the main channel thereof, to the place of beginning."

At the time of the negotiation of this land agreement the Indians of Fort Belknap Agency lived on Milk River in teepees and houses 14 miles east and west of the Agency. (Annual Report Comm. Indian Affairs, 1887, p. 141). Like the South Piegan, they were dependant primarily upon the weekly distribution of rations for their livelihood.

The Fort Belknap Agency at that time was not within the boundaries of the new reservation, so it was necessary to move both the Agency and the Indians southeastward onto the Fort Belknap Reservation in 1889. The new agency was established on the south bank of Milk River four miles south of Harlem.

A description of the Fort Belknap Reservation in 1890,

indicates that the Assiniboin were then living principally along the Milk River which formed the northern boundary of the reservation, while the greater number of the Gros Ventre lived in and near the Little Rocky Mountains which formed the southern boundary of the reservation, with a distance of 30 miles between the two settlements. (Report of Indians Taxed and not Taxed in the United States, 11th Census, 1890, p. 365). At that time the reservation of about 29 miles square afforded an average of 312 acres of land for each man, woman and child belonging to it. (Ibid., p. 367).

In 1950 the total enrolled population of Fort Belknap Reservation was 2,112, an increase of only 390 souls since 1890.

Quickly reviewing the problem of Gros Ventre land occupancy in the two decades prior to the extermination of the buffalo (1883-4), we find it greatly complicated by two factors (1) the contrary pressures of two more powerful allied tribes, the Blackfeet on the west and the Sioux on the east, and (2) the necessity for occupying in common lands with other friendly segments of tribes. It can be truthfully said that at no time during this period were the Gros Ventre the masters of or sole occupants of any sizeable tract of territory, and that they shifted about in the region between the Missouri and the Milk River east of the Bearpaw Mountains as much in response to pressures from other tribes as to the demands for food and the resources with which to make a living.

In the early '60s they were in the eastern part of this

area on the lower Milk River trying to save themselves from attacks by Blackfeet war parties. At that time they allied themselves with their former enemies the River Crow, who themselves were suffering from Sioux attacks. Together they hunted the region between the Missouri and Milk Rivers, probably generally east of the Little Rockies. Theirs was a peaceful relationship and the Gros Ventre certainly could be said to have invited the River Crow to share their hunting ground with them.

Then in 1868 the Gros Ventre seemed to prefer the southwesternmost of the Assiniboin groups, the Upper Assiniboin to the River Crow, intermarried with them and welcomed them as allies to share their hunting ground. But soon thereafter the more numerous, aggressive Sioux pushed into the Milk River Valley. The Gros Ventre and their Upper Assiniboin allies were forced to retreat westward in 1870 to the area between the Bearpaw Mountains and the Little Rockies, where they hunted with the Upper Assiniboin and sometimes the Mountain Crow, in the same territory if not in joint hunting operations. So much did the Gros Ventre fear the Sioux, who had taken over the eastern area which they formerly occupied in the angle of the Missouri and Marias, that in the middle '70s they were even afraid to go to the mouth of Milk River for supplies.

Then in the late '70s, as the numbers of buffalo diminished there came the flood of "British Indians" from north of the line seeking game after it had been destroyed in their own country. They - Assiniboin, Cree, and others hunted on Gros Ventre and Assiniboin lands until the buffalo were gone.

After the disappearance of the buffalo the Gros Ventre and Upper Assiniboin settled down solidly near the Fort Belknap Agency because they had no other choice. It was live on weekly rations or starve. So while the Indian tipis and cabins were huddled together near this one source of food, the rather nearly all of the land over which they had formerly hunted remained unoccupied. It was of no use to them under the conditions save as a means of bargaining with the whites for a chance to get a start in a new way of life on a reservation large enough to support them as farmers and stockmen.

183

CONCLUSIONS

1. The so-called "Blackfoot Nation of Indians" was a fiction. Neither in terms of common origin and language, nor in terms of possessing a common governmental organization could the four tribes of the North Blackfeet, Blood, Piegan and Gros Ventre be considered a nation. The North Blackfeet, Blood and Piegan tribes did possess traditions of common origin, and they spoke a common language; but they recognized no governmental authority higher than the head chief and council of each of the separate tribes. The Gros Ventre, an offshoot of the Arapaho, spoke a language different from that of the three other tribes, and possessed a separate governmental organization.

2. The Indians attached to the Blackfeet Agency in Montana comprise a portion of the Piegan tribe. To distinguish them from another portion of that tribe now residing on a reserve in Alberta, Canada, they should be identified as South Piegan Indians. Those Piegan Indians on the Alberta reserve should be identified as North Piegan Indians.

3. None of the four tribes of the so-called "Blackfoot Nation of Indians" were aboriginal occupants of land located within the boundaries of the present State of Montana. When first met by literate white men in the eighteenth century all of these tribes resided in the valley of the Saskatchewan River within the present Canadian Provinces of Alberta and Saskatchewan.

4. Until after the smallpox epidemic of 1781 all of these tribes continued to reside in the valley of the Saskatchewan River

in the present Canadian Provinces of Alberta and Saskatchewan. At that time the lands south of the 49th parallel later occupied by these four tribes were occupied by the Shoshoni, Flathead (Salish), Pend d'Oreille (Kalispell), Kutenai, and probably in part by the Crow Indians.

5. Between 1781 and 1810 the four tribes of the North-Blackfeet, Blood, Piegan and Gros Ventre, with the Piegan and Gros Ventre in the lead, pushed southward beyond the 49th parallel and, by force of arms, dispossessed the Shoshoni, Flathead, Pend d'Oreille, Kutenai, and probably the Crow Indians of their lands north of the Missouri.

How far south the Piegan and Gros Ventre hunted in summer or wintered prior to 1810 is questionable. But it does appear probable from the testimony of Lewis and Clark in 1805 that Gros Ventre hunting camps were on the main stem of the Missouri west of the mouth of Milk River. Whether or not the Piegan hunting camps extended their operations south of the tributaries of the Marias River during this period is uncertain.

It is certain that by 1805, from the testimony of Lewis and Clark, the Shoshoni, Flathead and Pend d'Oreille, who had been driven west of the Rockies by the warlike Blackfeet tribes and the Gros Ventre, were crossing the mountains and reasserting their traditional right to hunt buffalo on plains of present Montana in spite of powerful resistance by war parties of the Blackfeet tribes.

6. During the period 1810 to 1831 the area around the Three Forks of the Missouri and southward (Royce Area 398) was

debatable ground. It was frequented by large and aggressive "Blackfeet" war parties, but there is no positive evidence of hunting camps from any of the four tribes of the so-called "Blackfoot" Nation of Indians in this area at that time. The tribes from west of the Rockies continued to hunt in this area and farther north.

Throughout this period the Blackfeet, Blood and Piegan continued to trade with the Hudson's Bay Company and Northwest Company at their posts on the Saskatchewan River, primarily on the North Saskatchewan. This must have encouraged these tribes to spend much of their time north of the 49th parallel during this period. The Gros Ventre also traded on the Saskatchewan, but toward the close of this period all or a considerable portion of them went upon an extended visit to their kinsmen, the Arapaho, southward on the plains between the Platte and Arkansas Rivers.

7. During the period 1831-1850 American fur traders established and maintained posts on the Missouri River in the neighborhood of the mouth of Milk River. The fact that they received buffalo robes in trade whereas the Hudson's Bay Company did not, gave them a distinct advantage over their rivals in the British Possessions. The southward shift following the establishment of Fort Piegan, the first American trading post on the Missouri in Blackfeet country affected the Piegan primarily. The Blood and Blackfeet continued to winter and trade in the British Possessions while bringing their buffalo robes to the American posts. The Piegan wintered on Sun River and southward. During this period

we first hear of Piegan living in the area around the Missouri headwaters. This was the Small Robes band, a once large and independent band living apart from the other hunting bands of the tribe. They dared to make friends with the Flathead and to hunt with them in the headwaters region. So this debatable land became a common hunting ground. Smallpox (1837) and a disastrous defeat by the Crow in 1846 greatly reduced the numbers of this band, so that near the close of this period or shortly thereafter they withdrew northward and eastward into Royce Area 399.

In this period the Pend d'Oreille and Kutenai continued to hunt buffalo on the plains farther northward in Royce Area 565 at least as far eastward as the Sweet Grass Hills. So the tribes of the so-called "Blackfoot Nation" were not exclusive occupants of that region. Furthermore, the eastern portion of Royce Area 565, as far west as the lower Milk River to its mouth was occupied by the Assiniboin.

8. At the Treaty of Fort Laramie a portion of land south and east of the Missouri was described as Blackfoot Territory. This was not Royce Area 398, but is shown on De Smet's map made at the treaty council. Neither the Blackfeet tribes, nor the Flathead from west of the Rockies who might have disputed the assignment of this land to the Blackfeet were parties to this treaty.

9. Throughout the early nineteenth century the Blackfeet tribes continued to hunt on both sides of the 49th parallel. It is interesting to note that in the summer of 1853 Stanley found the Piegan (southernmost of the Blackfeet tribes) hunting north of that

line. And when Doty went to bring them in to the 1855 treaty council he also found them hunting in the British Possessions. At that time the Piegan and Blood tribes appear to have wintered in the United States and hunted northward into the British Possessions in summer. The reduced Small Robes were south of the Missouri. The North Blackfeet spent most of their time north of the 49th parallel and took little interest in American affairs. The four chiefs who represented them at the treaty council must have represented a minority of their tribe, and hence by Indian standards that tribe could not be considered to have made a treaty with the United States. At that time the distinction between the North Piegan (residing primarily north of the 49th parallel) and the South Piegan (residing primarily south of that line) was already apparent to Doty. He also recognized that the Gros Ventre were "not a portion of the Blackfoot nation." They resided to the eastward of the Piegan in the country bordering Milk River.

      The treaty of 1855 designated more land for the Blackfeet tribes than they then occupied. It is very doubtful if they occupied any of the common hunting ground (Royce Area 398) at that time or in later years, or if they then occupied Royce Area 399 east of the Judith River. At the same time it failed to recognize the right of the Pend d'Oreille and Kutenai to hunt buffalo east of the Rockies in Royce Areas 574 and 565, a right those tribes continued to exercise after the treaty.

The major objective of the treaty was the establishment of intertribal peace among the tribes hunting on the northwestern plains. The articles dealing with intertribal peace, agreed to by the chiefs, were nullified soon thereafter by their young warriors the Blood Indians starting against the Crow within 10 days of the treaty signing.

10. During the period 1862-1877 the North Blackfeet, Blood and North Piegan tended to spend more and more of their time north of the international boundary. This culminated in Treaty No. 7 with the Canadian Government at Blackfoot Crossing in 1877, at which all of these groups ceded their lands north of the 49th parallel to the crown, swore their allegiance to the Queen, and accepted reservation lands in present Alberta. The South Piegan did not participate in this treaty.

11. The Executive Order of 1873, as a result of which the land between the Musselshell and the Missouri and its western tributary, Sun River, was ceded, was one in which the Gros Ventre had no interest based upon occupancy. It had been land formerly occupied by the Piegan, from which they had withdrawn northward some eight years earlier.

12. At the time of the Act of April 15, 1874, which moved the southern boundary of the reservation northward to Birch Creek, none of the four tribes occupied the portion of the ceded area south of the Teton River. (See Royce Area 574.) But the South Piegan did occupy the portion of this area between the Teton River and Birch Creek. These Indians are on record as having opposed the

cession of this occupied portion, and their opposition was known to officials in Washington before the order was issued. They are also on record as having stated that they did not oppose the cession of that portion of Royce Area 574 south of the Teton River, i.e. the portion they did not then occupy.

13. Between 1874 and 1884 the South Piegan occupied that portion of Royce Area 565 from the Rockies to the neighborhood of the Bearpaw Mountains over which they hunted buffalo. They were not the exclusive occupants, however, because tribes living in Canada came southward to hunt here also, and in increasing numbers after the buffalo disappeared north of the boundary in 1879. During this period the small Gros Ventre tribe hunted in the portion of Royce Area 565 between the Little Rockies and the Bearpaw Mountains. However they shared this area with the Upper Assiniboin, and, as buffalo became scarce near the end of this period with Assiniboin, Cree and other groups from Canada.

14. After the buffalo disappeared, both the South Piegan and Gros Ventre were compelled by the necessity of living primarily upon Government rations, issued weekly at their Agencies, to settle down within a few miles of their Agencies - the South Piegan on Badger Creek and Birch Creek near the Blackfeet Agency, and the Gros Ventre on Milk River near Fort Belknap Agency. As early as 1883 these tribes expressed their desire to Senator Vest and Delegate Maginnis to exchange their surplus lands for seeds, farming equipment, etc. - the means with which to make a living on their gameless land. This was the land occupied by these tribes at the

time of the 1888 Land Agreements. Although the South Piegan accepted a reservation of their own, the Gros Ventre agreed to go upon a reservation with the Upper Assiniboin who had shared their hunting ground and had participated in the Land Agreement with them. In the case of the South Piegan no other tribe was involved in the Land Agreement or placed upon the reservation with them. In their case also the land occupied at the time of the cession was well within the area of the Blackfeet Reservation. In the case of the Gros Ventre it was necessary for them to move onto the Fort Belknap Reservation, from their homes near the abandoned Fort Belknap Agency farther up Milk River.

15. Between 1888 and the time the South Piegan negotiated their second Land Agreement in 1895, these Indians were issued cattle, farming implements, etc., and they spread northward over the reservation to establish homes in the river valleys. However, they did not establish homes in the mountainous area of the reservation which was the portion ceded. They made use of that portion of their reservation for hunting, fishing and obtaining timber. Under the terms of the Agreement they reserved their hunting, fishing and timber rights in the ceded area.

BIBLIOGRAPHY

Published Materials:

Annual Reports of the Commissioner of Indian Affairs, 1854-1896

Atkinson, Gen. Henry

    Expedition up the Missouri, 1825. House Doc. No. 117. 19th Congress, 1st Session. Washington, 1826

Atwood, W. W.

    Physiographic Provinces of North America, New York, 1940

Bradley, Lieut. James H.

    The Bradley Manuscript. Montana Historical Society Contributions, Vols. 3, 8, 9, Helena, 1900, 1917, 1923.

Catlin, George

    Letters and Notes on the Manners, Customs and Condition of the North American Indians. 2 Vols., London, 1841

Chittenden, Hiram M.

    The American Fur Trade of the Far West, 2 Vols., New York, 1935

Chittenden, H. M. and Richardson, A. T. (Editors)

    Life, Letters and Travels of Father Pierre Jean De Smet. 4 Vols. New York, 1905

Cocking, Mathew

    An Adventurer from Hudson Bay. Journal of Mathew Cocking from York Factory to the Blackfeet Country, 1772-1773. Ed. by Laurence J. Burpee. Transactions, Royal Society of Canada. 3rd series, Vol. 2, Ottawa, 1909

Cox, Ross

    Adventures on the Columbia River, New York, 1832

Culbertson, Thaddeus A.

    Journal of an Expedition to the Mauvaises Terres and the Upper Missouri in 1850. Ed. by John Francis McDermott. Bureau of American Ethnology, Bulletin 147. Washington, 1952

Curtis, Edward S.

    The North American Indian, Vol. 18, Norwood, Mass., 1928.

Denig, Edwin T.

    Indian Tribes of the Upper Missouri. Ed. by J. N. B. Hewitt. 46th Annual Report, Bureau of American Ethnology, Washington, D. C., 1930

    Of the Assiniboines. Ed. by John C. Ewers, Bulletin Missouri Historical Society, Vol. 8, No. 2, St. Louis, 1952

    Of the Crow Nation. Ed. by John C. Ewers, Bureau of American Ethnology, Bulletin 151, Anthropological Paper No. 33. Washington, 1953

Ewers, John C.

    The Blackfoot War Lodge; Its Construction and Use. American Anthropologist. New Series, Vol. 46, No. 2, 1944

    Identification and History of the Small Robes Band of the Piegan Indians. Journal Washington Academy of Sciences. Vol. 36, No. 12, 1946

    The Horse in Blackfoot Indian Culture, with Comparative Material from other Western Tribes. Bureau of American Ethnology, Bulletin 159, 1940

Ferris, W. A.

    Life in the Rocky Mountains. Ed. by Paul C. Phillips, Denver, Colorado, 1940

Flannery, Regina

    The Gros Ventres of Montana. Part I, Social Life. The Catholic University of America, Anthropological Papers, No. 15, Washington, D. C., 1953

Grinnell, George Bird

    Blackfoot Lodge Tales. New York, 1892

    The Story of the Indians. New York, 1895

Hamilton, William T.

    A Trading Expedition among the Indians in 1858. Montana Historical Society Contributions, Vol. 3, 1905

My Sixty Years on the Plains, Trapping, Trading and Indian Fighting. New York, 1905

The Council at Fort Benton. Forest and Stream, Vol. 68, No. 17. 1907. pp. 648-650

Hayden, Ferdinand V.

Contributions to the Ethnography and Philology of the Indian Tribes of the Missouri Valley. Transactions, American Philosophical Society, New Series. Vol. 12, Pt. 2, Philadelphia, 1862

Helena Weekly Independent, May 22, 1874

Hendry, Anthony

York Factory to the Blackfeet Country. The Journal of Anthony Hendry, 1754-1755. Ed. by Laurence J. Burpee. Transactions, Royal Society of Canada. 3rd Series, Vol. 1. Ottawa, 1907

Henry, Alexander

Travels and Adventures in Canada, and the Indian Territories between the years 1760 and 1776. New York, 1809

Henry, Alexander and Thompson, David

New Light on the Early History of the Greater Northwest. Ed. by Elliott Coues. 4 Vols., New York, 1897

Hodge, Frederick Webb, Ed.

Handbook of American Indians North of Mexico. Bulletin 30. Bureau of American Ethnology. 2 Vols., Washington, 1907

Hornaday, William T.

The Extermination of the American Bison. Annual Report, U. S. National Museum for 1886-1887. Washington, 1889

Innis, H. A.

Peter Pond, Fur Trader and Adventurer. Toronto, 1930

Isham, James

James Isham's Observations on Hudson's Bay, 1743. Ed. by E. E. Rich, Champlain Society, Toronto, 1949

Kappler, Charles J.

    Indian Affairs, Laws and Treaties. Laws. Vol. I, Washington, 1904

Koch, Peter

    Historical Sketch of Bozeman, Gallatin Valley and Bozeman Pass. Montana Historical Society Contributions, Vol. II, 1896

Kroeber, Alfred L.

    Ethnology of the Gros Ventres. American Museum of Natural History, Anthropological Papers, Vol. I, Part 4, New York, 1908

Kellogg, Louise Phelps, Ed.

    Memoir of Duluth on the Sioux Country, 1678-1692. Early Narratives of the Northwest. New York, 1917

Larocque, Francois

    Journal of Larocque from the Assiniboine to the Yellowstone, 1805. Canadian National Archives Publication No. 3. Ottawa, 1910

Larpenteur, Charles

    Forty Years a Fur Trader on the Upper Missouri, the Personal Narrative of Charles Larpenteur. Ed. by Elliott Coues. 2 Vols. New York, 1898

La Verendrye, P. G. V.

    Journals and Letters of Pierre Gaultier de Varennes de la Verendrye and his sons. Ed. by Laurence J. Burpee, Champlain Society Publication 16. Toronto, 1927

Le Sueur, Jacques

    Le Sueur's Voyage up the Mississippi. Wisconsin Historical Society Collections. Vol. 16. Madison, 1902

Lewis, Meriwether and Clark, William

    Original Journals of the Lewis and Clark Expedition. Ed. by Reuben Gold Thwaites. 8 Vols. New York, 1904-1905

    History of the Expedition under the Command of Lewis and Clark. Ed. by Elliott Coues. 4 Vols. New York, 1893

MacGregor, James G.

 Behold the Shining Mountains. Edmonton, Alberta, 1955

Mackenzie, Alexander

 Voyages from Montreal on the River St. Lawrence, through the Continent of North America. . . 1789 and 1793. Toronto, 1927

Maginnis, Martin

 H. R. 5427. 48th Congress, 1st Session, 1884

Maximilian, Alexander Phillip, Prinz zu Wied-Neuwied

 Travels in the Interior of North America. Early Western Travels. Ed. by Reuben Gold Thwaites. Vols. 22-24. Cleveland, 1906

M'Gillivray, Duncan

 The Journal of Duncan M'Gillivray of the Northwest Company at Fort George on the Saskatchewan, 1794-1795. Ed. by Arthur S. Morton. Toronto, 1929

Mitchell, David D.

 Blackfeet Indians. In Schoolcraft, Henry R., Historical and Statistical Information Respecting the History, Conditions and Prospects of the Indian Tribes of the United States. Vol. 5, 1855

Montana Historical Society Contributions, Vols. 2-10, Helena, 1896-1940

Morris, Alexander

 The Treaties of Canada with the Indians of Manitoba and the North-West Territories, Toronto, N.D.

Morse, Jedidiah

 A report to the Secretary of War of the United States on Indian Affairs. New Haven, 1822

Ordway, John

 Sergeant Ordway's Journal. Ed. by Milo Quaife. Wisconsin Historical Society Collections, Vol. 22. 1916

Owen, John

    Journal and Letters of Major John Owen, 1850-1871.
    2 Vols. Ed. by Paul C. Phillips. Helena, 1927

Partoll, Albert J. (Editor)

    The Blackfoot Indian Peace Council. Historical Reprints,
    Sources of Northwest History, No. 3. Montana State University,
    Missoula, 1937. (Publication of the original Proceedings in
    the National Archives.)

Raynolds, W. F.

    Report on Exploration of the Yellowstone River. Washington,
    1868

Report of Indians Taxed and Not Taxed in the United States. 11th
    Census, 1890. Dft. Ex. No.

Royce, Charles C.

    Indian Land Cessions in the United States. 18th Annual
    Report, Bureau of American Ethnology, Part 2, 1899

Schaeffer, Claude E.   197

    The First Jesuit Mission to the Flathead, 1840-1850.
    Pacific Northwest Quarterly, Vol. 28. July 1937

    Bird Nomenclatures and Principles of Avian Taxonomy of the
    Blackfeet Indians, Journal Washington Academy of Sciences,
    Vol. 40, No. 2, 1937

Schoolcraft, Henry R. (See Mitchell, David D.)

Stanley, John Mix

    Report of Mr. J. M. Stanley's Visit to the Piegan Camp at
    the Cypress Mountain. Pacific Railroad Survey Report of Ex-
    plorations and Surveys to Ascertain the Most Practicable Route
    of a Railroad from the Mississippi River to the Pacific Ocean.
    Vol. 1, Washington, 1855

Stevens, Isaac I.

    Isaac I. Stevens' Narrative of 1835-1855. Pacific Railroad
    Survey Report, etc. Vol. 12, Book I, Washington, 1860

Stuart, Granville

    Adventure on the Upper Missouri. Montana Historical Society Contributions. Vol. 1, 1876

Swanton, John R.

    The Indian Tribes of North America, Bureau of American Ethnology, Bulletin 145, Washington, 1952

Sharp, Paul F.

    Whoop-Up Country. Minneapolis, Minnesota, 1955

Teit, James

    Salishan Tribes of the Western Plateau. Ed. by Franz Boas. 45th Annual Report, Bureau of American Ethnology. Washington, 1930

Thompson, David

    David Thompson's Narrative of his Explorations in Western America, 1784-1812. Ed. by J. B. Tyrrell. Champlain Society Publication No. 12. Toronto, 1916

Thwaites, Reuben Gold (Ed.)

    The Jesuit Relations and Allied Documents. Travels and Explorations of the Jesuit Missionaries in New France, 1610-1791. 73 Vols., Cleveland, 1896-1901

Turney-High, Harry H.

    The Flathead Indians of Montana. Memoirs, American Anthropological Association, No. 48. Menasha, Wisconsin, 1937

    Ethnography of the Kutenai. Memoirs, American Anthropological Association, No. 56. Menasha, Wisconsin, 1941

Umfreville, Edward

    Present State of Hudson's Bay, Containing a Full Description of that Settlement and the Adjacent Country; and Likewise of the Fur Trade. London, 1790

Victor, Frances F.

    Eleven Years in the Rocky Mountains and Life on the Frontier. Hartford, Connecticut, 1877

Wheeler, Olin D.

    The Trail of Lewis and Clark, 2 Vols. New York, 1904

Wissler, Clark

    Material Culture of the Blackfoot Indians. American Museum of Natural History, Anthropological Papers. Vol. 5, Pt. 1, New York, 1910

    The Social Life of the Blackfoot Indians. American Museum of Natural History, Anthropological Papers, Vol. 7, Pt. 1, 1911

    Population Changes among the Northern Plains Indians. Yale University Publications in Anthropology. No. 1. New Haven, 1936

<u>Unpublished Documents</u>:

Documents in Indian Office Records. The National Archives.

    Code of Laws Adopted by Blackfeet, Blood and Piegan Indians. April 23, 1875. Blackfeet Agency Montana

    Commissioner of Indian Affairs to Secretary of the Interior, April 3, 1884

    Cooley, D. N. to James Harlan, April 12, 1866

    Doty, James to Isaac I. Stevens, December 20, 1854

    Doty, James to Isaac I. Stevens, December 29, 1854

    Doty, James, Report of Secretary Doty on his Mission to the North Camps, September 1855. (Part of the Blackfoot Treaty Proceedings.)

    Dusold, Andrew, Report to Blackfeet Agent Wood, Feb. 12, 1875

    Lea, L. to D. D. Mitchell, May 26, 1851. Indian Office Letter Book, No. 44

    Mannypenny, George W. to Commissioners Blackfoot Treaty, May 3, 1855

May, R. F. to Edward P. Smith, January 22, 1874

May, R. F. to Edward P. Smith, March 24, 1874

May, R. F. to Edward P. Smith, March 24, 1874

Meagher, Thomas F. to Commissioner of Indian Affairs, December 14, 1865

Mitchell, David D. to Commissioner Indian Affairs, October 13, 1849

Mitchell, David D. to Commissioner of Indian Affairs, November 11, 1851

Proceedings of Commissioners Blackfeet Land Agreement, Doc. 51,494. 1895

Price, H. to Secretary of the Interior, April 3, 1884

Sheridan, General Phillip H. to Adjutant General of the Army, July 1, 1870

Sully, General Alfred to Commissioner Indian Affairs, Census of Blackfeet Bands. July 16, 1870

Sully, General Alfred to Commissioner Indian Affairs, January 31, 1870

Sully, General Alfred to Commissioner Indian Affairs, February 26, 1870

Sully, General Alfred to Commissioner Indian Affairs, July 20, 1870

Report of Negotiations of Commissioners, The Northwest Commission. February 11, 1887

Wood, John to Commissioner Indian Affairs, February 15, 1875

Wood, John to Commissioner Indian Affairs, February 2, 1875

Wood, John to Commissioner Indian Affairs, May 14, 1875

Treaties in the National Archives

    Fort Laramie Treaty (negotiated 1851)

Treaty with the Blackfoot Nation (negotiated 1855)

Treaty with the Blackfeet, Fort Benton, 1865 (unratified)
Dft. Ex. 183

Treaty with the Blackfeet, Fort Benton, 1868 (unratified)
Dft. Ex. 183

Treaty with the Gros Ventre, Fort Hawley, 1868 (unratified)
Dft. Ex. 183

Treaty between Piegan and Gros Ventre, 1874 (May 16) Dft.
Ex. 210

Treaty between Piegan and Assiniboine, 1874 (May 16) Dft.
Ex. 210

Documents in Montana Historical Society, Helena, Montana

The Bradley Manuscript. Book A

Martin Maginnis Papers. May, R. F. to Martin Maginnis,
May 25, 1874

Documents in Museum of the Plains Indian, Browning, Montana

The Blackfeet Archives

Agent Wood's Letter Book. Letter of October 8, 1875

Agent Young's Letter Book. Letters of
February 1, 1879
May 8, 1879
August 1, 1879
January 6, 1882

Map References:

Physiographic characteristics:

Dr. Erwin Raisz' map, Landforms of the United States in W. W. Atwood's, Physiographic Provinces of North America, 1940

Period 1650 reconstruction:

Maps 1, 2, 3 in John R. Swanton, The Indian Tribes of North America, 1952

Period 1785:

   Peter Pond's map of the Canadian Northwest in H. A. Innis, Peter Pond Trader and Adventurer, 1930

Period 1851:

   Father De Smet's map used at the Fort Laramie Treaty Council. (Original in the Library of Congress.)

Period 1855:

   Map used by the Commissioners and Indians at the Blackfoot Treaty Council. (Original in the National Archives.)

Period 1865:

   Map of Montana showing the Lands of the Blackfoot Nation and the New Reservation Proposed in the Treaty of Fort Benton. (Original in the National Archives.)

Period 1884:

   Map showing contrast between proposed Fort Belknap Reservation in H. R. 5427, contrasted with land desired by Indians. (Original in the National Archives.)

COMMISSION FINDINGS

See also Findings in *Sioux Indians IV* in the Garland American Indian Ethnohistory Series.

204

BEFORE THE INDIAN CLAIMS COMMISSION

THE BLACKFEET AND GROS VENTRE TRIBES OF INDIANS, Residing Upon the Blackfeet and Fort Belknap Reservations in the State of Montana,
 	
                    Petitioners,
 	
THE ASSINIBOINE TRIBES OF INDIANS, Residing upon the Fort Belknap and Fort Peck Reservations, Montana, and
THE SIOUX TRIBE OF THE FORT PECK RESERVATION, Montana,
 	
                    Intervenors,
 	
        v.
 	
THE UNITED STATES OF AMERICA,
 	
                  Defendant.
	Docket No. 279-A

Decided: March 31, 1967

FINDINGS OF FACT

The Commission makes the following findings of fact:

1. Petitioners, The Blackfeet and Gros Ventre Tribes of Indians, timely filed their claim pursuant to the Indian Claims Commission Act of August 13, 1946 (60 Stat. 1049). The claim is for additional compensation for reservation lands ceded by petitioners to defendant by the agreement of cession ratified by Congress on May 1, 1888 (25 Stat. 113).

2. Petitioners are bands or tribes of Indians, commonly known as the Blackfeet and Gros Ventre Tribes, attached to the Blackfeet and Fort Belknap Indian agencies in Montana. The Blackfeet were for many years included in the Blackfoot Nation of Indians. Included in the petitioner,

Blackfeet Tribe, are the former Blood and Piegan Tribes of Indians. The Gros Ventre Tribe, once known as the Falls Indians, were formerly associated and affiliated with and a part of the Blackfoot Nation. Each of the petitioner tribes has a tribal organization recognized by the Secretary of the Interior as having authority to represent said tribes.

3. The Blackfoot Nation was composed of three tribes, the Blackfeet, the Blood, and the Piegan. All of these were of Algonkian origin and were closely related by blood, language and tradition. The Gros Ventre were Arapahoe in origin. Some time prior to the Treaty of October 17, 1855 (11 Stat. 657) with the Blackfoot Nation the Gros Ventre were pushed out of their ancestral home in eastern Wyoming and Montana by the Sioux and Assiniboine, and had become associated and affiliated with and a part of the Blackfeet Nation.

The Blackfoot Nation in early times had roamed over a vast region of country extending from the North Fork of the Saskatchewan River in Canada to the headwaters of the Musselshell River and from the Rocky Mountains on the west to 106 degrees of longitude on the east. They were a nomadic people and depended upon the buffalo for their existence. Their country was the home of vast herds of buffalo which ranged on the plains of the Musselshell and Judith, the Missouri, the Milk, and the Saskatchewan Rivers in countless numbers.

While these Indians were truly nomadic, there were certain sections of their territory which in time became recognized as their home territories. The Blackfeet proper and the Bloods occupied principally the country about the sources of the Marias and Milk Rivers, while the

Piegans occupied generally the country between the Milk River on the north and the Marias and Teton Rivers on the south. The Gros Ventre occupied the country bordering on the Milk River from its mouth to the territory of the Piegans.

4. On October 17, 1855, a treaty was made between the United States and the Blackfoot Nation by which a reservation area was set aside for the Blackfeet. It was described as follows:

> . . . the tract of country lying within lines drawn from the Hell Gate or Medicine Rock Passes, in an easterly direction, to the nearest source of the Muscle Shell River, thence down said river to its mouth, thence down the channel of the Missouri River to the mouth of Milk River, thence due north to the forty-ninth parallel, thence due west on said parallel to the main range of the Rocky Mountains, and thence southerly along said range to the place of beginning, . . .

On July 5, 1873, an Executive Order transferred the area between the Musselshell and Missouri to the public domain. This order altered the boundaries of the reservation as set up in the 1855 Treaty so as to leave the following:

> Commencing at the northwest corner of the Territory of Dakota, being the intersection of the forty-ninth parallel of north latitude and the one hundred and fourth meridian of west longitude; thence south to the south bank of the Missouri River; thence up and along the south bank of said river to a point opposite the mouth of Medicine or Sun River; thence in a westerly direction, following the south bank of said Medicine or Sun River, as far as practicable, to the summit of the main chain of the Rocky Mountains; hence along said summit in a northerly direction to the north boundary of Montana; hence along said north boundary to the place of beginning, excepting and reserving therefrom existing military reservations.

It will be noted from the above description that by this Executive Order of July 5, 1873, there was added the area of land from the Milk

River line eastward to the Dakota line. The added area contained 4,332,440 acres. This description includes what came to be known as Royce Areas 565 and 574, Montana.

An Act of Congress approved April 15, 1874 (18 Stat. 28) established a reservation as delimited in the Executive Order of July 5, 1873, except the following area was excluded:

> Commencing at a point on the south bank of the Missouri River, opposite the mouth of the Marias River; thence along the main channel of the Marias River to Birch Creek; thence up the main channel of Birch Creek to its source; thence west to the summit of the main chain of the Rocky Mountains; thence along said summit in a southerly direction to a point opposite the source of the Medicine or Sun River; thence easterly to said source, and down the south bank of said Medicine or Sun River to the south bank of the Missouri River; thence down the south bank of the Missouri River to the place of beginning, . . .

The area excluded under the above Executive Order description came to be known as Royce Area 574, Montana 1.

By Executive Order of August 19, 1874, the President restored to the public domain all that portion of the reservation as established by the Executive Order of July 5, 1873, which was not included within the boundaries of the reservation as established by the above Act of April 15, 1874. The area restored was Royce Area 574, Montana 1, referred to immediately above.

Thereafter, by Executive Order dated April 13, 1875, there was added to the reservation established by Act of April 15, 1874, a certain area on the southeast boundary of the former reservation, of approximately 5,865,900 acres (Royce Areas 622 and 623). Subsequently, under

Executive Order of July 13, 1880, the said addition was reduced by approximately 4,622,750 acres (Royce Area 622) and added to the public domain, thus leaving as a net addition in that quarter an area of 1,243,240 acres (Royce Area 623).

This addition of 1,243,240 acres plus the 4,332,440 acres added by the Executive Order of July 5, 1873, and retained under the Act of April 15, 1874, made a total net addition of 5,575,680 acres to that portion of the original 1855 reservation then remaining. However, there was involved under the Act of 1888 only 4,332,440 acres of the 5,575,680 additional acres. Area 623 lying south of the Missouri River was not ceded.

5. The land which is the subject matter of this suit is located in northern Montana, north of the Marias and Missouri Rivers to the Canadian boundary and eastward from the east boundary of the present Blackfeet Indian Reservation to a line due north from the mouth of the Milk River to the Canadian boundary. This territory is known as Royce Area 565, Montana 1. Under a stipulation entered into by petitioners and defendant and made a matter of record herein it was agreed that the above described territory contained 13,338,589 acres (Tr., p. 830).

Petitioners, based upon a percentage of population figure with regard to the Fort Belknap area, have reduced the acreage by 316,979 acres, making a total in which they claim a 100% interest of 13,021,610 acres. Petitioners also assert alternative claims which will be discussed in the opinion along with the alternative descriptions involved in such claims.

6. Intervenors are the Assiniboine Tribe and the Sioux Tribe of the Fort Peck Reservation in Montana. The Assiniboine Tribe is composed of two groups - one residing on the Fort Peck Reservation and the other on the Fort Belknap Reservation, also in Montana.

The Assiniboine Tribe of the Fort Peck Reservation, the Assiniboine Tribe of the Fort Belknap Reservation, and the Sioux Tribe of Fort Peck each has a governing body duly recognized by the Secretary of the Interior as authorized to speak for it and to represent it in the matter of this claim.

Each of the intervenors, Assiniboine and Sioux Tribes, is authorized to maintain this suit under Section 2 of the Indian Claims Commission Act (60 Stat. 1049).

Intervenors each allege an undivided one-fourth interest in the lands ceded by the Agreement of May 1, 1888, as tenants in common with the Blackfeet and Gros Ventre. They base their claim on the theory that the Act of April 15, 1874 (18 Stat. 28) created a joint reservation of some 14,969,156 acres, thereby destroying the 1855 treaty title of the Blackfeet and Gros Ventre and investing intervenors with a one-half interest along with the Blackfeet and Gros Ventre. This area is known as Royce Area 692, Montana 2, and this larger acreage also is the subject of one of petitioners' alternative claims.

7. The Act of April 15, 1874 (18 Stat. 28) upon which intervenors rely for their alleged recongized title reads in its entirety as follows:

> Be it enacted by the Senate and House of Representatives of the United States of America in Congress assembled, That the following described tract of country, in the Territory of Montana, be, and the same is hereby, set apart for the use and occupation of the Gros Ventre, Piegan, Blood, Blackfoot, River Crow, and such other Indians as the President may, from time to time, see fit to locate thereon, viz: Commencing at the northwest corner of the Territory of Dakota, being the intersection of the forty-ninth parallel of north latitude and the one hundred and fourth meridian of west longitude; thence south to the south bank of the Missouri River; thence up and along the south bank of said river, to a point opposite the mouth of the Maria's River; thence along the main channel of the Maria's River to Birch Creek; thence up the main channel of Birch Creek to its source; thence west to the summit of the main chain of the Rocky Mountains; thence along the summit of the Rocky Mountains to the northern boundary of Montana; thence along said northern boundary to the place of beginning.

8. It appears that between 1868 and 1870 the Assiniboines voluntarily occupied a part of the 1855 Blackfoot Reservation. There was no formal order made placing them on the reservation but they were permitted by defendant to remain and draw rations. Previous to the occupation by the Assiniboines of a part of the Blackfoot Reservation they had been driven from their Fort Laramie Treaty lands by the Sioux Indians.

After taking up residence on the reservation of the Blackfeet, Blood, and Piegan Tribes in the period from 1868 to 1870, the Assiniboines became separated into two bands, the Long Hair Band living chiefly in the western part of the reservation with the Gros Ventres and being known as the Upper Assiniboines, and the Canoe Band living in the vicinity of the mouth of the Milk River and being known as the Lower Assiniboines.

In 1873, a separate agency was established on this reservation at Fort Belknap, and to it were assigned the Gros Ventre and the Upper

Assiniboines. In the same year the Milk River Agency was removed to Fort Peck on the Missouri River near the mouth of the Milk River and to this agency were assigned the Lower Assiniboines and the Sioux then upon the reservation.

9. The annual report of A. J. Simmons, Agent at Fort Browning, later Milk River Agency, dated August 31, 1871, contains the first mention of the Sioux upon the Blackfeet Reservation. Agent Simmons reported as follows:

***

> The tribes belonging here and under my charge are the Assinaboines, Gros Ventres of the Prairie, River Crows, and more recently large bands of Santee and other Sioux, who, having roamed for a number of years without being under the supervision of the Department, or receiving anything therefrom, have now with its consent, attached themselves to this agency. These Sioux number as follows: Santees proper, under Standing Buffalo's brother, about 2,500; Yanktons, Yanctonais, Cutheads, and others, under Medicine Bear as principal chief, about 4,300.
>
> Every effort in my power has been made to induce them to go to the Sioux agencies east, but without effect. They close their ears to my words of advice in this regard, and assign some cogent reasons for their conduct. They declare they will remain in this country, and urge that they may receive supplies and be treated as other Indians are at the agency. I have issued flour and other supplies to them for the last four months, during which time they have behaved remarkably well.

***

In addition to the Agent's report there was correspondence from General P. H. Sheridan, the Secretary of War, and a man by the name of Winfred S. Hancock, all of which indicated the Sioux occupancy and the fear that any attempt to remove them by force would precipitate an uprising.

The situation apparently remained in this posture, with periodic recommendations that the Sioux be removed, until the creation of the Northwest Indian Commission which was instructed to remove the Sioux to the Great Sioux Reservation in Dakota, if possible. There is no evidence of a formal order placing the Sioux on the lands in suit.

The minutes of the Commission made during the council with the Sioux at Fort Peck on December 27, 1886, indicate that the Commission was unable to follow the instructions regarding removal and instead reassured the Sioux that they recognized their rights in the land and that they would be given a reservation and paid a sum of money each year for a number of years.

It was during the course of these negotiations that the Agreements of December 28 and 31, 1886 and January 21, 1887, were concluded with the Indians of the Gros Ventre, Piegan, Blood, Blackfeet, and River Crow Reservation in Montana. This Agreement, despite its heading, was signed by Assiniboine and Sioux as well as the other Indians.

These Agreements ceded the land in suit and established the Indian parties thereto on their reservations as delimited by the treaty. They were ratified by Congress on May 1, 1888.

10. The Commissioners who negotiated the agreements made the following report dated February 11, 1887:

***

    The first question to engage the attention of the Commission was as to the advisability and practicability of attempting the removal of the Sioux of Fort Peck to the Great Sioux Reservation, in Dakota, our instructions contemplating such a step if deemed expedient.

After a thorough investigation of the matter the Commission decided that it was unadvisable to make the attempt. The Indians were decidedly opposed to such change, and manifested a good deal of surprise and uneasiness at the mere suggestion of the plan. It was learned that the few who went to the Standing Rock Agency last spring would have returned had they been allowed to do so, and some did return. *** The Sioux at the Fort Peck Agency have occupied the country there for nearly a quarter of a century, and claim equal rights with the other Indians in the Blackfeet Reservation, which claim is not disputed by any of the other Indians occupying the reservation. By reference to the Act of Congress establishing the reservation (18 Stat., p. 28) it will be observed that the reservation was set apart for certain tribes or bands specified by name, "and such other Indians as the President may, from time to time, see fit to locate thereon." The Sioux were placed upon the Blackfeet Reservation by the Government over twenty-three years ago, and it does not appear that their right of occupancy has ever been questioned. By long residence they have become greatly attached to the country, and would not voluntarily abandon it. The Assinaboines of the Fort Peck Agency, who number about 1,100, are for the most part settled at Wolf Point, about 20 miles from the agency. The Sioux have their habitations in the immediate vicinity of the agency.

***

The promise of stock cattle was the principal inducement which led to the cession of the vast territory relinquished to the Government. The agreement was satisfactory alike to the Indians and their friends present during the negotiations; and we believe that if strictly carried out the Indians will require no further aid from the Government.

***

Negotiations were immediately opened with the Fort Belknap Indians and after three days counciling the agreement was accepted and signed by a large majority of the male adults attached to the agency. A reservation was selected, embracing the region of country between Milk River and the Little Rocky Mountains, and extending from Snake Creek to Peoples Creek on the north, and from one extremity of the Little Rockies to the other on the south. The Indians were unwilling to remove, either to the Fort Peck Agency or to any distant reservation, but they consented, unanimously, to take the lands above described for their permanent home.

***

Leaving Fort Belknap Agency on the 23d of January, the Commission returned to Sun River Crossing, 5 miles northeast from Fort Shaw, en route to the Blackfeet Agency, 100 miles distant from the latter place.

***

On the 5th of February the storm abated to such extent as to allow the Commission to continue its journey to the Blackfeet Agency.***

***

The chiefs began by complaining of ill-usage and bad faith on the part of the Government in past time, and charged that an immense tract of country had been wrested from them without any compensation in return, and that they had been left to starve, while their white neighbors had grown rich out of their misfortunes. They demanded $3,000,000 for the relinquishment of their interest in the surplus lands of the reservation and stubbornly refused to accept an offer of $125,000 per annum for ten years, which was made to them. Finally, however, after long and patient reasoning with them, they agreed to accept $150,000 per annum for the period mentioned.

Upon mature deliberation we decided to accede to their demand. The sum agreed upon is, proportionately, greater than the amount agreed upon with the Indians of the other two agencies, Fort Peck and Fort Belknap, but the argument was used, and it can hardly be disputed, that the needs of these Indians are in a large measure greater than those of the other Indians. ***

***

Furthermore, these Indians, no doubt, have the most ancient claim upon the ceded territory, at least as far eastward as the mouth of Milk River. They occupied it as far back as their history is known, and they naturally feel that they have a stronger claim to it than any of the other Indians. They were earnest and persistent in demanding recognition on that account.

While this did not go far in influencing our decision, it undoubtedly made the Indians more stubborn and exacting in their demands.

***

By the terms of the agreement a tract of country, estimated to contain 17,500,000 acres, is ceded to the United States. Three separate reservations are retained for the Indians.

***

11. The following are the terms of the agreements executed by the Blackfeet, Blood, and Piegan; Gros Ventre; Sioux; and Assiniboine as ratified by the Act of Congress of May 1, 1888 (25 Stat. 113). Only the treaty articles through VIII are quoted herein.

Whereas, John V. Wright, Jared W. Daniels, and Charles F. Larabee, duly appointed commissioners on the part of the United States, did, on the twenty-eighth and thirty-first days of December, anno Domini eighteen hundred and eighty-six, and the twenty-first day of January, anno Domini eighteen hundred and eighty-seven, conclude an agreement with the various tribes or bands of Indians residing upon the Gros Ventre, Piegan, Blood, Blackfeet, and River Crow Reservation in Montana Territory, by their chiefs, head-men and principal men, embracing a majority of all male adult Indians occupying said reservation, which said agreement is as follows:

Agreement concluded December twenty-eighth and thirty-first, eighteen hundred and eighty-six, and January twenty-first, eighteen hundred and eighty-seven, with the Indians of the Gros Ventre, Piegan, Blood, Blackfeet, and River Crow Reservation in Montana, by John V. Wright, Jared W. Daniels, and Charles F. Larabee, Commissioners.

This agreement, made pursuant to an item in the act of Congress entitled "An act making appropriations for the current and contingent expenses of the Indian Department, and for fulfilling treaty stipulations with various Indian tribes, for the year ending June thirtieth, eighteen hundred and eighty-seven, and for other purposes," approved May fifteenth, eighteen hundred and eighty-six, by John V. Wright, Jared W. Daniels, and Charles F. Larabee, duly appointed commissioners on the part of the United States, and the various tribes or bands of Indians residing upon the Gros Ventre, Piegan, Blood, Blackfoot, and River Crow Reservation, in the Territory of Montana, by their chiefs, head-men, and principal men, embracing a majority of all the male adult Indians occupying said reservation, witnesseth that--

Whereas, the reservation set apart by act of Congress approved April fifteenth, eighteen hundred and seventy-four, for the use and occupancy of the Gros Ventre, Piegan, Blood, Blackfoot, River Crow, and such other Indians as the President might, from time to time, see fit to locate thereon, is wholly out of proportion to the number of Indians occupying the same, and greatly in excess of their present or prospective wants; and whereas the said Indians are desirous of disposing of so much thereof as they do not require, in order to obtain the means to enable them to become self-supporting, as a pastoral and agricultural people, and to educate their children in the paths of civilization: Therefore, to carry out such purpose, it is hereby agreed as follows:

ARTICLE I

Hereafter the permanent homes of the various tribes or bands of said Indians shall be upon the separate reservations hereinafter described and set apart. Said Indians acknowledging the rights of the various tribes or bands, at each of the existing agencies within their present reservation, to determine for themselves, with the United States, the boundaries of their separate reservation, hereby agree to accept and abide by such agreements and conditions as to the location and boundaries of such separate reservation as may be made and agreed upon by the United States and the tribes or bands for which such separate reservation may be made, and as the said separate boundaries may be hereinafter set forth.

ARTICLE II

The said Indians hereby cede and relinquish to the United States all their right, title, and interest in and to all the lands embraced within the aforesaid Gros Ventre, Piegan, Blood, Blackfoot, and River Crow Reservation, not herein specifically set apart and reserved as separate reservations for them, and do severally agree to accept and occupy the separate reservations to which they are herein assigned as their permanent homes, and they do hereby severally relinquish to the other tribes or bands respectively occupying the other separate reservations, all their right, title, and interest in and to the same, reserving to themselves only the reservation herein set apart for their separate use and occupation.

ARTICLE III

In consideration of the foregoing cession and relinquishment the United States hereby agrees to advance and expend annually, for the period of ten years after the ratification of this agreement, under direction of the Secretary of the Interior, for the Indians now attached to and receiving rations at the Fort Peck Agency, one hundred and sixty-five thousand dollars; for the Indians now attached to and receiving rations at the Fort Belknap Agency, one hundred and fifteen thousand dollars, and for the Indians now attached to and receiving rations at the Blackfeet Agency, one hundred and fifty thousand dollars, in the purchase of cows, bulls, and other stock, goods, clothing, subsistence, agricultural and mechanical implements, in providing employees, in the education of Indian children, procuring medicine and medical attendance, in the care and support of the aged, sick, and infirm, and helpless orphans of said Indians, in the erection of such new agency and school buildings, mills, and blacksmith, carpenter, and wagon shops as may be necessary, in assisting the Indians to build houses and inclose their farms, and in any other respect to promote their civilization, comfort, and improvement: **Provided**,

That in the employment of farmers, artisans, and laborers, preference shall in all cases be given to Indians residing on the reservation who are well qualified for such position: <u>Provided further</u>, That all cattle issued to said Indians for stock-raising purposes, and their progeny, shall bear the brand of the Indian Department, and shall not be sold, exchanged, or slaughtered, except by consent or order of the agent in charge, until such time as this restriction shall be removed by the Commissioner of Indian Affairs.

ARTICLE IV

It is further agreed that whenever in the opinion of the President the annual installments provided for in the foregoing article shall be found to be in excess of the amount required to be expended in any one year in carrying out the provisions of this agreement upon either of the separate reservations, so much thereof as may be in excess of the requirement shall be placed to the credit of the Indians of such reservation, in the Treasury of the United States, and expended in continuing the benefits herein provided for when said annual installments shall have expired.

ARTICLE V

In order to encourage habits of industry, and reward labor, it is further understood and agreed, that in the giving out or distribution of cattle or other stock, goods, clothing, subsistence, and agricultural implements, as provided for in Article III, preference shall be given to Indians who endeavor by honest labor to support themselves, and especially to those who in good faith undertake the cultivation of the soil, or engage in pastoral pursuits, as a means of obtaining a livelihood, and the distribution of these benefits shall be made from time to time, as shall best promote the object specified.

ARTICLE VI

It is further agreed that any Indian belonging to either of the tribes or bands, parties hereto, who had, at the date of the execution of this agreement by the tribe or band to which he belongs, settled upon and made valuable improvements upon any of the land ceded to the United States under the provisions of this agreement, shall be entitled, upon application to the local land office for the district in which the lands are located, to have the same allotted to him or her, and to his or her children, in quantity as follows: To the head of the family, one hundred and sixty acres; to each child over eighteen years of age, eighty acres; to each child under eighteen years of age, forty acres; and the grant to such Indians shall be adjusted upon the survey of the lands so as to conform thereto. Upon the approval of said allotments by the Secretary of the Interior, he shall cause patents to issue therefor in the name of the allottees, which patents shall be of the legal effect and declare that the United States does and will hold the lands thus allotted for the period of twenty-five years, in trust for the sole use and benefit of the Indian to whom such allotment shall have been made, or, in case of his decease, of his heirs, according to the laws of the Territory of Montana, and that at the expiration of said period the United States will convey the same by patent to said Indian, or his heirs as aforesaid, in fee, discharged of said trust and free of all charge or incumbrance whatsoever. And if any conveyance shall be made of said lands, or any contract made touching the same, before the expiration of the time above mentioned, such conveyance or contract shall be absolutely null and void: <u>Provided</u>, That the laws of descent and partition in force in said Territory shall apply thereto after patents therefor have been executed and delivered: <u>Provided further</u>, That any such Indian shall be entitled to his distributive share of all the benefits to be derived from the cession of lands to the United States under this agreement, the same as though he resided within the limits of the diminished reservation to which he would properly belong.

ARTICLE VII

The outboundaries of the separate reservations, or such portions thereof as are not defined by natural objects, shall be surveyed and marked in a plain and substantial manner, the cost of such surveys to be paid out of the first annual installments provided for in Article III of this agreement.

ARTICLE VIII

It is further agreed that, whenever in the opinion of the President the public interests require the construction of railroads, or other highways, or telegraph lines, through any portion of either of the separate reservations established and set apart under the provisions of this agreement, right of way shall be, and is hereby, granted for such purposes, under such rules, regulations, limitations, and restrictions as the Secretary of the Interior may prescribe; the compensation to be fixed by said Secretary and by him expended for the benefit of the Indians concerned.

12. No council minutes of the meetings with the Fort Belknap and Blackfeet Agency Indians were kept because of physical difficulties. The same was true of the Assiniboine council at the Wolf Point Agency. However, minutes were kept of the Sioux council at the same agency. The following are excerpts from those minutes.

***

* * * Many people have denied that the Sioux have any right or title to this land here; they say that they do not belong here, but down in Dakota. When the Government sent us here we were told that we could make such agreement with you as we thought best -- to remain or go away, just as you liked. During our stay here we have talked with many people--the military officers, your agent, late agent, and other friends, and it is the united opinion that it is better for you to remain.

We also think it is better, and therefore shall not advise you to remove. And in treating with you we state in the outset that we recognize your right to this land, and we propose to treat with you as having equal rights in this reservation with all the other Indians; that is, the Assiniboines, Gros Ventre, and Blackfeet. I know that you have sometimes been uneasy yourselves because white men are continually saying that you have no right or title here, and that you should be sent from your present homes, and I know it will make you feel good-- your heart strong--to hear us say that we think and believe that you have rights, and equal rights, in this vast domain, with all the other Indians located upon it, and that we propose to award to you a share of it, sufficient for you and your children now and for years to come.

***

Our proposition is to leave to you and the Assiniboines at Wolf Point a reservation here. To the Indians at Belknap, a reservation that they may select, and to the Indians at Blackfoot, a reservation they may select. In addition to this we also propose to give you and the Assinaboines at Wolf Point, and to each of the other bands or tribes, a certain sum of money each year for a term of years, so that you will have the means to provide yourselves comfortable homes, gather around you stock, cattle, and sheep, and give you a good start in life.

***

13. Based upon the preceding findings of fact and the record as a whole, it is the conclusion of this Commission that the petitioner, the Blackfeet Nation, owned a one hundred percent (100%) interest in the remainder of their 1855 reservation which was ceded under the Act of May 1, 1888 (25 Stat. 113). This area contained 13,338,589 acres including the Fort Belknap Reservation and that portion of the Fort Peck Reservation which extended west of the line running north from the mouth of Milk River to the Canadian boundary. Since the Gros Ventre Tribe benefited from the Fort Belknap Reservation to the extent of 316,979 acres, this 13,338,589 acres has been reduced to 13,021,610 acres.

14. The Act of May 1, 1888 (25 Stat. 113) defined the interest of the Blackfeet Nation in that portion of the 1874 reservation which lay east of the Blackfeet 1855 treaty boundary and which was ceded under the said Act of May 1, 1888. Based upon a percentage of population as compared with the Sioux and Assiniboine Tribes, that interest amounted to 54.3% of the 1,630,567 acres ceded.

Therefore, the petitioner, Blackfeet Nation, is entitled to 885,398 acres of the area as its proportionate share, thereby making a total cession by the Blackfeet Nation of 13,907,008 acres under the Act of May 1, 1888 (25 Stat. 113).

15. Based upon the preceding findings of fact and the record as a whole it is the conclusion of this Commission that the intervenors, the Sioux Tribe and the Assiniboine Tribe, acquired recognized title to a proportionate share of the 1874 reservation under the Act of

May 1, 1888, and that by the same Act they joined in the cession of a stipulated 14,969,156 acres of what became known as Royce Area 692, Montana 2, and their proportionate part of this area based upon a percentage of population is 45.7%. The division between the Sioux and Assiniboine Tribes, based upon their respective populations in 1888, would be 43.2% to the Sioux and 56.8% to the Assiniboine.

Under the stipulation filed herein the total acreage ceded under the Act of May 1, 1888, was 14,969,156 acres. Then 45.7% of 14,969,156 acres would be 6,840,904 acres. The share of the Sioux Indians therein would be 43.2%, or 2,955,271 acres. The remainder, or 3,885,633 acres, would be the proportionate share of the Assiniboine.

Valuation

16. Nearly all of the subject area lies within the drainage basins of the Marias and Milk Rivers, tributaries to the Missouri River. Most of the drainage basin of the Marias River is a flat glacial plain, broken only by the uplift of the Sweet Grass Hills. This uplift is some seven or eight townships in area and is the extrusion of the batholith that has found the Sweet Grass Arch which extends roughly between Great Falls, Montana and Lethbridge, Alberta. The Sweet Grass Hills rise to an elevation of 6,983 feet. The elevation at Cut Bank, Montana, is 3,751 feet.

The drainage basin of the Milk River consists principally of a flat glacial plain formed by the last Pleistocene ice sheet. The eastern part of the Milk River Plains is undulating to hummocky. This is the result of less glaciation and of glacial moraine formation.

Southeast of Havre, between Milk and Missouri Rivers, the plain is extensively broken by the Bear Paw Mountain uplift. This area and the associated foothills and benchlands occupy some forty-five townships of land. At the highest point, the Bear Paw Mountains rise to 6,906 feet. Southeast of the Bear Paw Mountains there occurs another small mountainous area called the Little Rocky Mountains. Eastward of this small mountain uplift, between the junction of the Milk and Missouri Rivers, there is a sizeable area of rough land, with some interspersed badlands formations, known as the Larb Hills area. This area covers some twenty-one townships. It received little or no glaciation and has heavy residual soils that have weathered into rough lands.

The valley of the Milk River is a flat, alluvial valley which is mostly unbroken with low and generally smooth escarpments. However, the valley of the Missouri has considerable rough lands and breaks along its course. Between the mouths of the Marias and the Milk Rivers, the Missouri is deeply entrenched below the plains and the breaks of the river extend back as far as five to ten miles on both sides of the river.

The extreme eastern portion of the area, beyond the confluence of the Milk River and the Missouri, is drained by a series of short streams. In this area, the Missouri is not deeply entrenched and its escarpment is not much broken. The Missouri here flows through a wide and flat flood plain.

17. Almost the entire subject area was covered by the Pleistocene ice sheet. As a result, most of the area is a glacial plain, smooth to undulating. Because of this glaciation, the locally underlying geological

formations generally do not determine the soil characteristics. A small part of the subject area received little or no glaciation, and in those areas the underlying geologic formations are important in determining the soil characteristics. The glacial drift which occurs over almost the entire area varies in depth from ten to sixty feet.

The prairie soils that cover most of the area are known to soil science as the "Brown" soils. These soils have a top soil of medium-brown color, a medium or loam texture, and a depth varying from six to fourteen inches. These soils are good grassland soils. The prairie loam soils which have formed upon the glacial drift consist mainly of those grouped under three soils. These are Joplin loam, Scobey loam, and Williams loam.

In the Marias plains, the top soil varies from medium to light brown in color, and from five to ten inches in depth. These are fairly good grassland soils. As the Marias plains slope upward to the Sweet Grass Hills, the soil depth increases and the color darkens, a result of higher rainfall as the elevation increases. In some parts of the plains of the Marias and Milk Rivers, there occur local areas of "Solonized" soils. These soils have a columnar top soil structure which tends to seal when wet. These soils make inefficient use of water and may be bare of any vegetation. This type of soil does not occur extensively enough within the area to be of any significance or of any economic importance.

Those soils of the Milk River plains that have formed upon residual materials, as in parts of Blaine, Phillips, and Valley Counties may be heavy-textured and not as good for tillage as the Joplin, Williams, and Scobey loams. The heavier soils are, however, good grassland soils. The residual soils of northern Blaine, Phillips, and Valley Counties are better grassland soils than are the Joplin loam soils of the Marias plains.

In the Bear Paw Mountains, the elevation has resulted in higher precipitation and resulting good soil formation. Nearly all of the Bear Paw Mountains and surrounding uplift have adequate soils for good range production.

South of the Bear Paws, the soils are residual, formed on the Pierre shales and other marine shales. These soils are moderately fertile and are classed as fair in range forage production. This also applies to the land south of the Little Rocky Mountains though the soils south of the Little Rocky Mountains appear somewhat better and more productive than those south of the Bear Paws.

The soils of the Badlands Basin of South Valley County are also residual, formed principally upon the Lance formation. These heavy soils are derived from marine shale deposits and are fair grassland soils where not too eroded. These soils are the least productive grassland soils of the entire area.

In the northeastern part of the subject area, in the present Sheridan, Daniels, and Roosevelt Counties, some of the best Scobey and Williams loam soils of the area are found. This part of the area was quite heavily glaciated, resulting in a drift mostly favorable for good soil formation. Due to the favorable growing season and precipitation, a good grassland resource is present there.

18. The subject area has a northern climate. Summer days are long, warm and sunny. Winter days are short and sometimes quite cold. Moisture evaporation rates are much lower than those of southern climates. The duty of water is much higher in the production of vegetative growth. Lower evaporation rates extend the use of surface water for livestock. Summer temperatures range between 50 and 95 degrees. Winter temperatures fall between minus 20 and 45 degrees. Wind velocities are typical of the northern plains, five to twenty miles per hour except during storms. Winter "Chinook" winds are fairly common in the western part of the area. These warm, dry winds quickly clear the rangelands of snow cover and are very helpful from the standpoint of winter use of rangeland by livestock.

At Havre, the long-run average annual precipitation is 13.9 inches. This amount of precipitation is adequate for the development of good soil and range land resources. In the drier parts of the area, the aver. precipitation may be as low as eleven inches. This would not be favorab for native plant growth and soil development were it not for the very favorable seasonal distribution. Seventy-five percent of the average annual precipitation falls during the months of the growing season. The heaviest precipitation falls in the month of June, with an average of about three inches for that month.

As a result of this precipitation pattern, native grasses achieve most of their growth during the months of May, June and July, and cure well on the stem during the warm and dry month of August. Thus, with dry winters and light snow cover, the grasses are not leached or matted down, and remain available for feed during the winter. The range land grazing season of the area is ten to twelve months.

The growing season of the entire area is adequate for good range forage production. The northernmost part of the area along the Canadian border has an average frost-free season of 120 days. About two-thirds of the subject area has an average of 140 frost-free days, ample for grain and hay crops.

19. The major portion of the subject area consists of grassland in native range land types. The mixed-prairie grasslands of the northern plains consist of a native range plant association which is a combination of midgrasses and shortgrasses. This range land type provides a very highly productive combination as the midgrasses are cool weather grasses and the shortgrasses are warm weather grasses. The principal midgrasses of the area are western wheat grass and needle grass, which are of medium height in their growth habits. These form the overstory of the prairie grasslands. The principal shortgrass which forms the understory of the combination is the blue grama grass, a strong sod former. Other important grasses of this area are the Junegrass, sandgrass and slender wheat grass.

In the southern portion of the area, on the residual soils south of the Bear Paws and the Little Rockies, brush grasslands are found. This area has a dominant overstory of shrubs but a considerable understory of native range land grasses. In the Badlands Basin of South Valley County, the range land is a shrub type with the big sagebrush and saltbrush as the overstory and wheat grasses as the dominant understory.

In the mountainous parts of the area, the range land type is a grassland with some locations having a marked shrub or tree aspect. The grasses in the mountainous areas are principally bluebunch wheatgrass or a combination of the plains grasses and the mountainous bunch grasses. These grasses form very productive range lands.

20. By 1870, Montana had a population of 20,595. By 1880, it had increased to 39,159 and by 1890, to 142,924. The discovery of gold and the presence of steamers on the Missouri River had given impetus to the development of the area. By 1867 steamers were plying between St. Louis and Fort Benton along the Missouri River which forms the south boundary of the subject tract. In 1877, twenty-five steamers arrived at Fort Benton. In 1878, forty-six steamers arrived there. In 1881, five lines of steamers, comprising from 25 to 30 boats, made their headquarters at Bismarck, Fort Benton being the western terminus of these lines.

In 1877, the value of exports from Montana, by the Missouri River, of ore, bullion, wool, robes, skins and hides, was approximately $1,270,600.00. In 1881, imports by way of the Missouri, amounted to 34,760,000 pounds with a value of $5,214,000.00.

Steamboat traffic on the Missouri did not begin to wane until the advent of the Great Northern Railroad into the area in 1887.

21. By 1880, the Secretary of the Interior had announced his opposition to preservation of large Indian reservations. The proposal

was made that division of land be made among the Indians in severalty with the remainder of the land to be sold to whites. It was argued that this land pattern would bring the two races into closer relationship and promote the more rapid assimilation of the Indian.

As early as 1883, pressure began to build up for cession of the Blackfeet Reservation. Reacting to pressure of important persons and groups interested in expansion, Territorial Governor Crosby recommended a reduction in size of the Blackfeet Reservation. He again made this recommendation in 1884.

The Great Northern Railway substantially traversed the subject area by 1887, running to Havre and then down to Great Falls, Montana. There was also rail transportation available in adjacent Canada. This added to the pressure to obtain a cession of the Blackfeet area.

229

The influential citizens and the Sun River Sun, a Montana newspaper, exerted pressure on Congress to get the Blackfeet Reservation opened. The reason for this pressure lay in the serious overstocking of the existing Montana range by 1884.

This pressure resulted in the Congress authorizing the Secretary of the Interior to negotiate with the Indians of northern Montana for a reduction of their reservation. This culminated in the Act of May 1, 1888 wherein the cession under consideration was made.

22. Prior to the cession of the Blackfeet Reservation the cattle and sheep industry had begun.

The destruction of the buffalo paved the way for cattle operators to move onto the Montana plains. Cattle and sheep were first brought into Montana to meet the needs of the mining camps. These early herds were located in the western valleys near the mining areas. At the height of the mining activity, large herds were driven in to meet the demand for meat. When the population began to stabilize in the mining regions, the demand declined, a surplus of cattle accumulated and, by 1870, the range of the western valleys had become seriously crowded. It was then that the movement to the eastern plains began. In that year Robert S. Ford and Thomas Dunn took one thousand cattle into the Sun River Valley. In 1873, Conrad Kohrs and John Bielenberg moved large herds into the same region.

Camp Baker was constructed in 1879 in the Smith River Valley to provide protection to the herds which were being raised there and in the upper Musselshell, and provided a market for some of the beef as well. During the late 1870's, a movement of cattle and sheep from Oregon and California was pushing its way into the eastern Montana plains

The extension of the Union Pacific Railroad through Cheyenne in 1867 and the cession by the Crow Indians of a huge portion of their reservation in 1868 led to a great influx of cattle into the grazing area offered by Montana. This northward migration proceeded steadily through the 1870's with additional encouragement in the early 1880's by the building of the railroad into Montana. During the early 1880's cattle were being shipped to St. Paul by the Canadian Pacific Railroad.

The growth of large herds in the areas immediately adjacent the Blackfeet Reservation resulted in pressure from the cattle industry to have the Blackfeet Reservation opened.

The reservation was not immune from use by cattlemen, however. In 1880, 1000 head of cattle and 50 head of horses were moved into the area of the Bear Paw Mountains. Another 100 head came into the Bear Paws in 1885. 5000 head were moved to the foot of the Little Rockies in 1885. By 1886, accounts of cattle moving into the area were numerous.

The area of the Blackfeet Reservation was well adapted to sheep and the industry developed rapidly. By 1884, it was estimated that there were 100,000 sheep in Chouteau County.

23. With the close of the Civil War tremendous herds of Texas longhorn cattle that had accumulated during that war began to be moved out by means of the railroads in Kansas, Missouri, and Nebraska. These trail herds began in 1866 and in 1867 when the demand and prices were up more than 1000 carloads left Abilene, Kansas. The Secretary of Agriculture in response to Senate Resolution No. 289 in reporting on "The Great Boom in Range Cattle" covering the 1880-1885 period, on this phase of the matter said that

> *** Actual demands reached such a volume in 1871 that 600,000 cattle were driven north and to the railroad in that year. The heavy range use in western Kansas and Nebraska that began with these drives never ceased until the grass was plowed under, although dropping prices decreased the profits and hence the number of drives. By 1885 a total of more than 5 million cattle had been driven northward from Texas.

Many of these Texas herds were soon headed for the Wyoming and Montana free open range. The number of cattle in the Wyoming Territory had increased from 90,000 in 1874 to 450,000 in 1879 and 530,000 in 1880; however, a lack of railroad connections, a change from placer to deep vein mining, and a shift from the use of oxen to horses and mules in freighting, brought the boom to a close, and the Montana ranchers for the same reasons soon found a surplus of about 17,000 head, chiefly four and five year olds. They could be purchased for $10.00 a head.

Open range ranching in central and eastern Montana was held up since this region was still Indian country and had no railroad connections to the market in the east until the Northern Pacific Railroad was completed in 1883. The great possibilities of the region as an open range were fully appreciated by those interested in the cattle business. It was well watered, and its short buffalo grass cured on the stem during July and August made excellent feed. Its thickets of small trees and bushes along the deep bedded creeks afforded natural shelter for stock while its buttes and mesas broke the force of the winter winds.

24. Between 1880 and 1886 every available bit of range in central and northeastern Wyoming and central and eastern Montana (below the Missouri River) was filled to overflowing. It was estimated that in 1880 Montana contained 250,000 head of stock including dairy cattle and work oxen with the central and eastern portions practically unoccupied. By the fall of 1883 the number had increased to 600,000 and those central and eastern ranges had been rapidly taken over. By 1886 the ranges of both Wyoming and Montana had reached the point of saturation.

Many large cattle companies were organized during this period (1880-86); in 1883 alone twenty companies were capitalized at more than twelve million dollars and the membership of the Wyoming Stockgrowers' Association increased from 267 in 1883 to 363 in 1885, at which time its members owned some two million head of stock. While the Montana Stockgrowers' Association organized in 1884 with 63 members, and never equalled in size that of the Wyoming Association, it took a very active part in protecting the rights of the stockmen of Montana during that period of time.

25. Cattle raising under the open range system, dependent as it was upon weather conditions, had always been recognized as hazardous and the periodic severe winters were soon forgotten by the stockmen despite the warnings of some of the old-timers and the boom gained momentum. The culmination of this boom period occurred during the winter of 1886-87.

The following description of that winter was taken by an author from the files of territorial newspapers:

> *** The story of the calamitous winter of 1886-87 has been told many times. It closed down from the northwest fully six weeks earlier than usual, holding the cattle ranges in its iron grip for more than four months, relaxing at last only to leave ruin and destruction in its wake. The first storm began on November 4 with a very low temperature and a terrible blizzard. The fine snow packed into the coulees and depressions and covered the river bottoms. The storm finally spent itself but the extreme cold continued. Then followed blizzard after blizzard, throughout the months of November, December, January, and even into February, with the temperature often dropping to forty degrees below zero. The snow in many places lay four to five feet on the level

and the drifts were of monstrous size. With what little
grass there was buried under successive layers of snow, it
is easy to foretell the results.

The newspapers of Wyoming, Montana, and Dakota were
filled with stories of the terrible suffering and loss of
stock.

Many of the large companies went into the hands of the receiver in the summer of 1887 and had the remnants of their herds disposed of as their creditors demanded payment. The catastrophe of 1886-87 demonstrated to cattlemen, both large and small, the dangers of open range feeding and over-expansion, and adjustments were made. Large herds were no longer turned loose without shelter to graze and drift where they willed. Herds were smaller and were kept under careful control, shelter being provided for the weaker animals and hay cut for emergency feeding.

Cattle decreased in Montana from 1,050,000 in 1886 to 990,000 in 1887; in Wyoming from 970,000 in 1886 to 960,000 in 1887. However, the 1888 figures show an increase in Montana to an estimated 1,015,000 head.

The House Report (1889) in discussing the nature of the open range operation said:

*** The range-cattle business in the Western States and
Territories is carried on chiefly upon the public lands.
With the exception of a small percentage of lands, the
title of which has been secured under the provisions of
the homestead and pre-emption laws and desert land acts of
the United States or the timber-culture acts, the cattle
upon the northern ranges feed upon the public lands of the
United States, their owners being simply tenants by suf-
ferance upon such lands.

It was well known that land acquired in checkerboard patterns from the railroad during this period couldn't be controlled or exclusively used. Every owner of a herd of cattle or band of sheep insisted on using it, and in actual practice, did so with impunity. The Swan Land and Cattle Company purchased 555,890 acres of land from the Union Pacific Railroad Company in 1884 and after making two annual $150,000 payments on the purchase price voluntarily relinquished 253,226 acres to the railroad. John Clay, who was manager of this company for several years, set forth the reason for the relinquishment as follows:

> *** The Carbon Co. railroad lands (intermediate sections) to the extent of 283,226 acres were allowed to revert to the railroad. Two payments had been made and eight more were due. We got no use of these lands. Everybody with a flock of sheep or a bunch of cattle ranged over them. In those days you had only the redress of damages for trespass and as the sheepmen kept an attorney by the year, and the juries would only give a cent damages, it was a wearisome business and unprofitable. *** The lands were let go under my advice because it incurred a payment of $150,000.00 for which there was then no return. ***

26. During this open range era both the agriculturist and the rancher were having their difficulties. The line of frontier farmers steadily moved into Dakota, Montana, and Wyoming and at first they did little to bother the cattleman, but as time went on they increased in numbers and by acting together began to construct fences around their homestead tracts. These fences interfered with many of the stockmen's waterholes and freedom of the range. By the late nineties the open range had largely disappeared except a small area in northeastern Montana where it lingered on for another decade. The "homesteaders" had prevailed upon the legislatures to enact stock laws which prohibited

the stockman's cattle and sheep from destroying their crops without
payment of damages. The open range era was considerably limited and
the ranching methods had undergone a complete change.

27. For many years the westward movement of the population was
halted at the edge of the Great Plains by the presence of Indians and
by the different nature of the land from what the farmer from the
humid east was familiar with.

The homestead law of 1862 encouraged the farmer to move into the
Great Plains where he settled along the river bottoms beginning in the
1860's. At first the cattlemen were not disturbed, but by the latter
half of the 1880's the number of homesteaders had increased to the
point where they were taking up watering places that cattlemen had used
for years. Since it was impossible to run cattle without watering places
the fencing of waterholes by homesteaders led to friction and bloodshed
between the two groups.

It had long been recognized that the homestead policy of 1862
was not suited to the Great Plains area. The rainfall which was sufficient for grass was insufficient for crops. In 1878 Major J. W. Powell
had recommended to Congress certain changes in the homestead law with a
view to making it more adaptable to conditions on the Great Plains.
Although these recommendations were not adopted in toto they did lead
to the creation of the Geological Survey and a commission to further
study and report on the homestead situation in the Great Plains.

This Commission spent the summer of 1879 conducting an investigation on the Plains. The cattlemen who were asked about certain aspects of Powell's report with regard to creating pastoral homesteads of 2,560 acres, leasing of the range, etc., were opposed to any change. They wanted a continuation of the open range policy.

By 1884, after seeing homesteaders file on bottom lands and hay lands which they had been using; after seeing the more prudent cattlemen acquiring title to such lands, and seeing water holes fenced, many of these same cattlemen were in favor of a leasing program.

Homesteaders, along with other problems of the range cattle industry set the stage for the winter of 1886-87, described heretofore, which brought the industry to its knees and forced a recognition on the part of cattlemen that the free and easy days were fading. Thereafter the industry generally recognized and accepted the fact that proper range management was necessary in order to exist. The presence of sheep in ever increasing numbers made the need for range control most apparent.

28. The parties hereto agree and the Commission finds that the subject area had a highest and best use as grazing land for the raising of cattle and sheep.

The Commission, based upon the findings of fact and the record as a whole, finds that there existed as of May 1, 1888, a demand for the subject lands in large tracts for the purpose of grazing livestock.

29. Sales of comparable land were nonexistent within the subject area prior to May 1, 1888. The following sales from the general area were introduced by petitioners:

(1) The Musselshell Cattle Company made seven purchases from the Northern Pacific Railway Company, consisting of a total of 23,026.66 acres for a total price of $33,269.11, an average price of $1.44 per acre. The contracts were signed at various times from 1886 to 1889. These lands lay on the Musselshell River drainage about fifty miles northwest of Billings, Montana, and were prairie grasslands similar to those in the subject area. These were sales of smaller tracts making a total of 23,026.66 acres and were not contiguous.

(2) The Montana Cattle Company purchased 58,101.05 acres for $1.00 an acre in 1875, 1896, 1897 and 1899. Those lands were located in the Musselshell and Yellowstone River drainages approximately sixty miles due west of Billings. All of those lands were prairie grasslands of the range land type. The purchase was from the Northern Pacific Railway Company.

(3) David Auchard purchased 56,356 acres for an average price of $1.16 an acre from the Northern Pacific Railway Company in 1891, 1893, 1894, 1896, and 1897. Those lands were located about forty miles northwest of Great Falls. They compared in range land types to the Bear Paw Mountains and Sweet Grass Hills of the subject area.

(4) Alonzo Van Duzee purchased 12,808 acres for a contract price of $1.00 per acre in 1899. Those lands were located about fifteen miles northeast of the present city of Dickinson, North Dakota. These were prairie grasslands quite comparable to the subject area and were purchased from the Northern Pacific Railway Company.

(5) Mr. Arthur C. Huidekoper purchased 11,520 acres under a contract with the Northern Pacific Railway Company dated December 3, 1883, for an average price of $2.00 per acre. The land of this sale was located in the drainage of the Little Missouri River, just east of the Montana-North Dakota line and about forty miles south of the present site of the town of Medora, North Dakota. This was range land of the prairie rough land type.

(6) W. D. Washburn purchased 113,917.93 acres under a contract with the Northern Pacific Railway Company dated February 28, 1899, for an average price of $1.00 per acre. This land was located just east of the Missouri River in west-central North Dakota. At the time of the sale it was prairie grassland.

(7) Mr. John R. McGinley purchased 29,373.93 acres from the Northern Pacific Railway Company in September, 1899, for $49,935.09. This was an average price of $1.70 per acre. This land was located in central North Dakota and was in the farm belt with a rainfall of 16 to 18 inches.

30. Petitioners also introduced certain Canadian sales from the Southern Alberta Land District:

(1) On April 22, 1896, the Alberta Railway and Coal Company sold 28,661.7 acres to James A. Cunningham for $1.00 per acre. This land is located on the Milk River Ridge, about fifteen miles east of the town of Cardston, Alberta, Canada, and was range land.

(2) The Department of Interior of the Dominion of Canada sold twenty-five sections to the Cochrane Ranch Company on May 30, 1895, at a price of $1.25 per acre. That land was located between the Waterton and Belly Rivers in southern Alberta, west of the southern portion of the Blood Indian Reservation and twelve miles north of the Montana-Alberta border. It was principally foothill grassland comparable in type and productivity to the Sweet Grass Hills and the Bear Paw Mountains.

(3) The Alberta Railway and Coal Company sold to Jesse Knight and Oscar Raymond Knight 21,920 acres of land in one piece and 10,471 acres in another for an average price of $2.50 per acre. These transactions occurred in September, 1901. The land involved in these sales was range land of the prairie grassland type. This land was located near Cardston, Alberta. This sale is not sufficiently established by the evidence as to consideration.

(4) The Alberta Railway and Coal Company on July 10, 1901, sold 200,000 acres to Jesse Knight for a consideration of $2.00 per acre. This land was located west of the present town of Warner, Alberta, on the Milk River Ridge and was prairie grassland. This sale is not sufficiently established by the evidence as to size or consideration.

(5) The Calgary & Edmondton Land Company, Ltd. sold 36,245 acres of land to the Cochrane Ranch Company on May 2, 1904, for a consideration of $45,307.00, an average of $1.25 per acre. This was prairie grassland.

31. In addition to sales from the general area petitioners also presented certain supplemental methods of valuation for the purpose of

confirming the opinion of their expert witness as to the value of the subject area as arrived at on the basis of the sales presented in evidence.

The first of these methods was capitalization of income. Petitioners' expert presented as a basis for their supplemental method certain leases by the State of Montana in Meagher County which lies south of the subject area. The first of these leases were made in 1895 and by 1896 there were 37,440 acres of range land leases in Meagher County. These leases ran for five-year terms at an average rental rate of 10.31 cents per acre. Since the State of Montana had no taxes or upkeep to pay, this figure was taken as the net rental on the reasoning that leases by the State of Montana have, historically, been lower than private leases, with the differential being approximately equal to the taxes and upkeep that a private landlord would have to pay from his rental income.

In the absence of adequate information on the subject the petitioners' expert chose 8% as a general average interest rate on land mortgages during 1888. A capitalization of the 10.31 cents at 8% produces an approximate value of $1.30 per acre for Meagher County range land which was considered as being comparable to the subject area on an average.

32. A second supplemental method of confirming the value arrived at by means of sales in the general area as employed by petitioners' expert consisted of a statistical average of value per animal unit of capacity of the subject area.

This process involves the determination of the value of the ranching property and lands as of the date of taking. This value is assigned by petitioners' expert as being $30 during the period in question.

This $30 estimate per animal unit value of ranching lands as of 1888 when multiplied by the 509,970 CYL'S (see Finding No. 33) the result divided by the 14,969,156 acres of the subject area yields a per acre value of $1.02.

33. The commonly accepted method of determining the productivity or grazing capacity of range lands is the animal unit month, known as the A.U.M. This is the acreage of grazing land required to sustain one animal unit for one month. An animal unit in livestock is commonly accepted to be a cow, a mature steer or five ewes. A mature horse is rated as 1.2 and a yearling cow as .65. The term "cow year long", known as a C.Y.L. is a calculation of the number of animals an area would support for year around grazing.

In order to apply the above criteria it is necessary to determine the various types of range within a given area. Petitioners' expert shows in Item No. 9 of the Addenda to his report, Petitioners' Exhibit 114, his classification of the various types of range land within the subject area. His estimate of the carrying capacity of the subject lands as of 1888 is shown by the following table:

Rangeland type	Acreage	Acres per A.U.M.	A.U.M.'s
Prairie grassland (west)	8,983,246	2½	3,595,500
Sagebrush grasslands	1,502,750	3½	429,360
Missouri River breaks	665,700	5	133,140
Badlands basins	481,300	5	92,260
Bearpaw Mountains	1,030,920	1½	687,280
Sweetgrass Hills	176,805	1½	117,870
Prairie grasslands (east)	2,128,435	2	1,064,220
Totals	14,969,156		6,119,630

The above figures show an average of 2.44 acres per A.U.M. or approximately 30 acres per animal per year and a total of 509,970 CYL. This means that, according to petitioners' expert, the subject area could have carried 509,970 head of cattle over the grazing season, which he states to be approximately 10 months of the year.

34. A third supplemental valuation process used to confirm the valuation derived from the sales was a valuation based upon range land types. This method consisted of comparing the several principal range land types in the actual sales with the similar range land types of the subject area. Where carrying capacities were significantly different for similar range land types of the actual sale and of the subject area, the value was interpolated on a capacity basis.

The following table shows the results of this method:

Rangeland Type	Acreage	Value per acre	Total value
Prairie Grassland (west)	8,983,246	$1.20	$10,779,895.00
Sagebrush Grassland	1,502,750	.85	1,277,377.00
Badlands Basin	481,300	.60	288,780.00
Missouri River Creeks	665,700	.60	399,420.00
Bear Paw Mountains	1,030,920	2.00	2,061,840.00
Sweet Grass Hills	176,805	2.00	353,610.00
Prairie Grassland (east)	2,128,435	1.50	3,192,652.00
Total acreage	14,969,156	Total value	18,353,534.00

These estimates result in a price of $1.23 per acre for the subject lands.

35. Petitioners' expert submitted his opinion of the value of the subject lands as a unit of 14,969,156 acres, based upon comparable sales data and productivity, as being $16,466,071.00, or approximately $1.10 per acre.

36. Defendant's expert appraiser listed three generally accepted methods of land appraisal. The first of these was comparable sales of land. The second was the capitalization or income approach, and the third was reproduction, less depreciation of buildings and improvements. The latter two methods were dismissed as being unsuitable for measuring the value of the subject land.

The sales used by defendant's appraiser for comparison were the following:

(1) The purchase in 1880 of between 3 and 4 million acres of land by Munson and Gunter of Denison, Texas, located in northern and western Texas was financed with Reconstruction Government script which had been obtained at $16.00 per section or 2½ cents per acre. Most of this land was sold between 1880 and 1890 in small tracts at 25 to 50 cents per acre. Land without surface water was 25 cents per acre and that with surface water was 50 cents.

(2) The purchase of 3,000,000 acres in 1881 by the XIT Ranch located in the Texas Panhandle at an agreed value of 50 cents per acre in return for the construction of the Texas State Capitol. The ultimate cost of this land exceeded $1.00 per acre because of the construction difficulties encountered.

(3) The purchase in 1881 of 120,000 acres for 20 cents per acre by Charles Goodnight of land located in the Texas Panhandle bordering the Palo Duro Canyon.

(4) The purchase in 1884 of 1,059,560 acres of land at .472 cents per acre from the Santa Fe Railroad by the Aztec Land and Cattle Company. This land was located in New Mexico and Arizona.

(5) The purchase in 1883 of 580,000 acres of land at 17 cents per acre known as the Amarilla Spanish Grant. This land was located in northern New Mexico and southern Colorado and had a U. S. patent.

(6) The Swan Land and Cattle Company in 1884 purchased from the Union Pacific Railroad 555,890 acres for $460,900 to be paid in 10 installments. After two payments were made 286,473.08 acres of this purchase were cancelled, leaving 269,416.92 acres. These were checkerboard lands and carried control of additional acreage of the public lands. They were located in Wyoming. The price paid for this land is subject to question.

(7) The purchase of 2,430,000 acres of land by J. W. McCammon in 1886 from the Northern Pacific Railway Company for the sum of $2.00 per acre. This purchase was made under a rather complicated agreement involving the preferred stock of the railway company receivable at par though purchased at a lesser price which varied. The land was located in North Dakota and was principally agricultural land.

Defendant's expert felt that all of these lands were equal or superior to the subject land.

37. Subsequent to the introduction of the evidence concerning the above sales defendant's expert prepared a list of "hindsight" sales. These sales varied in date from 1895 to 1904:

(1) Northern Pacific Railway Company to Marcus Daly, contract dated February 9, 1899, on which the assignee, the Big Blackfoot Milling Company, subsequently purchased about 900,000 acres of timbered land located in Flathead, Sanders, Lincoln, Powell, Granite, and Missoula Counties, Montana, at 50 cents per acre with an additional 50 cents per thousand board feet for stumpage.

(2) Northern Pacific Railway Company to 77 buyers on contracts dated 1895 to 1903 for 1,053,033 acres of land for $1,000,371.65, or 95 cents per acre. These contracts averaged about 13,000 acres-plus per contract, the largest sale to one person being 86,875.40 acres. This land is located in Dawson, Custer, Yellowstone, Fergus, and Meagher Counties, Montana.

(3) Northern Pacific Railway Company to W. D. Washburn, a ten year contract dated February 28, 1899, for the sale of 113,917.93 acres of land for $113,917.93, or $1.00 per acre. This land was located in North Dakota.

(4) Northern Pacific Railway Company to Hackney-Boynton Land Company, Contract No. 20239, dated March 14, 1901, sale of 1,174,680.64 acres for $1,233,414.48, or $1.05 per acre. This was located in North Dakota.

(5) Northern Pacific Railway Company to Hackney-Boynton Land Company, Contract Nos. 20239-21323, dated August 31, 1904, sale of

1,003,778.24 acres for $409,871.90, or about 41 cents per acre. This was North Dakota land lying between the Missouri and James Rivers.

The above lands were considered by defendant's expert to equal or exceed the quality of the subject lands.

38. In addition to citing the sales mentioned above defendant's expert also used the capitalization or income method as a supplementary approach to confirm his appraised price of 27 cents-plus per acre.

This capitalization approach was based upon the estimate of defendant's witness as to a reasonable return to the purchaser of the subject tract through a leasing program at a figure of four cents per acre. This leasing program at four cents per acre was considered to be a losing one for about the first twenty years because of overhead, according to defendant's witness.

39. Defendant's witness placed a value of approximately 27 cents per acre on the 14,969,156 acres of the subject area which were ceded on May 1, 1888, for a total unit value of $4,050,000.00.

40. Defendant introduced the testimony of a range economist who placed a value of 24 cents per acre on the subject lands as of 1888. This figure was determined by taking the price of beef on the Chicago market in 1888, figuring the production of a model ranching operation and the income from that production, and deducting certain fixed costs of operation to arrive at the amount of money available for land charge. This figure was then divided by the number of animal units on the ranch to obtain the return for use of the land. This figure was then divided

by the carrying capacity of the range to obtain the return per acre. This in turn was divided by a figure representing interest and taxes to arrive at the final value per acre of 24 cents.

41. Defendant's expert witness prepared a sampling of the subject area based upon notes made by the men who surveyed the subject area. This sampling was made in a pre-determined pattern within the subject area prior to reading the survey notes. The sample consisted of 120 townships, with nine of them being partial townships because of the irregular boundary. The size of the sample was approximately 2,764,800 acres. As shown by Defendant's Exhibit No. 156 the sample was fairly arranged to take in both the width and breadth of the subject area.

Based upon our interpretation of these survey notes and keeping in mind the highest and best use of the area as grazing land, the following results are shown:

```
Total sample                            120 townships
Total acres (approximate)               2,764,800
Townships classified good grazing       76
    "           "      fair    "        28
    "           "      poor    "        16
                                        ─────
                        Total           120

Percentage good grazing                 63 1/3
    "      fair    "                    23 1/3
    "      poor    "                    13 1/3
                                        ─────
                        Total           100%

Percentage of good to fair grazing      86 2/3
```

42. The present day oil and coal resources of the subject area were unknown as of the valuation date on May 1, 1888, and so had no value to a prospective purchaser on that date.

There are still some 1,854,153 acres of public domain in the State of Montana. Of this amount some 750,000 acres lie within the subject area. Most of this area of 750,000 acres, except for the badlands basin of south Valley County and the shaly buttes of the lower breaks of the Missouri River, was capable of use as grazing lands, although having a smaller rainfall than the average. Even the worst of this land formed a sheltered winter grazing possibility.

43. Economic conditions during the period from 1870 to about 1895 were of a stable nature generally although depressed. As shown by Petitioners' Exhibit No. 114, Addenda No. 5, the general price level had started down sharply after 1865 and while it slowed momentarily about 1870, it continued its downward trend until 1895 when it hit bottom at an index of about 32.

During this period the panics of 1873, 1883, and 1893 occurred and it wasn't until the later 1890's when the banking system had improved and gold production increased that sufficient monetary reserves were available to stabilize the market and begin the upward trend. This trend, with the exception of the period 1910-1915 continued until about 1920.

This was a period of subsistence agriculture rather than commercial agriculture and while produce prices remained stable they were at a low level.

As shown by Addenda No. 6 of Petitioners' Exhibit No. 114 cattle prices on the Chicago market remained fairly consistent from 1870 through 1900 when they ranged from a high of $6.34 per hundred weight in 1870 to a low of $3.90 per hundred in 1889. The price range from 1880 to 1890 was as follows:

1880	$ 4.75
1881	5.25
1882	6.25
1883	5.60
1884	5.90
1885	5.35
1886	4.75
1887	4.20
1888	4.70
1889	3.90
1890	4.15

As can be seen from the above range of prices and the generally low level of the economy, the sale of the subject tract in 1888 would have been more difficult than in 1882 for instance when cattle prices were at their peak of the 1880-1890 decade.

44. Based upon the preceding findings of fact and upon the record as a whole, it is the conclusion of this Commission that the subject area as a unit of 14,969,156 acres had a value on May 1, 1888, of $11,975,324.80, or at the rate of 80 cents per acre.

45. The consideration promised under the Agreement of May 1, 1888, amounted to $4,300,000 for a cession of 14,969,156 acres. This amounts to approximately 29 cents per acre for land with a unit value of $11,975,324.80, or at the rate of 80 cents per acre on May 1, 1888.

46. Based upon the preceding findings of fact and the record as a whole, it is the conclusion of this Commission that a consideration

of 29 cents per acre for land having a value of 80 cents per acre on May 1, 1888, is unconscionable on its face and that defendant is liable to petitioners and intervenors for the difference between the amount of consideration paid the parties and the value of their respective interests on May 1, 1888, as found by this Commission in Findings Nos. 13, 14 and 15 made herein.

47. The respective shares referred to in Finding of Fact No. 46 are as follows:

(1) The Blackfeet Nation ceded their interest in a total of 13,907,008 acres with a value of $11,125,606.40 as of May 1, 1888.

(2) The Assiniboine Tribe ceded their interest in a total of 3,885,633 acres with a value of $3,108,506.40 as of May 1, 1888.

(3) The Sioux Tribe ceded their interest in a total of 2,955,271 acres with a value of $2,364,216.80 as of May 1, 1888.

48. Based upon the preceding findings of fact, and the record as a whole, it is the conclusion of this Commission that:

(1) The Blackfeet Nation shall have and recover from defendant the sum of $11,125,606.40, subject to the amount of consideration paid or which may be credited any party and to offsets, if any, to which defendant may be entitled under the Indian Claims Commission Act.

(2) The Assiniboine Tribe of the Fort Peck and Fort Belknap Reservation in Montana shall have and recover from defendant the sum of $3,108,506.40, subject to the amount of consideration paid or which may be credited any party and to offsets, if any, to which defendant may be entitled under the Indian Claims Commission Act.

(3) The Sioux Tribe of the Fort Peck Reservation in Montana shall have and recover from defendant the sum of $2,364,216.80 subject to the amount of consideration paid or which may be credited any party and to offsets, if any, to which defendant may be entitled under the Indian Claims Commission Act.

An order to the above effect will be entered.

/s/ Arthur V. Watkins
Arthur V. Watkins
Chief Commissioner

/s/ Wm. M. Holt
Wm. M. Holt
Associate Commissioner

/s/ T. Harold Scott
T. Harold Scott
Associate Commissioner

BEFORE THE INDIAN CLAIMS COMMISSION

THE BLACKFEET AND GROS VENTRE TRIBES OF)
  INDIANS, Residing Upon the Blackfeet)
  and Fort Belknap Reservations in the   )
  State of Montana,   )
                        Petitioners,   )   Docket No. 279-A
)
THE ASSINIBOINE TRIBES OF INDAINS,   )
  Residing Upon the Fort Belknap and   )
  Fort Peck Reservations, Montana,   )
     and   )
THE SIOUX TRIBE OF THE FORT PECK   )
RESERVATION, Montana,   )
                        Intervenors,   )
)
         v.   )
)
THE UNITED STATES OF AMERICA,   )
)
                        Defendant.   )

Decided: MAR 31 1967

Appearances:
  Glen A. Wilkinson and John W. Cragun
    for Wilkinson, Cragun and Barker,
    Attorneys for Petitioners

  Frances L. Horn, Jerry C. Straus and
  George E. Lyman, Of Counsel

  Marvin J. Sonosky,
    Attorney for Intervenors

  John S. White,
    Of Counsel

  William D. McFarlane, with whom was
  Mr. Assistant Attorney General
  Edwin L. Weisl, Jr.,
    Attorneys for the Defendant

OPINION OF THE COMMISSION

Scott, Associate Commissioner, rendered the decision of the Commission.

Petitioners, Blackfeet and Gros Ventre Tribes of Indians, have timely filed their claim in this cause for a cession of land in northern Montana made to defendant under the terms of the Agreement of May 1, 1888 (25 Stat. 113). They allege their claim under Section 2(3) and (5) of the Indian Claims Commission Act of 1946 (60 Stat. 1049). Each of petitioner tribes has a tribal organization recognized by the Secretary of the Interior as having authority to represent said tribes.

Intervenors are the Assiniboine Tribe and the Sioux Tribe of the Fort Peck Reservation in Montana. The Assiniboine Tribe is composed of two groups - one residing on the Fort Peck Reservation and the other on the Fort Belknap Reservation in Montana.

The Assiniboine Tribe of the Fort Peck Reservation, the Assiniboine Tribe of the Fort Belknap Reservation and the Sioux Tribe of Fort Peck, each has a governing body duly recognized by the Secretary of the Interior as authorized to represent it before this Commission.

Intervenors allege a one-half undivided interest in 14,969,156 acres in northern Montana which was ceded under the Agreement of May 1, 1888, by them and by petitioners. This allegation is based upon their contention with regard to the legal effect of the Act of April 15, 1874 (18 Stat. 28).

The background of this case is long and must be set forth in some detail in order to properly assess the various claims asserted and to understand the position of the parties herein.

When this claim was first filed by petitioners they alleged only a proportionate interest in the area of land ceded by the Agreements

of 1886 and 1887 as ratified by the Act of May 1, 1888 (25 Stat. 113).
Defendant duly filed an answer to the allegations contained in the petition and at a later date filed a motion for summary judgment based upon the doctrine of res judicata by reason of the judgment entered by the Court of Claims on April 8, 1935, in Docket E-427 entitled Blackfeet, et al., v. The United States, reported in 81 C. Cls. 101.

This Commission sustained defendant's motion as to one claim and denied said motion as to three others (See 2 Ind. Cl. Comm. 302, 322-323). The present claim is one of the three claims allowed to stand under that decision.

This decision by the Commission was upheld on appeal to the Court of Claims in its decision rendered March 2, 1954 and reported at 127 C. Cls. 807.

Petitioners and defendant then filed a stipulation in which it was agreed that the acreage involved in the subject area amounted to 14,969,156 acres. Just prior to this stipulation the Commission had set the case for hearing, denied a motion by defendant for a continuance, and defined the issues to be tried at the hearing while reserving to defendant its right, at the discretion of the Commission, to present ethnological testimony. Immediately thereafter the Commission severed the three remaining claims and assigned Docket No. 279-A to the present claim. Petitioners filed an amended petition to which defendant was required to reply. Defendant then filed a motion to consolidate certain cases and in the course of their reply thereto petitioners indicated that their claim was based on recognized rather than aboriginal title. Defendant then filed certain motions which were argued before the Commission and denied by it. Defendant then filed its answer. The Commission reset the case for hearing and shortly thereafter petitioners filed a motion to amend their amended petition to include the Assiniboine Tribes of Fort Belknap and Fort Peck, Montana. After oral argument, when it was indicated that the amendment would be denied, petitioners filed a plea of intervention on behalf of the said tribes.

A hearing was then held on the valuation phase of the case under the pleadings as they then stood. Subsequently the Commission denied petitioners' motions to amend and to intervene. Defendant then moved to reopen the hearings to present ethnological testimony and rebuttal exhibits. Petitioners opposed this motion. Petitioners then filed notice of appeal from the Commission's order denying the plea in intervention on behalf of the Assiniboine. Defendant filed a supplementary response to petitioners' opposition to its motion to reopen the record, etc. The Commission denied defendant's motion, thereby excluding the ethnological evidence, and ordered the filing of briefs. Defendant again sought to reopen the record and was denied. In the meantime attorneys for petitioners perfected their appeal from the order denying the intervention. Briefs were then filed in the Court of Claims.

Attorneys for petitioners then discovered an apparent conflict between the interests of the Blackfeet Nation on the one side and the Assiniboine on the other. They resigned from the Assiniboine case and the present counsel then undertook the case.

Attorneys for petitioners then moved the Commission to reopen the case on their theory that the Blackfeet and Gros Ventre owned 100% of the area held by them under the terms of the 1855 Treaty (11 Stat. 657) between them and defendant and which was ceded under the Agreement of 1888. Defendant opposed this motion and the matter was argued. Petitioners prevailed and additional valuation evidence was heard on the smaller area claimed by petitioners under the theory of 100% ownership.

On June 7, 1963, the Court of Claims rendered its decision with regard to the right to intervene by the Assiniboine Tribe. The Court held that the interest of the Assiniboine in the subject matter arising from their participation in the agreements ratified by the Act of 1888, was such as to entitle them to intervene in this case and remanded it with directions to grant the motion and permit their intervention as parties petitioner.

Thereafter counsel for the Assiniboine Tribe filed a motion for leave to intervene on behalf of the Sioux Tribe of the Fort Peck Reservation on the authority of the Court of Claims decision in the Assiniboine appeal. After responses from the parties and oral argument the Commission entered an order granting the motion and making the said Sioux Tribe a party petitioner along with the Blackfeet Nation and Assiniboine tribes.

A further motion by defendant to make the petition more definite and certain was denied and the last of eight briefs herein was filed on June 8, 1966.

Broadly speaking, the issues before the Commission are those of ownership of the lands involved, the interests created in the parties under the Acts of 1874 and 1888, if any, and the value of the lands ceded.

Defendant's contention in its brief of November 6, 1961, with regard to a lack of proper parties appears to be based primarily on its theory of the origin of the Blackfeet, Blood, and Piegan tribes and their relationship with the Canadian government. It would seem sufficient to point out that these are the groups dealt with by the defendant in the various treaties, agreements, and acts involved in this case and that they meet the requirements of the Indian Claims Commission Act (60 Stat. 1049) with regard to jurisdiction. The Blackfeet Nation has been found by the Court of Claims to have been a confederated tribe composed of Blackfeet, Blood, Piegan, and Gros Ventre Indians. (Blackfeet, et al., v. United States, 81 C. Cls. 101, 117)

Defendant's second contention concerns the effect of the doctrine of res judicata based upon the case of Blackfeet, et al., v. United States, 81 C. Cls. 101 (1935).

Defendant, while acknowledging the decision of the Commission in Docket 279 wherein this same defense was overruled (2 Ind. Cl. Comm. 302, 316-317), insists that such decision was incorrect. It is defendant's position that the land involved in this case was necessarily involved in the Court of Claims case because a portion of it, based on population figures, was offset against the recovery had for the portion of the 1855 treaty land sued for therein.

We see nothing in this argument that wasn't answered in the prior opinion of the Commission referred to above. This case is a suit between the same parties on a different claim which could not have been litigated under the terms of the jurisdictional act in 81 C. Cls. 101, as previously stated by this Commission in 2 Ind. Cl. Comm. 302, 317.

Defendant's contention under point three in its brief of November 6, 1961, that petitioners did not have recognized title to the area in suit is based upon its argument that the Treaty of 1855 (11 Stat. 657) was a treaty of peace and did not vest title in petitioners. In the light of the decision by the Court of Claims, as well as the language of the treaty itself, this contention can have no validity.

The language of the Court at 81 C. Cls. 101, 123-124 is sufficiently specific to indicate that they considered that they were dealing with recognized title. The recognized title of petitioners under the 1855 treaty is obvious and it seems unnecessary to belabor the point. So far as this Commission is concerned we are dealing with recognized title in petitioners to that part of the 1855 treaty lands set apart for them under the Treaty of October 17, 1855 (11 Stat. 657) and which is in litigation in this case.

The detailed analysis made by the Court of Claims of the case of United States v. Northern Pacific Railroad Company, 311 U.S. 717, in the Crow Tribe of Indians v. The United States, 151 C. Cls. 281, 293-297, appears to dispose of the defendant's contention that the Blackfeet Treaty of October 17, 1855, did not create a "reservation" for the Blackfeet.

While the principal discussion in that case concerned the Fort Laramie Treaty under which the Crow Nation claimed recognized title, the Blackfeet Treaty of 1855 was also included, and the decision of the Court of Claims in the *Crow* case, supra, is equally applicable thereto. There is no allegation by petitioners concerning "reservation" title but rather they contend for "recognized" title. The distinction between the two types of title was drawn by the Court of Claims in the Crow case, supra, after the Supreme Court had held in Northern Pacific that the treaties of Fort Laramie and with the Blackfeet in 1855 did not create technical reservations.

Based upon the reasoning in the Crow case the Commission is of the opinion that the Northern Pacific case did nothing to disturb the recognized title held by the Blackfeet under the Treaty of October 17, 1855 (11 Stat. 657).

Defendant's fourth point in its brief of November 6, 1961, concerns the consideration promised under the May 1, 1888 Agreement (25 Stat. 113) to petitioners. This question would be better passed for the moment and will be considered after a discussion of the position of intervenors in this matter.

The discussion up to this point has concerned petitioners and defendant directly and intervenors only indirectly as it might bear on their ultimate interest.

There is also a three-way contest between petitioners and intervenors and defendant. It is this phase of the case which lends itself to a presentation of the rather involved factual situation surrounding the transactions between the various parties.

The case takes this turn because of the delay between the beginning of the litigation and the entrance of the intervenors. The original briefs, evidence and arguments concerned only petitioners and defendant, then with the participation of intervenors it became necessary to file new briefs and the emphasis shifted from a question of 100% title under the 1855 treaty and value of the land between petitioners and defendant to intervenors' theory of a statutory reservation created under the Act of April 15, 1874 (18 Stat. 28) whereby they claim to have received a one-half interest in a different area of land created by that Act.

Intervenors have been found entitled to maintain their claim under the terms of the Indian Claims Commission Act (60 Stat. 1049). They are presently in this suit by virtue of a decision of the Court of Claims whereby this Commission was reversed and the case remanded with directions to permit the intervention of the Assiniboine Tribe as parties petitioner. Upon the remand, counsel for the Assiniboine moved the Commission for an order granting the Sioux Tribe of Fort Peck permission to intervene. This motion was granted and we now have the Assiniboine Tribe of Fort Peck and Fort Belknap and the Sioux Tribe of Fort Peck as intervenors.

Having previously determined in this opinion that petitioners held their 1855 treaty lands by recognized title acquired under that treaty, we must then determine whether such title was divested by any means prior to the Agreement of May 1, 1888 (25 Stat. 113). If it was not, then it seems obvious that intervenors could not have acquired an interest in those lands before the Agreement of May 1, 1888.

a reservation containing an area of 33,830 square miles, or 21,651,200 acres, indicates that the moving cause for the ratified agreement of 1888 was a disintegration of this enormous reservation area and its segregation into distinct reservations for the Indian tribes of northern Montana, and this is precisely what was done; the Sioux, Assiniboine, Gros Ventre, and Blackfoot Nations composed of Piegan, Blood, and Blackfeet Indians received a delimited reservation, and the United States received a cession of 17,500,000 acres of land thrown open to public settlement. (Emphasis supplied)

***

On page 131 of the same case the Court continues:

***

On the basis of the invalidity of the treaties of 1865 and 1868 it is admitted that the surplus lands ceded to the plaintiffs under the treaty of 1855 and thrown open to settlement by the act of April 15, 1874, totaled 15,289,344 acres. The remaining issue with respect to this area revolves around whether the increased acreage added to plaintiffs' reservation totaling 5,575,680 acres, should be deducted from the total acreage of 15,289,344 as a basis of judgment for plaintiffs' loss. Plaintiffs' reservation having been increased in acreage, their loss was proportionately decreased when their surplus lands were taken under the act of 1874, for the increased area was included in plaintiffs' cession of their reservation in 1888 for which they secured consideration. (Emphasis supplied) The issue would be one of easy solution were it not for the provisions of the act of May 1, 1888 (25 Stat. 113). This act, embodying agreements between the United States and the tribes of Indians heretofore mentioned, accomplished the cession of the plaintiffs' entire reservation and its division into separate reservations ceded to the Sioux, Assiniboine, Gros Ventre, and Blackfoot Tribes. In other words, the United States acquired by the agreement of 1888 the plaintiffs entire reservation, then totaling 21,651,200 acres, made up of 16,075,520 acres of plaintiffs' original reservation and the 5,575,680 acres added thereto by the United States. 17,500,000 acres of the reservation were thrown open to settlement and 4,151,200 acres segregated into reservations of which the plaintiffs acquired a reservation of 3,099,298 acres.

The agreement of 1888 created a landed unit to which the plaintiff Indians contributed their reservation and the United States 5,575,680 acres. The Indians in virtue of

This Act of Congress set aside the same area as the Executive Order with the exception of what came to be known as Royce Area 574, Montana 1. The remaining area is Royce 565, Montana 1, and is the same as Royce Area 692, Montana 2, with the exception of the reservations shown therein. At this date it contained no individual reservations.

On August 19, 1874, the President issued an Executive Order restoring Royce Area 574 to the public domain.

On April 13, 1875, another Executive Order added 5,865,900 acres to Royce 565. This addition is shown on Royce Areas 622 and 623, Montana 2. Thereafter, on July 13, 1880, an Executive Order restored Area 622 to the public domain, leaving Area 623 which contained 1,243,240 acres as an addition to the 1874 reservation.

This addition of 1,243,240 acres, plus the addition under the Executive Order of July 5, 1873, and which was retained under the Act of April 15, 1874, of 4,332,440 acres, made a total addition of 5,575,680 acres to the original lands recognized by the Treaty of 1855 as belonging to the Blackfeet Nation.

Not all of this addition was ceded under the Act of May 1, 1888, (25 Stat. 113) but was considered in the Blackfeet case in the Court of Claims for the purpose of offsets against the recovery had for the area taken under the Act of April 15, 1874 (81 C. Cls. 101).

The area in suit here which was dealt with in the Act of May 1, 1888 (25 Stat. 113) is shown on Royce Area 692, Montana 2, and the cession therein has been stipulated by the parties to contain 14,969,156 acres.

This is the same area, with the exception of the Fort Belknap, Fort Peck, and Blackfeet reservations, which for lack of a better term is referred to as the 1874 reservation.

Petitioners' requested findings of fact and briefs present three alternative claims.

The first is for the value of a 100% interest in 13,021,610 acres. This constitutes a claim for the original part of the 1855 treaty reservation which they allege was still remaining at the time of the Act of May 1, 1888, less the portion of the Fort Belknap reservation occupied by the Gros Ventre Indians. It was stipulated that the area contained 13,338,589 acres. The Fort Belknap reservation was 622,748 acres and the Gros Ventre Indians occupied 50.9% thereof during the period 1888-1890, making a total acreage for their benefit of 316,979 acres. This 316,979 acres deducted from 13,338,589 acres leaves a net acreage of 13,021,610.

The first alternative claim is for 54.3% interest in 14,969,156 acres, which is the stipulated acreage of the area ceded by the Act of May 1, 1888. Petitioners allege that they constituted 54.3% of all the inhabitants of the 1874 reservation at the time of the Act of May 1, 1888. (See page 15, Petitioners' Findings of May 4, 1960)

The second alternative claim is for a 100% interest in the 14,969,15[6] acres ceded under the Agreement of May 1, 1888. (See page 48, Petitioners' Brief of March 30, 1966)

As can be seen the alternative claims of petitioners are geared to cover whatever decision this Commission may reach concerning the intervenors' allegation as to the legal effect of the Act of April 15, 1874 (18 Stat. 28).

The Court of Claims has on three previous occasions considered more or less indirectly the question now before us. This serves as a source of confusion as much as enlightenment because of the indirect nature of their decisions with regard to the 1874 Act. These cases have involved the Blackfeet Nation, the Assiniboine Tribe, and the Crow Tribe. These cases need analysis for the purpose of determining the arguments of all three participants herein with regard to the doctrine of collateral estoppel or res judicata as well as to determine their indirect bearing upon the issues before us since all of the parties herein were not parties to each of those cases.

The first case to be considered is that of The Blackfeet, et al., v. The United States, 81 C. Cls. 101 (1935). This case was tried under a jurisdictional act of 1924 and involved almost the same facts as this case except that the land sued for therein was taken by the Act of April 15, 1874, rather than that of May 1, 1888. It was in this case that the "Common Hunting ground," Royce Area 398, Montana 1, was sued for, as well as Royce Areas 399 and 574, Montana 1. Recovery was had for the latter two areas, but damage for loss of hunting rights was denied.

Defendant in this case alleged that the treaties of 1865 and 1868 with the Blackfeet and Gros Ventre were valid and binding agreements whereby the lands sued for under the 1874 Act had already been ceded and petitioners had no claim under the 1874 Act.

The Court stated as follows on page 128 of 81 C. Cls. 101:

***

We think the defense is vulnerable in another important respect. If the treaty of 1868 delimited the plaintiffs' reservation and accomplished the cession of their surplus lands, the legislation which thereafter attempted to establish a similar reservation was unnecessary. It was not until July 5, 1873 (1 Kapp. 855), that the Government by direct act set aside a reservation for the plaintiffs and other Indians, and this reservation so set aside by Executive order added to the reservation delimited in 1868, 4,332,440 acres. In 1874 by legislation a different reservation was delimited for the plaintiffs and the total area decreased to the extent of 2,115,993.6 acres. Again, in 1875, the reservation was increased which resulted in the end in a total increase of the reservation to the extent of 5,575,680 acres. This legislation, enacted at a time when the policy of the Government was to deal directly with tribal Indian lands, can hardly be said to have been enacted upon the basis of a congressional belief that an unratified treaty concluded in 1868 conferred a right to place foreign Indians upon plaintiffs reservation.

266 On the contrary, the large increase in acreage which finally entered into the question seems to indicate that Congress recognized a very substantial increase was essential to care for the augmented population of the reservation which was in 1888 placed thereon. The agreement of May 1, 1888 (25 Stat. 113) resulted from the authorized negotiations of 1887 wherein the Secretary of the Interior was to secure, if possible, an agreement from the Indians of northern Montana and Fort Berthold, Dakota, for a reduction of present reservations, or removal to new ones (24 Stat. 29, 44). The Secretary concluded negotiations which are evidenced by the agreement ratified (Emphasis in original) by Congress May 1, 1888. The ratified agreement of 1888 disposes of the lands delimited as a reservation for the plaintiffs in 1874 and specifically recites that said reservation being in excess of the needs of the nation, a desire exists to dispose of so much of the reservation as is not required by the Indians in order to acquire sufficient funds to maintain the nation and promote its civilization. (Emphasis supplied)

No provision of any act in this series of legislation refers to the unratified treaty of 1868, and the fact that Congress in 1874 permitted the plaintiff Indians to occupy

Petitioners' rights in the land in suit began with the Treaty of October 17, 1855, and included a much larger area than is sued for herein. There were two treaties negotiated with petitioners' predecessors in 1865 and 1868. These treaties were not ratified and did not become binding since ratification was a prerequisite to their validity.

After the arrival of intervenors' ancestors in the area of the Blackfeet lands, the President issued an Executive Order on July 5, 1873, which changed the boundaries of these lands. This change excluded the area now known as Royce Area 399, Montana 1, and left the areas known as 574 and 565, Montana 1. The Executive Order also added to the 1855 Blackfoot lands an additional 4,332,440 acres between the eastern boundary of the 1855 lands, being a line running from the mouth of Milk River to the Canadian border, and the Dakota border. The Missouri River was the south boundary of this addition and the Canadian border was the north boundary.

The Executive Order of July 5, 1873, stated as follows:

> It is hereby ordered that the tract of country, above described, be withheld from entry and settlement as public lands, and that the same be set apart as a reservation for the Gros Ventre, Piegan, Blood, Blackfeet, River Crow, <u>and other Indians</u>, as recommended by the Secretary of the Interior and Commissioner of Indian Affairs. (Emphasis supplied)

Congress then passed an Act on April 15, 1874 (18 Stat. 28) which created the 1874 reservation and stated that it was "set apart for the use and occupancy of the Gros Ventre, Piegan, Blood, Blackfeet, River Crow, <u>and such other Indians as the President may, from time to time, see fit to locate thereon</u>." (Emphasis added)

<u>this agreement, wherein consent was given to allocate the unit among the plaintiffs and the foreign Indians as the United States might see fit, put all the tribes upon an equal basis.</u> The plaintiffs acquired their proportionate <u>share of the added lands and the foreign Indians their proportionate share in the entire area, which of course included the plaintiffs contribution.</u> The Government was intending an equitable and just division of the estate and to this end it realized the rights of the plaintiffs. The plaintiffs constituted 54.3 percent of the entire Indian population placed upon the lands, and the foreign Indians 45.7 percent. Predicated upon this percentage of reciprocal rights acquired and surrendered, the plaintiffs failed to derive a monetary benefit in the added lands in excess of the proportion of their population to that of the entire landed estate. (Emphasis supplied)

*** The lands added to the reservation by the United States totaled 5,575,680 acres, 54.3% of the same equals 3,027,594.24 acres. To this extent, in equity and fairness, the contribution of the United States entered in the creation of joint estate for the joint benefit of all the Indians.

***

The above quotation was made in length for the purpose of context. The emphasized portions are the ones considered as indicating most clearly the thinking of the Court as it reached its decision. The judgment constitutes collateral estoppel between petitioner and defendant but does not affect the intervenors and is cited for the purpose of aiding the clarity of our decision.

It would seem from the context of the Court's opinion, especially from the emphasized portions, that the Court did not consider that the 1874 Act created any rights in tribes other than the petitioners, or to express it affirmatively, the "foreign Indians" acquired whatever rights they might have under the Act of May 1, 1888.

More compelling than the above statement of the Court in its opinion is what the Court was requested but refused to do. A motion was filed by attorneys for petitioners in that case in an attempt to have the Court reduce the offset of 3,027,594 acres charged against petitioners from the 5,575,680 acres added by the defendant to the 1874 reservation.

Petitioners made the following argument in support of their motion:

> When the Act of April 15, 1874 was passed these plaintiffs were already in possession of 16,075,520 acres, which they owned and title to which was guaranteed to them by the Treaty of 1855. This was included in the reservation provided by said act and to which said Indians were not parties. This added 4,332,440 acres to plaintiffs' reservation and the Executive orders of 1875 and 1880 resulted in the further addition to this reservation of 1,243,240 acres, producing a total acreage therein of 21,651,200 acres. (Op., p. 22) <u>By the same act of 1874 other Indians were given rights, without the consent of said plaintiffs, amounting to an undivided interest in this entire reservation equal to 45.7% thereof, or 9,894,598.4 acres, while plaintiffs rights in said reservation amounted to 54.3%, or 11,756,601.6 acres.</u> It will thus be seen that while plaintiffs, as a result of the aforesaid acts of the defendant, to which they were not parties, indirectly contributed 16,075,520 acres to the total of this reservation, under the operation of the act of 1874 its interest therein was reduced to 11,756,601.6 acres. Therefore, under the act of April 15, 1874, plaintiffs' interest in the land to which they held title under the Treaty of 1855 was diminished by 4,318,919 acres without their consent and without any act on their part.
>
> Consequently, it is believed that the Court should not have charged these plaintiffs with any portion of the addition of 5,575,680 acres to this reservation, or 3,027,594 acres, or any part thereof. This at the value placed thereon by the court amounts to $1,513,797.00, and the accompanying motion asks that the gross judgment be increased by this amount. (Emphasis supplied)
>
> (Defendant's Exhibit No. 5)

This argument is basically the same one which intervenors now advance to the effect that the Act of April 15, 1874 created a statutory reservation in which they acquired an interest prior to its cession under the Act of May 1, 1888.

The Court, at page 139 of 81 C. Cls. 101, acknowledged this and another motion filed by petitioners and states that petitioners therein had vigorously challenged the basis of the award and sought to demonstrate that the set-offs allowed by the Court in the matter of the government's contribution of lands disposed of under the Act of 1888 were erroneous and requested that the findings be amended and a new trial granted. The Court said that these motions as well as those filed by defendant had caused a review of the entire record and that the Court was of the opinion that the basis invoked to arrive at the amount of the judgment to be awarded was not inequitable but was justified by the record. This amounts to a repudiation of petitioners' argument although such argument was not mentioned directly. This repudiation is consistent with the position of present petitioners that the Act of 1874 did not disturb their ownership under the terms of the 1855 treaty.

The second case in which the Court of Claims had occasion to discuss the Executive Order of July 5, 1873, the Act of April 15, 1874, and the Act of May 1, 1888, was <u>The Crow Nation or Tribe of Indians of Montana</u> v. <u>The United States</u>, 81 C. Cls. 238 (1935). There is general agreement among the parties that this case correctly held that the River Crows had no interest in the 1874 reservation. Once again the case is not binding on petitioners or intervenors since they were not parties. However, the reasoning of the Court in reaching its decision may be of assistance in this case before us.

A similarity of the factual background of one group of Crows with that of the petitioners and intervenors arises from the fact that this group left the main body of Crows on their Fort Laramie Treaty lands and went to the Milk River where they joined with the Gros Ventres and occupied part of the lands of the Blackfeet Nation sometime before 1873. They became known as the River Crows as opposed to the Mountain Crows who remained on the Fort Laramie lands.

In 1873 when the Executive Order reservation was set up the order named the Gros Ventre, Piegan, Blood, Blackfeet, River Crow "and other Indians" as being those for whom the reservation was created. This and the Act of April 15, 1874, which also named the River Crow "and such other Indians as the President may, from time to time, see fit to locate thereon", gave rise to a claim by the Crow Nation for an interest in common with the other named Indians in the 1874 reservation.

The Court of Claims dismissed this claim, as well as the others asserted in the case, and in the course of its opinion made the following statements on page 278:

> *** The River Crows had their own reservation along with the Mountain Crows and the two tribes composed the Crow Nation; <u>the order of 1873 and the act of Congress of 1874 gave to the River Crows only the right to reside upon the reservation, so set apart by Executive order, and did not confer upon them any definite title or particular interest in the land</u>. It was in the nature of a tenancy by sufferance or residential title. The object and aim of it was to prevent hostilities among the tribes hunting and fishing in this territory, and to control the liquor traffic on the Missouri River. <u>This recalcitrant tribe, which had removed from its own reservation, gave nothing as a consideration for any interest in this new reservation</u>. In all subsequent proclamations of the President which were ratified by act of Congress the River Crows were never recognized as having an interest in the area so set apart by this Executive Order of 1873. It was simply a license or permission granted by

271

the Government which could be withdrawn and ceased to
exist when the River Crows returned to the Crow Nation
reservation. <u>The Executive order reserves to the
President the right to put other Indians on the reservation and this could not be done if a statutory title,
as tenants in common, was given to these five tribes alone.</u>

In 1879 the River Crows finally returned to their reservation and from then on remained thereon. There is nothing
in the proclamation of the President and the acts of Congress
ratifying the permission to reside on the reservation north
of the Missouri River, to show more than a temporary residence;
and the greater part of the lands so set apart as a reservation
to the Gros Ventres, Piegans, Bloods, Blackfeet, River Crows,
and other Indians was taken subsequently for the public domain
by the agreements of 1886 (24 Stat. 29, 44) and 1887 (25 Stat.
113), and ratified in 1888. The record does not disclose the
exact period when the Assiniboines and Sioux Indians were
placed on this reservation, but they were residing there after
the River Crows had departed and when the 1886-1888 agreements
were made. The agreements were made with the tribes on the
reservation at the time. The designation of the territory
as a "reservation" of the Gros Ventres, Piegans, Bloods, Blackfeet, and River Crows was descriptive only, and carried no
title to the lands other than the right to reside thereon, and
this right disappeared upon removal therefrom. (Emphasis supplied)

The reasoning of the Court in the above quoted portion of the opinion makes it very clear that it considered that neither the Executive order of July 5, 1873, nor the Act of April 15, 1874, carried any title to the reservation.

The third case in which the same general facts have been reviewed is <u>The Assiniboine Indian Tribe</u> v. <u>The United States</u>, 77 C. Cls. 347 (1933). This case sheds very little light on the problem confronting the Commission in the instant case. Intervenors contend that certain language of the Court in that case establishes that they acquired an interest in the subject area under the Act of 1874. When quoted in full the context of the statement does not appear to support intervenors contention.

The Court found as follows on page 357 of 77 C. Cls. 347:

Pursuant to an act of Congress in 1886 and 1887 an agreement was concluded by duly appointed commissioners with the various tribes of Indians residing upon the Gros Ventre, Piegan, Blood, Blackfoot, and River Crow Reservation in the Territory of Montana. This agreement was ratified by the act of May 1, 1888. By this agreement these Indians relinquished to the United States all their right in the land embraced in the reservation heretofore set apart to them and not specifically set apart and reserved in separate reservations set forth in the agreement, and the United States agreed to expend, and did expend, large sums for the benefit of the Indians in the manner and for the purpose set out in said agreement. The chiefs, headmen, and the principal men of the bands of Indians, including the Assiniboines attached to and receiving rations at the Fort Peck Agency, consented to and signed this agreement.
(Emphasis supplied)

This is a general finding made because of the Assiniboine's claim of immemorial possession to the area of the Blackfeet Reservation. It was designed to show, inter alia, that the Assiniboine had failed to protest the 1888 act. As such it is hardly conclusive evidence of a matter not then before the Court. For this reason we cannot agree that it establishes intervenor's claim under the Act of 1874.

It is the conclusion of the Commission that while the above cases have certain elements, particularly the Blackfeet case, which would constitute collateral estoppel as between petitioners and defendant, it is of small importance because these same matters are sufficiently established in this record.

For this reason the Commission has cited these cases for the purpose of disposing of certain allegations and for their help in arriving at our own conclusion rather than for the primary purpose of res judicata or collateral estoppel. They do not, of course, dispose of all of the allegations of the present parties, particularly those of the intervenors.

The intervenors' case rests basically upon the interpretation of the Act of April 15, 1874. We are inclined to agree with intervenors' argument that a statutory reservation was created thereby. Congress could create a statutory reservation regardless of the recognized title of the Blackfeet Nation under the 1855 treaty.

We are fully award that a decision that the 1874 act created a statutory reservation appears to conflict with the ruling of the Court of Claims in the Crow case, supra. We believe, however, that the conflict is more apparent than real. A statutory reservation may be created while bestowing a limited right on the Indians occupying it, or, as in the case here, making the acquisition of rights subject to a condition subsequent. Federal Indian Law, page 607.

On page 608 of the revised edition of Federal Indian Law the Act of 1874 is cited as an example of a statutory reservation. If it is in fact a statutory reservation then it would seem that it must have carried a property right of one kind or another with it under the language of the Act. The language used was unequivocal. It stated "*** that the following described tract of country, in the Territory of Montana, be, and the same is hereby, set apart for the use and occupation of the Gros Ventre, Piegan, Blood, Blackfoot, River Crow, and such other Indians as the President may, from time to time, see fit to locate thereon, ***."

The words "use and occupancy" as used in the context of the above-quoted portion of the Act of 1874 are the exact words used to describe the rights of the Indians in the aboriginal lands to which the United States had the fee. This right consistently has been held to be compensable, both under jurisdictional acts and under the Indian Claims Commission Act. It was a compensable property right at the time of the Crow case in 81 C. Cls. 101, supra. The use of these words in an Act of Congress, regardless of whether they referred to lands upon which the Indians named therein had an aboriginal right, are sufficient to create a compensable interest in Indian tribes or groups who are the beneficiaries of such Act.

At the time of the Crow case, supra, it probably would have been immaterial whether such rights were created by Executive Order or by statute. The precise nature of the effect of an Executive Order reservation with regard to creating rights in the beneficiaries was not at all clear. The prevailing opinion seemed to be that the rights created thereunder, at least in the absence of contrary language, were permanent in nature.

However, since there was no set number of tribes, groups, or bands which might be placed upon this reservation, there arises the question as to what interest the tribes named in the Act of 1874 took under that Act. If the President had the right to place other tribes on this reservation, then there never could be an irrevocable interest created in any tribe or group until such time as an ultimate disposition was made of the reservation.

275

This is undoubedly the underlying rationale of the Court of Claims decision in the <u>Crow</u> case, supra. For the tribe which was not present on the land at the final disposition could hardly be said to have had an interest in the land when such interest could become finally determined only at the time of disposition. In other words, we have come full cycle to the statement of the Court in the <u>Crow</u> case, supra, that "The Executive Order reserves to the President the right to put other Indians on the reservation and this could not be done if a statutory title, as tenants in common, was given to these five tribes <u>alone</u>." (Emphasis supplied)

This statement refers to the Executive Order of 1873, but must encompass the terms of the Act of 1874 as well. The logic of the above-quoted statement appears indisputable whether applied to the Executive Order or the Act.

We come then to the conclusion that the Act of Congress of April 15, 1874, did in fact create a statutory reservation in which the interests of the beneficiary tribes were confirmed only by their proper presence on the reservation at the time of its disposition.

As shown heretofore the tribes on the reservation and dealt with at the time of its ultimate cession on May 1, 1888, were the Blackfeet Nation, including the Gros Ventre, the Sioux, and the Assiniboine.

The Sioux and Assiniboine, while present in the area of the reservation at the time were not named in the Executive Order of 1873 or the Act of 1874. They must then have been placed on the reservation by the President either directly or at his direction. The evidence shows that there was no formal order which did this.

The implication from the evidence is that the government acquiesced in their presence because of a fear of the consequences of removal, particularly in the case of the Sioux. Both the Sioux and Assiniboine voluntarily attached themselves to the reservation because of the agencies at which they could receive supplies. The evidence further shows that no preparation was made for their presence at the agencies until after the fact.

This brings us again to the decision of the Court of Claims in the case of <u>Blackfeet, et al., Nation</u> v. <u>United States</u>, 81 C. Cls. 101 (1935). The Court stated at pages 131-132 of its opinion:

***

The agreement of 1888 created a landed unit to which the plaintiff Indians contributed their reservation and the United States 5,575,680 acres. The Indians in virtue of this agreement, wherein consent was given to allocate the unit among the plaintiffs and the foreign Indians as the United States might see fit, put all the tribes upon an equal basis. <u>The plaintiffs acquired their proportionate share of the added lands and the foreign Indians (acquired) their proportionate share in the entire area, which of course included the plaintiffs' contribution.</u> The Government was intending an equitable and just division of the estate and to this end it realized the rights of the plaintiffs. The plaintiffs constituted 54.3 percent of the entire Indian population placed upon the lands, and the foreign Indians 45.7 percent. Predicated upon this percentage of reciprocal rights acquired and surrendered, the plaintiffs failed to derive a monetary benefit in the added lands in excess of the proportion of their population to that of the entire landed estate . *** (Emphasis supplied)

The Court also stated:

*** the large increase in acreage which finally entered into the question seems to indicate that Congress recognized a very substantial increase was essential to care for the augmented population of the reservation which was in 1888 placed thereon *** (p. 128) and at pages 139-140:

> *** It must not be overlooked that the act of May 1, 1888 *** while not in form a treaty, was one in legal effect. The <u>plaintiffs</u> by assenting to the terms of the act approved the division of the proceeds, recognized the rights of the foreign Indians involved, and voluntarily for a good consideration <u>granted the rights which accrued to all</u>. (Emphasis supplied)

It seems clear from the above quotations that the Court of Claims determined the rights of the Sioux and Assiniboine Indians to have been created under the Agreement of May 1, 1888, and not under the Act of 1874. While the intervenors were not parties to that case and not bound thereby, the language cited is extremely persuasive in the present case.

This holding in the Blackfeet case appears to be consistent with the decision in <u>Healing</u> v. <u>Jones</u>, 210 Fed. Supp. 125; aff'd 373 U.S. 758, cited by petitioner. This is a case between the Hopi and Navajo Tribes arising from an Executive Order reservation established in 1882 for the Hopi, "*** and such other Indians as the Secretary of the Interior may see fit to settle thereon".

The three-man District Court stated as follows at pages 138-139:

> The words "may see fit" connote a future contingency, to be fulfilled only by an exercise of discretion. Those words thus contemplate the exercise of Secretarial authority which did not come into existence until the executive order was issued.
>
> ***
>
> As previously pointed out, the "such other Indians" clause could only be effectuated by subsequent Secretarial action.

The Court then continued its exhaustive opinion wherein it discussed at page 156 the affirmative action taken by Commissioner Rhoads and Secretary of the Interior Wilbur on February 7, 1931, whereby they segregated the Hopi and Navajo and fenced separate areas for them.

On page 169 of the opinion the Court stated that:

> In our opinion, the course of administrative action and accompanying pronouncements from February 7, 1931 to July 22, 1958, with exceptions which we discount for reasons stated, warrant the finding, which we make, that all Navajos residing in the 1882 reservation in July, 1958 were impliedly settled therein by the Secretary of the Interior in the exercise of his authority to settle other Indians in that reservation.
>
> The question remains whether, in settling Navajos in the reservation, the Navajo Indian Tribe itself was impliedly settled in the 1882 reservation.
>
> Throughout the period from February 7, 1931, when Navajo rights of use and occupancy were first administratively recognized, to July 22, 1958, Navajos entered the 1882 reservation for purposes of residence without limitation as to number. Nor was any effort made to pick and choose between Navajos who might enter, all who came being administratively welcome. This course of administrative conduct is explainable only on the hypothesis that the Navajo Indian Tribe itself had been settled in the 1882 reservation.

The Court in this case found sufficient evidence of administrative actions to support its finding of settlement of the Navajo Tribe by the Secretary of the Interior on the 1882 reservation. This was an affirmative act done in 1931 and followed by further evidence of acquiescence in the habitation of the Navajo on the reservation.

The parallel found in this case is the Act of May 1, 1888, which ratified the agreements of 1886 and 1887 and thereby ratified the participation by the Sioux and Assiniboine in those Agreements. This is the first affirmative action taken by defendant towards recognizing an interest in the Sioux and Assiniboine to the 1874 reservation as distinguished from defendant's negative action by its failure to remove them from the reservation after they had voluntarily attached themselves thereto.

It seems clear that the action of defendant in 1888 is sufficient to constitute a recognition of the rights of the Sioux and Assiniboine in the reservation created by the Act of 1874. It was a course of action begun by a voluntary attachment by the Sioux and Assiniboine and culminating in an affirmative act on the part of defendant which was sufficient to indicate that they considered the Sioux and Assiniboine to have acquired a tribal or group interest in the reservation.

Again the question is at what point did these two tribes acquire their respective interests? It would seem that the terms of the Act of 1874 with regard to the discretionary placement of other Indians on the reservation would force the conclusion that a tribe's interest would date from the time of the affirmative act which recognized it as belonging on the reservation. In this case it would be the Act of May 1, 1888, which recognized the rights of the Sioux and Assiniboine and at the same time compensated them for those rights.

As pointed out heretofore, it was necessarily the Act of May 1, 1888 which determined the interests of the various tribes on the reservation. Until the reservation was terminated there was no way to determine the respective interests of the tribes located thereon. So long as there existed the right of the President to place additional Indians on the reservation then no one group, with the possible exception of the Blackfeet, had a vested interest in any determinable part.

The corollary problem is, what percentage interests finally were created in the various tribes residing on the reservation in 1888? This matter is complicated by the recognition of Blackfeet title under

The Treaty of 1855. We have determined that the Act of 1888 created the title of the Sioux and Assiniboine. It did not create the title of the Blackfeet Nation. That title existed as recognized title from the date of the 1855 treaty. If the Act of 1874 created a statutory reservation, did it also deprive the Blackfeet Nation of its title created under the 1855 treaty? We think that it did not.

This Commission has held in prior cases that the continued occupation by Indian tribes of lands ceded under a valid treaty is a permissive occupation and does not change the date of taking from the actual cession date to the date of removal. This principle is still one to which this Commission adheres in appropriate cases. However, in the case now before us the factual situation is somewhat different.

The Blackfeet Nation owned by recognized title a majority of the area encompassed in the statutory reservation created by the Act of 1874.[281] That Act included the River Crow Indians who ultimately departed the reservation and returned to live with the Mountain Crow prior to the Act of 1888. Under this Commission's interpretation of the effect of the 1874 Act the Crow lost their opportunity to acquire a vested interest therein under the Act of May 1, 1888. This then leaves the Blackfeet Nation, which was named in the Act of 1874, as the only group with an interest in their 1855 treaty lands prior to the recognition of the rights of the Sioux and Assiniboine under the 1888 Act. This was not a permissive occupation by the Blackfeet Nation. They occupied the 1874 statutory reservation under the same quality of title after the Act of 1874 as they did under the 1855 treaty. To hold otherwise would appear to be a distinction without a difference. There was no reduction of their interest until Congress ratified the agreements with the Sioux and Assiniboine on May 1, 1888, and thereby confirmed an interest in those two tribes. For this reason the Blackfeet retained their 100% interest in their 1855 treaty lands until May 1, 1888, regardless of the creation of a statutory reservation under the Act of 1874.

The next question concerns the interest acquired by the several parties in the Blackfeet reservation and the additional 5,575,680 acres of land attached to the eastern end of the original Blackfeet reservation under the Act of 1874 and subsequent Executive orders.

On the two occasions when the question has arisen the Court of Claims has determined that the Blackfeet and Assiniboine did acquire an interest under the 1888 Act. The Blackfeet were charged with their proportionate share of the added lands while the Assiniboine were charged with the payments which they received under the 1888 Act. This is a clear indication that the Court considered the Blackfeet to have acquired an interest only in the additional lands since they already owned their 1855 treaty lands. On the other hand it is equally clear that the Court considered that the Assiniboine had an interest in the whole area ceded because there was no division of the proceeds under the 1888 cession as between additional lands and Blackfeet 1855 treaty lands. The consideration was paid as a whole to all of the parties to the agreements and upon the basis that all of the parties had an interest in all of the area, including the original Blackfeet lands. We are of the opinion that this was a proper interpretation of the effect of the agreements which culminated in the Act of 1888.

On that basis it is our decision that the Blackfeet Nation contributed and ceded the majority of its interest in the 1855 treaty lands which under the stipulation and concessions made herein amounted to a net acreage of 13,021,610 acres. In addition thereto they owned 54.3% of the additional acreage which was ceded under the Act of 1888. This amounted to 54.3% of 1,630,567 acres which was the acreage actually ceded from the land lying east of the Blackfeet 1855 treaty boundary. 54.3% thereof amounts to 885,398 acres. This constitutes a total acreage figure ceded by the Blackfoot Nation of 13,907,008 acres and is their proportionate part of the area which the defendant acquired under the Act of 1888. The Blackfeet Nation owned by recognized title its 1855 lands and these lands, with the exception of the Blackfeet reservation and a portion of the Fort Belknap reservation, were ceded by the Blackfeet Nation under the 1888 Act. There can be no question but that the Blackfeet title to the 1855 treaty lands was intact at the time of the Act of 1888. As was found by the Court of Claims in the Blackfeet case, supra, they contributed those lands to the landed unit created by the Act of 1888. The proceeds from the cession of this land were paid more or less equally to the participating tribes and no distinction was made in favor of the Blackfeet for their contribution. The motives of defendant at the time were to reduce what it considered to be excessive reservation areas and to open up such land to the public. In its attempts to accomplish this end its conduct resulted in an overreaching with regard to the duty owed the Blackfeet to protect and preserve their property. As a result of this the Blackfeet Nation paid a part of its resources over to the Sioux and Assiniboine for their benefit. The fact that the Blackfeet acceded to this arrangement does not excuse defendant from its obligation to deal fairly and honorably with dependent Indian tribes. There was no obligation on the part of the Blackfeet to support the Sioux and Assiniboine. As stated on page 135 of the Blackfeet case, supra, the preoccupation of defendant with implementing its Indian policy and providing for the subsistence of the Indians led to a disregard for lands as such, or their value. That the results of the 1888 Act arose from a preoccupation with administration of public affairs does not lessen the import of that Act on the fortunes of the Blackfeet Nation.

As pointed out earlier the total acreage figure to which we find the Blackfeet entitled amounts to 13,907,008 acres. This figure exceeds the acreage figure stipulated by the parties as being the acreage ceded under the Act of May 1, 1888. We are not going beyond the petitioner's pleading in finding this acreage figure. The ultimate acreage figures will far exceed the stipulated amount because they arise as the result of our interpretation of the legal effect of the Act of 1874 and the Act of 1888 and the resultant loss to the Blackfeet by having contributed a part of its resources to fulfill the obligations of defendant to the Sioux and Assiniboine under the Act of 1888.

The interest of the Assiniboine in the whole 1888 cession is considered to be settled by our decision as to the effect of the 1888 Act as well as by the decision of the Court of Claims in the Assiniboine case, supra. The Assiniboine interest cannot exist without a Sioux interest also existing. They both participated in the agreements leadin to the Act of 1888. They must stand or fail together. It is our decision that both intervening parties have an interest in the lands ceded under the 1888 Act. The extent of that interest must be explored further.

Intervenors contend that their interest consists of an undivided one-fourth share each. They base this contention on the law of property which is perfectly valid in the case of individuals who take an interest under an instrument which does not specify the particular share of each. In such a case the interest is presumed to be in common and therefore equal.

To apply such a rule to Indian lands would lead to an unjust result in most cases. Indian rights in land are tribal in nature and not individual. If we tried to equate tribal rights with individual rights and thereby create an equal interest in an area among the tribes using and occupying it, we would be ignoring the basic fact of Indian use and occupancy. We would be creating a common law concept of title in an area where such concept had never grown by custom or usage. The smallest tribe would be entitled to as much as the largest one. To do this would be contrary to reason since a subsistence use of land necessarily implies a use in proportion to numbers. Where there is no evidence of intention to the contrary and no language stating what interest shall be taken, we think the proper and just manner of dividing tribal interests in a given area is by population as of the date of cession, or an average population near that date, whichever is more reasonable under the particular circumstances.

The cases cited by intervenors to sustain their contention with regard to a joint ownership of the 1874 reservation are not convincing. The Cheyenne-Arapahoe Tribes v. United States, 10 Ind. Cl. Comm. 1, 32, 99-100 (1961) was decided by this Commission to be a common claim on the basis of the facts of that case. The tribes had been a single entity at one time and were divided by defendant afterward. Also the evidence showed that the separate tribes each continued to occupy one-half of the original area after being separated by defendant. The final award was made on the basis of a stipulation by the parties reflecting the population of the tribes as of 1958.

The case of Otoe-Missouria v. United States, 5 Ind. Cl. Comm. 316, was also based upon a factual situation. The evidence was not sufficient to enable the Commission to determine the respective areas occupied by the various tribes and the only reasonable solution lay in finding a joint use.

In the present case we have population statistics for the tribes in the year 1888 and can easily make a computation of their respective shares.

As stated in Findings No. 13, 14, and 15 made herewith, and as explained previously the respective shares of the petitioners and intervenors, Assiniboine and Sioux, are as follows:

Blackfeet Nation	13,907,008 acres
Assiniboine	3,885,633 acres
Sioux	2,955,271 acres

Valuation

The valuation evidence in this case has also taken an unusual turn. Because of the alternative theories advanced by petitioners at various stages of the proceedings there are five valuation reports in this record. Intervenors have chosen to rely on the evidence of value as submitted by petitioners and have introduced none of their own.

The valuation evidence as set forth in the findings indicates that the subject area was best adapted for the purpose of grazing cattle and sheep. Both parties have agreed that this was its highest and best use as of May 1, 1888. While the evidence indicates that there are portions of the area which are not adaptable for any use, in general the climate, soil and grasses are well suited for year around grazing. The rainfall while too low for dry land farming is normally spaced during the growing season so as to encourage the growth of grasses early in the summer and then allow those grasses to cure on the stem so as to create adequate grazing during the winter months in the absence of unusually severe weather.

The native grasses themselves are adapted to provide good grazing. They vary from place to place within the subject area but in general each type of grass or grasses within the particular area have their place within the category of grazing grasses. Even in most of those spots where grass is not particularly abundant the cover is often adaptable for the grazing of sheep. The natural phenomonon known as the "chinook" wind adds to the desirability of the area for grazing.

These are warm, dry winds which clear the snow from the ground so that grazing is easier for the stock.

The growing season over about two-thirds of the subject area is an average of 140 days. This is adequate for grain and hay crops, either for personal subsistence or, where water is adequate, for the growing of hay for supplemental stock feeding.

The general development of Montana began primarily with the discovery of gold. By 1870 the population of the territory was 20,595 and by 1880 it had increased to about 40,000. The next decade saw a further increase to 142,924. The ability of the Missouri River to handle steamboats was a large factor in the development of the area. By 1867 steamboat traffic was established between St. Louis and Fort Benton. In 1881 there were 25 to 30 steamers plying the Missouri River, with their headquarters at Bismarck and Fort Benton as the western terminus.

These steamers carried $1,270,600 worth of exports from the territory in 1877 and in 1881 carried imports of the value of $5,214,000.

As the territory developed pressure began to build for a cession of the Blackfeet Reservation. The Secretary of the Interior was opposed to the preservation of large Indian reservations and had so indicated. By 1883 the people of Montana were applying pressure to the Territorial Governor to have the reservation reduced and he so recommended in 1883 and 1884. By 1887 the presence of the Great Northern Railroad running to Havre and Great Falls added to the demand for a reduction of the Blackfoot reservation. Finally the Congress authorized the negotiation of agreements with the Indians and the cession of May 1, 1888 was the result.

The background for this pressure lay in the cattle industry. With the destruction of the vast herds of buffalo there was released millions of acres of grazing lands in Montana's plains area. The initial herds of stock came in answer to the demand created by the miners who entered the gold fields. As those populations stabilized and demand dropped the herds increased and by 1870 there was a surplus of cattle in the western end of the territory. This resulted in a crowding of the range and created a need for further grazing lands. The cattlemen began a move to the east and in 1870 a herd of 1,000 head was moved into the Sun River valley. Soon thereafter other herds followed. During the late 1870's there came a movement of cattle onto the eastern Montana plains from Oregon and California.

The extension of the Union Pacific Railroad through Cheyenne, Wyoming in 1867 and the cession by the Crow Indians of a part of their reservation in 1868 increased the number of cattle coming into Montana.

This increase in the number of cattle led to eventual use of the Blackfeet Reservation although it was not yet open. In 1880 a herd of 1,000 head was moved into the area of the Bear Paw Mountains. In 1885 another herd of 5,000 head was moved to the foot of the Little Rockies. At about this same time it was estimated that there were some 100,000 sheep in Chouteau County.

The real crowding of the Montana range occurred through the movement of cattle from Texas after the Civil War. The accumulation of cattle in Texas during the war had been tremendous. After hostilities had ceased these herds started being moved by means of the railroads in Kansas, Missouri, and Nebraska. By 1885 more than 5 million cattle had been driven northward from Texas. The free range in Wyoming and Montana attracted many of these herds.

Although central and eastern Montana did not utilize the open range system as early as did Wyoming, the natural possibilities of Montana, as well as Wyoming and Dakota, were recognized. The grasses were adapted to open range grazing and the country afforded winter protection for the herds.

While there had been a pause in the cattle industry around 1880 because of a surplus of cattle, by 1886 every available bit of range in Montana below the Missouri River was occupied and the range was saturated in both Montana and Wyoming.

The boom had caused the organization of large cattle companies between 1880 and 1886. In 1883 alone some twenty cattle companies were capitalized at more than twelve million dollars and located in the area of Montana and Wyoming. In 1885 the members of the Wyoming Stockgrowers' Association owned a total of two million head of cattle.

The winter of 1886-87 saw the end of the boom in the cattle business. The hazards of open range grazing were well known but the seemingly endless profits caused even the experienced cattlemen to over extend. The severity of the winter of 1886-87 caused the death of thousands of cattle on the over grazed range. These losses forced many of the large cattle companies out of business. The remnants of their herds were sold to satisfy their creditors.

This experience forced adjustments in the open range system. Herds were reduced, shelter provided and hay cut for emergency feeding. Althou the figures may not be entirely accurate or consistent they do show a considerable decrease in the number of cattle in Montana after the winter of 1886-87.

This catastrophy caused a reassessment of the open range policy by Congress as well as by the cattlemen, although it produced no change in the land laws at that time. Congress was aware of the use of public land by the cattlemen through their control of small parcels acquired under the public land laws. There was also an awareness in general that the purchase of checkerboard lands from the railroad was not an answer to the cattleman's problem of sufficient grazing land. It was almost impossible to keep others from using the private land which lay next to public land in the checkerboard.

The problems of the cattlemen were compounded by the continuing advance of homesteaders into cattle country. The homesteader would file on a piece of land containing water or bottomlands where the cattleman had been accustomed to water his stock and cut hay. Once this homestead was fenced it could reduce the grazing range of the cattleman by a considerable amount. Eventually the legislature enacted fence laws to protect the homesteader and this spelled the end of the open range era for all practical purposes.

While the unsuitability of the homestead laws to the great plains was recognized there was no change made. The matter was studied and recommendations made but not acted upon. The cattlemen themselves were opposed to change during the earlier years. As time passed and the water and hay lands were disappearing some cattlemen came to recognize the need for range control through ownership. This loss of water holes and hay lands through private acquisition helped set the stage for the winter of 1886-87 and the increasing number of sheep on the range added to the necessity for controlled range. After 1886-87 it began to be generally recognized that proper range management was necessary to the continued existence of the cattle industry on a profitable basis.

For the above reason it is apparent that there did exist a demand for the practically virgin grazing land which lay within the Blackfoot Reservation at the time of its cession on May 1, 1888.

The next question facing the Commission is that of the fair market value of the subject tract on May 1, 1888.

There were no sales within the subject area as of the date of taking. Petitioners presented evidence of sales within Montana but outside of the subject area. These would seem to be the most nearly comparable sales in location and time, although most of them were somewhat later than the May 1, 1888 date of taking and were selective purchases. In addition to these sales petitioners also used certain Canadian sales of rather large areas. These sales were from a later period since the development of the area north of the border in Canada was later than that of the Territory of Montana, although by not too many years.

By way of justifying the use of these Canadian sales which dated from 1895 to 1904 petitioners introduced the testimony of a Canadian rangeland conservationist and management consultant from Calgary, Alberta Mr. Hanson, who at the time was chief forester for the Eastern Rockies

Conservation Board, testified at some length as to the comparability of the Canadian lands with the subject lands. It was his conclusion that the lands were in fact comparable. Since Mr. Hanson based his testimony upon information supplied by Mr. Saunderson, petitioners' other expert, and such information is embodied in certain of the findings of fact heretofore made, there is no specific finding concerning Mr. Hanson's testimony.

Mr. Hanson indicated that while he had made no specific investigation of a difference in the economic growth of Alberta and Saskatchewan as compared with the subject area he had, based upon what he considered to be reliable authorities, accepted a time lag of five years in the economic development of Alberta and Saskatchewan as compared with Montana. While this statement stands unsupported in the record, the Commission is disposed to accept it as being reasonable, based upon a matter of common knowledge that there was in fact a general lag in development between the two countries.

Petitioners' introduction of certain small sales within the subject area has been ignored since petitioners' expert witness did not consider them to be comparable and did not rely upon them in arriving at the unit value.

The sales from Montana and North Dakota introduced by petitioners as being comparable were all Northern Pacific Railway Company land sales. These were the only lands available in sufficiently large quantity to form an economic ranching unit.

While these are the only sales in the general area which are of any assistance in arriving at a market value for the subject area, they suffer somewhat from having been selective purchases due to the inability of a purchaser to acquire lands in blocks because of the checkerboard railroad grants. Conversely, the use by a purchaser of checkerboard lands of the intervening sections of public lands also detracts from their value as comparable sales.

However, the fact remains that these sales are the only ones available in the area of Montana for comparison and they do give an indication of the price at which a willing seller and a willing buyer could agree under the conditions as they existed at those dates.

The Northern Pacific sales, located in North Dakota and Montana, ranged in size from 11,520 acres to 113,917.93 acres. The price range was from $1.00 to a high of $2.00 per acre. As stated previously, many of these sales covered a period of years and were non-contiguous selective purchases.

The Musselshell Cattle Company purchases were made at various times from 1886 to 1889. Photographs of some of the land of this purchase show it to have been comparabel to the lands in the subject area. The average price paid was $1.44 per acre for a total of 23,026.66 acres. These sales were of the non-contiguous, selective type.

The Montana Cattle Company purchase was of the non-contiguous selective type and from the photograph of a part appears to have been comparable land. The contracts to purchase covered the years 1895, 1896, 1897 and 1899. These sales averaged $1.00 per acre for a total of 58,101.05 acres.

The Auchard purchases of 56,356 acres at an average price of $1.16 per acre were made in 1891, 1893, 1894, 1896, and 1897. The photograph of a part of this area shows foothill grasslands which appear to be of rather less quality than similar types found in the subject area.

The Van Duzee sale of 12,808 acres at $1.00 per acre was made in 1899 and lay near the present city of Dickinson, North Dakota.

The Huidekoper purchase of 11,520 acres in 1883 at an average price of $2.00 per acre consisted of odd sections and lay near the town of Medora, North Dakota.

The largest single purchase was that by W. D. Washburn of 113,917.93 acres in 1899 for a consideration of $1.00 per acre. This land lay in west-central North Dakota.

The last sale cited was of 29,373.93 acres by the Northern Pacific in 1899, for $49,935.09, or an average of $1.70 per acre. This, however, was farmland in central North Dakota and had an average rainfall of 16 to 18 inches.

The Canadian sales introduced by petitioners were five in number and ranged in date from 1895 to 1904. The price range was from $1.00 per acre to $2.50 per acre. The testimony of Mr. Hanson, as well as certain photographs introduced, was intended to establish the comparability of this land with that of the subject area. From the photographs introduced it would appear that as of the valuation date these Canadian lands were comparable with and perhaps better than the subject lands. They also had the advantage of being sold in blocks rather than checkerboards.

The first of the Canadian sales was by the Alberta Railway and Coal Company to James A. Cunningham of 28,661.7 acres at $1.00 per acre. This land was located on the Milk River near Cardston, Alberta and was sold in 1896.

The Canadian Government sold 16,000 acres at $1.25 per acre to the Cochrane Ranch Company in 1895. This land was located 12 miles north of the Montana-Alberta border.

The two sales by the Alberta Railway and Coal Company to Jesse Knight are shown to be of doubtful value for comparison with the subject land for the purpose of establishing a fair market value. The evidence leaves too much doubt as to the size and consideration involved in these two sales. No consideration was recited in the transfer documents which can be reasonably related to the price paid for the land itself. In the case of the smaller sale the evidence as to consideration is conflicting and in the case of the larger sale the evidence shows other considerations than money to have been involved. See petitioners' exhibit No. 114, pp. 71-74. For these reasons these sales will not be considered for the purpose of arriving at the fair market value of the subject tract.

The fifth sale introduced by petitioners was that of The Calgary and Edmondton Land Company, Ltd. to the Cochrane Ranch Company in 1904. This tract was 36,245 acres and sold at an average of $1.25 per acre.

By way of establishing the correctness of his conclusion as to value based upon the preceding sales, Mr. Saunderson used certain supplemental methods of valuation.

The first of these methods was a capitalization of income approach wherein he ascertained the cost of certain grazing leases made by the State of Montana in Meagher County in 1896. These leases averaged a net 10.31 cents in the State of Montana. He then assumed a rate of return in 1888 of 8%. Thus capitalized this return produced a value of $1.30 per acre.

This is admittedly a supplemental check on the basic method of comparability in sales and as such does not stand alone as a determination of value. This supplemental method suffers from the same disability as the primary method of comparable sales in that it is later in time as to the fact of the leases and in addition it is a net income to the state rather than a gross income to a private lessor.

The second supplemental method was that of a statistical average of value per animal unit of carrying capacity. This involves the use of the animal unit of capacity and the value of the ranching property in the general area. These figures are then divided-the CYL into the value of the property-to arrive at the animal unit of value. This figure which represents the animal unit of value for the general area is then used to multiply the number of CYL's for a given area and this result is in turn divided by the acreage of the given area to arrive at its value per acre.

In the instant case Mr. Saunderson has established the figure of $30.00 as being the value per animal unit of carrying capacity from 1870 to 1890. This figure is in turn multiplied by the estimated carrying capacity (CYL's) of the subject area, which is 509,970 CYL's and this result is divided by the acreage of the subject area, 14,969,156 acres, which gives a value of $1.02 per acre.

The efficacy of this method as a check on the comparable sales method of valuation is questionable since the same premises are necessary to either method. The establishment of the unit value of carrying capacity is dependent upon the same facts necessary to establish the fair market value of the subject area in 1888. This method as a check on the comparable sales method succeeds only in begging the question.

The third supplemental approach used by petitioners' witness was by valuation of rangeland types of the subject area based upon the sales of comparable range types contained within the tracts introduced herein as comparable sales. Where there were no comparable land types Mr. Saunderson interpolated on a carrying capacity basis to arrive at a supplemental value figure. This interpolation was used in the case of the sagebrush grassland, Missouri River breaks and badlands basins which totaled approximately 2-1/2 million acres of the subject area.

In order to interpolate, Mr. Saunderson needed a base figure. For this base he chose the prairie grasslands at $1.20 per acre. This figure presumably came from his comparison of the sales outside of the area with the same types of grazing land within the area. This figure is at variance with his previously used figure of $30,00 per acre since it represents in his calculations a price of $36.00 per acre at the rate of 2-1/2 AUM's per month or 30 acres per CYL times $1.20. It also varies from his overall value figure of $1.10 per acre.

Despite the same limitations which all of these valuation methods have, this would seem to be more nearly compatible with the primary method of comparable sales. In those cases where direct comparison between range types was possible this method, based as it is upon comparable sales, represents a refinement on the regular comparable sales method in that it compares type with type rather than an overall comparison. In this sense though it would be an unacceptable method in that it is essentially a totaling of the sum of the parts to arrive at a value for the whole. This is contrary to the accepted practice of the courts.

Mr. Saunderson's ultimate value for the 14,969,156 acres of the subject tract amounted to $16,466,071.00 or at the rate of $1.10 per acre for the land as a unit.

Defendant's expert witness, Mr. Darwin Harbin, submitted three separate appraisal reports. Mr. Harbin mentioned three accepted methods of appraising lands. Two of these, the capitalization of income approach and reproduction cost, he dismissed as being unsuitable for the present type of valuation. He then states that he will rely upon the comparable sales method. For these comparable sales Mr. Harbin chose sales located in Texas, New Mexico and Arizona, southern Colorado, Wyoming, and North Dakota.

The Munson and Gunter purchase of 1880 was not a bona fide sale in the accepted sense of the term. It was made with government script purchased at the rate of $16.00 per section, or 2-1/2 cents per acre. The sales were made in small homestead tracts, not in grazing-sized acreage and the purchase price based upon the use of the script was such as to permit a considerable profit on resale at 25 cents and 50 cents an acre. The Commission does not consider this sale as comparable since it was made with script and so does not reflect a true value based upon a free transaction between seller and purchaser either in its purchase or resale in homestead tracts.

The purchase by the XIT Ranch was done by trading and the ultimate cost of the land far exceeded the price agreed upon. It does not represent a bona fide sale under the definition of fair market value.

The Goodnight purchase in Texas at a rate of 20 cents per acre is without sufficient proof in the record to establish its validity. The reference in the expert's report to Defendant's Exhibit No. 41, page 55, shows only the bare statement that Goodnight purchased 170,000 acres at 20 cents per acre instead of the 120,000 acres quoted in the report. In any event the comparability of this land with the subject land suffers by reason of its distance from Montana.

The Aztec purchase amounted to a forced sale because of pressure exerted through Aztec's parent company against the Atlantic and Pacific Railroad. For this reason the sale was not one made on the open market.

The Amarilla grant sale by Catron to the U. S. Land and Colonization Company is not a valid sale because Catron was President and a Director of the U. S. Land and Colonization Company. He later repurchased all of the grant which lay in Colorado for the sum of $2,000.00.

The Swan Land and Cattle Company purchased from the Union Pacific Railroad 555,890 acres in 1884. This was grazing land located in Wyoming and was in the usual checkerboard pattern. Swan allowed about half of this acreage to revert to the railroad. It is difficult to tell what the actual price of this land was. There is a conflict in the testimony and pleadings. Mr. Harbin on page 603 of the transcript testified as follows about this sale:

> *** About a half million acres of Union Pacific lands, alternate sections, I haven't been able to tie down. I see various references. Some say 50 cents an acre, others a dollar an acre, and I figured it up in one place where I found a record that showed about 85 cents an acre, so I don't know. It was somewhere between 50 cents and a dollar and whether it was paid for with reduced value stock or bonds, I am not familiar. That may account for the difference in the values assigned by various writers. ***

In addition to the question as to actual price paid, these lands were subject to the usual infirmity of checkerboard sales as an index of fair market value in that such lands usually carried control of large areas of public lands in addition to the lands purchased.

The sale by the Northern Pacific Railway Company to J. W. McCammon of 2,430,000 acres in North Dakota, is useless as a comparable sale. It involved a stock transfer at par regardless of the purchase price and was not an open market transfer.

Defendant in one of its two supplemental valuation reports set out certain hindsight sales. These sales have been set out in the findings, although these, just as most of the prior sales used by defendant, must be rejected as not comparable in most cases.

The sale to Marcus Daly in 1899 by the Northern Pacific was made at 50 cents per acre with an additional 50 cents per thousand board feet for stumpage. This was obviously a timber sale and not a grazing land sale. In addition the ultimate consideration is not known.

The sales by the Northern Pacific to 77 buyers on contracts dated from 1895 to 1903 in which the sales averaged about 13,000 acres, with the largest sale being for 86,785.40 acres, show an average price of approximately 95 cents per acre.

The Northern Pacific sale to W. D. Washburn in 1899 of 113,917.93 acres at $1.00 per acre was of land in North Dakota.

The Hackney-Boynton Land Company sales by the Northern Pacific in 1901 are not comparable because of the colonization agreements involved.

In addition to these sales, Mr. Harbin furnished in his three appraisal reports a mass of information upon almost every conceivable aspect of the subject area. Much of his testimony concerns itself with the soils of the subject area and has as its primary thesis that over fifty percent of the area was composed of "Gumbo soil" and of no value. This Commission is faced, however, with the undeniable fact that the subject area was considered among the best grazing land in the country at the time.

As a matter of fact, Mr. Harbin, in his original appraisal report, Defendant's Exhibit No. 241, at pages 86 and 87, sets forth "A Tabulation of Ideal Stock Raising Conditions For Montana" and at the bottom of page 87 he makes the following statement: "The Blackfoot area comes about as near to furnishing such conditions as can be found anywhere in the United States as of May 1, 1888."

Despite the above statement concerning the desirability of the subject area as grazing land, and despite the fact that the average of his acceptable comparable sales would have exceeded such price, Mr. Harbin set a fair market value of $4,050,000, or approximately 27 cents per acre.

It appears that although he excluded all methods of valuation except comparable sales as being inapplicable to the present valuation, Mr. Harbin did in fact establish his valuation through the use of a capitalization of income approach based upon leasing the area to stockmen (see Defendant's Ex. 327, page 17, and Ex. 240, pp. 141-147, 167-171). In one of his supplemental reports, Defendant's Exhibit No. 327, pp. 12-14, he assigns values to the various types of land within the subject area to arrive at the same approximate 27 cents per acre for the somewhat smaller area valued therein. He assigns no reasons for the various values placed upon the different lands and timber. In any event it is immaterial that he failed to do so because the method is no more valid than when done by petitioner's expert. It still amounts to a summation of the value of the parts to reach the value of the unit and is contrary to accepted appraisal techniques insofar as the courts are concerned.

303

The 403 pages of the three appraisal reports submitted by Mr. Harbin contain a mass of information, as stated heretofore. However, in the face of his statement to the effect that the subject area afforded some of the best grazing land to be found in the United States on May 1, 1888, the vast majority of this information becomes secondary. This does not mean that the Commission does not appreciate having at its disposal the results of the efforts of both experts. While it is true that this is opinion evidence and the Commission is free to draw its own conclusions therefrom, the fact remains that this Commission does give due weight to these opinions and attempts to base its conclusions upon what it considers to be the relevant portions of the efforts of all experts in the case.

In this case, however, once the conclusion has been reached that the subject lands were among the best grazing lands in the United States as of the relevant date, the questions of topography, climate, including rainfall, temperature and growing season; and soil have been laid to rest. Any consideration of alternative use, or lack thereof, such as for farming, becomes immaterial. For these and similar reasons much of defendant's appraisal reports have not been made a part of the findings herein.

One particular part of defendant's appraisal report included an excellent sampling of the subject area by surveyors' notes. This was a fair sample of some 2,700,000 acres for which the pattern was established prior to assembling the survey notes. The results of this sampling, based upon our own conclusions drawn from reading these notes indicates that approximately 86% of the sample represented good to fair grazing land as of 1888. This represents 63% good grazing and 23% fair grazing, with approximately 13% found to be poor grazing.

The quality of this land, along with the obvious demand, belies the figure of 27 cents per acre as found by defendant's expert appraiser. For this and other reasons heretofore mentioned the Commission must reject the value of $4,050,000 placed upon the subject area by Mr. Harbin.

Mr. Saunderson's valuation and his basis therefor has been set out above. The sales cited by Mr. Saunderson are more nearly in the nature of comparable sales than are those cited by defendant. They are much closer to the area under consideration, including those in Canada. The Canadian sales suffer not from the fact of being Canadian but rather from the normal infirmities of uncertain consideration and later dates.

The primary difficulty with the Montana and North Dakota sales, aside from the time element, lies in their relatively small size, lack of contiguity, and their selective nature. These are all difficulties with which the Commission has been faced many times because often the only sales are of non-contiguous railroad lands. They do, however, furnish a basis, along with other evidence, for arriving at what we consider to be the estimated or imputed fair market value of the subject tract.

The external factors which would add or detract from the fair market value of the subject area as grazing land were nearly all positive. Rail transportation ran through the area as far as the town of Havre and then southwest to Great Falls. There was available rail transportation to the Chicago market by way of Canada also.

The demand for the land is demonstrated by the heavy pressure for its cession as well as by its unauthorized use by cattlemen occasioned in large measure by the overcrowded condition of the adjoining range. The evidence as to a slackening of this demand due to the cattle losses during the winter of 1886-87 is conflicting. Much of this evidence is a romanticized version of that famous winter. One set of figures shows a decrease of approximately 190,000 head of cattle, while another shows a decrease of 60,000 head from 1886 to 1887. Both sets of figures are estimates and both come from the Department of Agriculture. One set of figures would appear to be more reliable since it is an attempt to estimate the total number of livestock on farms from 1867-1935. These figures show an increase of cattle tin Montana from 990,000 in 1887 to 1,015,000 in 1888. It is this same set of figures which shows 1,050,000 cattle in 1886, a decrease of 60,000 head from 1886 to 1887. This is Defendant's Exhibit No. 36, page 117. Defendant's Exhibit No. 48, page 123 shows the larger decrease. However, it is a narrative account submitted for consideration in connection with potential legislation affecting the subject of the western range. It would appear that Exhibit No. 36 would be the more dependable evidence.

The recognition by cattlemen of the need for controlled grazing which was spurred by the losses of the winter of 1886-87 would have tended to increase the demand for lands which could be bought in single tracts for the purpose of protecting winter range as well as for raising supplemental feed for hard winters.

The location of the subject tract is not a matter of great import in this valuation. Its fitness as grazing lands is affected by its location in that the Chinook winds play a part in its desirability for winter grazing. The location of the Missouri River along the south border of the tract adds to its value because of supply transportation. The fact that it was not in the path of emigration is a positive factor in this instance since this type of cattle grazing requires large spaces. A greater population nearby would have added to its market potential for beef but the presence of rail transportation in the tract and in nearby Canada for shipping to the Chicago market offsets to a large extent the lack of population cents nearby.

Transportation within the area was a matter of small importance to its use as grazing lands. Well known trails for the movement of cattle to the area existed and were used by herds coming up from the south. Once the cattle arrived they were turned loose on the range to graze until ready for the market.

Economic conditions within the cattle industry would have been somewhat depressed at the date of taking due to the cattle losses occasioned by the winter of 1886-87 in combination with the management practices which caused a sell-off of the herds in order to maintain profits for the stockholders of the large foreign controlled cattle companies.

Economic conditions in general were stable but depressed during the period in question. The panic of 1873 was followed by that of 1883 and yet a third in 1893. The period from 1870 to 1895 was one of "bottoming out". The price level started down in 1865 and did not begin its upturn until 1895 when a better developed banking system and an increase in gold production bolstered the monetary reserves.

Cattle prices during the critical period just before the date of taking were at a low ebb. The price in 1887 was $4.20 per hundredweight, the lowest of the decade to that time. As a matter of speculation it might be said that such prices for cattle would have had the effect of creating a demand for grazing range to hold over cattle for improving prices. In fact, the figures do show an increase in cattle in Montana from 1887 to 1888. Whether this resulted from a refusal to ship or natural increase we cannot be sure.

It seems more reasonable under the circumstances to assume that the decreasing market price in 1887 would have had an adverse effect on the price of grazing land in the spring of 1888. The recognition of ranchers in general that controllable range had become a necessity to efficient stock raiding would have been tempered by a lack of money due to falling cattle prices.

The use by petitioners' expert of the land sales heretofore mentioned for purposes of comparison with the subject tract, especially those sales occurring after the date of taking, has raised vigorous opposition from defendant. Without going into detail concerning each sale, it may be said that the objections raised by counsel for defendant are, in general, valid. The difficulty, which is typical of these cases, lies in determining the ultimate comparability of these sales with the subject tract.

We know to begin with that we must take into consideration the size of the area to be valued. It is of course much larger than any of the sales, or all of them together, for that matter. This then limits the market and throws comparatively small sales off as an indicator of market value.

We do not have to consider costs incident to subdivision in this instance because the area has a highest and best use as grazing land and any subdivision for that purpose would be of minimal importance.

It appears, too, that the matter of interest costs incident to holding the land prior to disposal would present less of a financial burden on a prospective purchaser. The demand for economic grazing units, despite the adverse factors mentioned, would have been sufficient to enable a purchaser to dispose of the area in a much shorter time than if he were selling in small parcels. The time necessary to development for sale in small parcels would not have been a cost factor to a purchaser in the form either of the actual cost of such development or the expenditure of interest during the time necessary to do the planning and work involved in such development.

Although the natural drainage of the subject area between the Milk and Marias rivers appears to be good as does that of the portion of the area east of the Milk River, it would still be necessary to furnish water for stock use in parts of the area. It does not appear from the evidence that this constituted a great problem or one that would have adversely affected the market value of the subject tract to a very great degree.

For the above reasons, and based upon the findings of fact made herein and upon the record as a whole, it is the opinion of this Commission that the subject tract of 14,969,156 acres had a fair market value on May 1, 1888 of $11,975,324.80, or at the rate of 80 cents per acre.

The matter of consideration paid under the Agreement of May 1, 1888, has been the subject of prior litigation between petitioners and defendant in <u>Blackfeet, et al., Nation</u> v. <u>United States</u>, 81 C. Cls. 101. Petitioners and defendant have accepted this fact, although they disagree as to the proper amount to be credited to defendant. The intervenors, Assiniboine and Sioux, have objected to the matter of consideration being determined at this time. We do not think that this objection was intended to prevent a determination by this Commission as to the issue of liability. Intervenors undoubtedly had reference to the issue as to the amount of consideration actually paid or credited to defendant in prior cases. These matters should be considered at a future hearing on consideration paid or which may be credited to any party and on offsets.

The Commission feels that there is insufficient evidence in the record at this time to make a final determination of consideration paid or which may be credited any party as opposed to the consideration promised. For this reason the judgment rendered herein is a gross judgment and subject to the amount of consideration paid or which may be credited any party as well as offsets, if any.

This Commission, in accordance with Finding of Fact No. 46 made herein, is of the opinion that an agreed consideration of $4,300,000 for lands having a value of $11,975,324.80 as of the date of taking is unconscionable on its face.

The issue of fair and honorable dealings was pleaded by petitioners but has become moot in the face of a finding of liability on the basis of unconscionable consideration.

In conclusion, it is the opinion of this Commission that under Section 2(3) of the Indian Claims Commission Act, and in accordance with the findings of fact this day entered herewith, that:

(1) The Blackfeet Nation shall have and recover from the defendant the sum of $11,125,606.40, subject to the consideration paid and to all offsets, if any, to which defendant may be entitled under the Indian Claims Commission Act.

(2) The Assiniboine Tribe of the Fort Peck and Fort Belknap Reservation in Montana shall have and recover from the defendant the sum of $3,108,506.40, subject to the consideration paid and to all offsets, if any, to which defendant may be entitled under the Indian Claims Commission Act.

(3) The Sioux Tribe of the Fort Peck Reservation in Montana shall have and recover from defendant the sum of $2,364,216.80, subject

to the consideration paid and to all offsets, if any, to which defendant may be entitled under the Indian Claims Commission Act.

An order to the above effect will be entered.

(Signed) T. Harold Scott
T. Harold Scott
Associate Commissioner

Concurring:

(Signed) Arthur V. Watkins
Arthur V. Watkins
Chief Commissioner

(Signed) Wm. M. Holt
Wm. M. Holt
Associate Commissioner

DATE DUE

MAR 17 1982	NOV 06 1996
OCT 17 1982	OCT 19 REC'D
NOV 9 1982 RET'D	
NOV 1982 RET'D DISCARD	NOV 19 1996
OCT 22 1991 RET'D	Dec 8 MPL
DEC 21 91	
JUL 30 RET'D	DEC 08 REC'D
NOV 30 1992 RET'D	DEC 22 2000
	NOV 25 REC'D
MAR 29 1993 RET'D	MAR 22 2005
MAY 06 1994	MAR 14 2005
FEB 15 REC'D	
MAY 05 1995	MAR 17 REC'D
MAY 05 REC'D	APR 19 REC'D
	MAY 15 2010

DEMCO 38-297